THE TROUBLE

律师的麻烦
美国律师的职业困境

〔美〕德博拉·罗德 著
王进喜 译

Deborah L. Rhode

WITH LAWYERS

译　序

美国斯坦福大学法学院的德博拉·L. 罗德（Deborah L. Rhode）教授，是批判美国法律职业治理和司法现状的最著名的学者之一。《律师的麻烦》一书以丰富的资料贴近现实，以素描的手法刻画问题，系统地总结了她对美国律师业多年的观察和思考，全面说明了美国律师业所面临的挑战。该书指出，美国律师行业在法律实务活动的条件、近用司法、法律职业多样性、律师规制、法律教育等方面，没有处理好基本问题。有些问题是市场驱动的，其他的则是法律职业自身造成的。本书揭示了如下问题：律师事务所的利润优先给律师带来的苦果，近用司法上的政治障碍，律师协会在非律师人员投资、多行业执业、律师惩戒等问题上的保守性和自利性，法学院在排名中的挣扎，法学院学生的困厄，法学教师学术上的自娱自乐，等等。当这些问题活生生地摆在面前的时候，律师的形象不再光鲜，人们对法律职业的高度期望落空。正如作者所说的那样，在美国的历史上，律师们一直站在关于社会正义的每一个重要运动的前列，现在是他们把更多的精力转向内部的时候了。诚然，期望罗德教授在这本小册子中对所有问题都给出明确的答案是不现实的，她本人也指出，这些问题的解决需要综合性方案,需要整个法律职业乃至社会改变态度,即产生进行必要改革的意愿。

本书对美国法治现实的批判,是我们观察美国法治的重要维度之一。在罗德教授就律师行业治理、法学教育等提出的问题中,我们是不是能看到自己的影子呢?特别是对美国法律职业、法学教育乃至法律制度的盲目崇拜者而言,这本现实主义的小册子应该可以起到去天真、存冷静的效果。

北京大学出版社的蒋浩、田鹤诸君为本书的编辑出版工作付出的心血,给我留下了深刻印象;中国政法大学博士研究生鱼新岩、硕士研究生王嘉炜、熊鹏等同学提供了书稿校对等宝贵协助,谨此说明并致以诚挚感谢。

是为序。

王进喜

2020 年 5 月 1 日

译者介绍

　　王进喜,男,1970年生,中国政法大学法学院教授,法律职业伦理研究所所长,律师学研究中心主任,法学博士,博士研究生导师;中国法学会律师法学研究会副会长,司法部律师惩戒委员会委员;美国西北大学法学院富布莱特研修学者(2002—2003),美国加州大学戴维斯分校法学院高级访问学者(2010—2011)。主要研究领域:法律职业伦理(法律职业行为法)、证据法。主要著作有:《法律职业伦理》(中国人民大学出版社2020年版)、《法律职业行为法(第二版)》(中国人民大学出版社2014年版)、《法律伦理的50堂课》(五南图书出版股份有限公司2008年版)、《美国律师职业行为规则理论与实践》(中国人民公安大学出版社2005年版)、《美国〈联邦证据规则〉(2011年重塑版)条解》(中国法制出版社2012年版)、《刑事证人证言论》(中国人民公安大学出版社2002年版)、《律师事务所管理导论》(译著,中国人民大学出版社2015年版)、《践行正义———一种关于律师职业道德的理论》(译著,中国人民大学出版社2015年版)、《加拿大律师协会联合会职业行为示范守则》(译著,中国法制出版社2016年版)、《面向新世纪的律师规制》(译著,中国法制出版社2016年版)、《科学证据与法律的平等保护》(译著,中国法制出版社2016年版)、《英国证据法实务指南》(译著,中国法制出版社2012年版)、《证据科学读本:美国"Daubert"三部曲》(译著,中国政法大学出版社2015年版)、《美国律师协会职业行为示范规则(2004)》(译著,中国人民公安大学出版社2005年版)等。

致　谢

本书的完成要感谢很多人。我非常感谢牛津大学出版社的戴维·麦克布赖德（David McBride），他一直支持这个项目，并在整个出版过程中为它提供了指引。我也对布鲁斯·阿克曼（Bruce Ackerman）、本杰明·巴顿（Benjamin Barton）、罗伯特·戈登（Robert Gordon）等人富有启发的评论表示感谢，并对阿伦·亨森（Aaron Henson）的出色研究表示感谢。斯坦福大学法律图书馆的工作人员保罗·罗密欧（Paul Lomio）、索尼娅·莫斯（Sonia Moss）、里奇·波特（Rich Porter）、蕾切尔·山姆伯格（Rachael Samberg）、塞吉奥·斯通（Sergio Stone）、乔治·维兹瓦里（George Vizvary）、埃里卡·韦恩（Erika Wayne）和乔治·威尔逊（George Wilson）在参考文献上提供了宝贵的帮助。我最感谢的是我的丈夫拉尔夫·卡瓦纳（Ralph Cavanagh），他的支持和指导，使这本书顺利出版。

目 录 | CONTENTS

第一章　导言	**Chapter 1 Introduction**
第二章　执业条件	**Chapter 2 Work Condition**
016 / 变革的驱动力	Driving Force of Reform
019 / 利润优先	Profit is Preferred
024 / 对实务活动的满意度	Satisfaction with Practical Activities
038 / 错位的优先事项	Misplaced Priorities
046 / 改革战略	Reform Strategy
第三章　近用司法	**Chapter 3 Access to Justice**
060 / 刑事辩护	Criminal Defense
074 / 民事司法制度中的障碍	Barriers of Civil Judicial System
第四章　法律职业的多样性	**Chapter 4 Diversity of the Legal Profession**
120 / 原则与实践的差距	The Gap between Principle and Practice
126 / 解释差距	Explain the Gap
130 / 种族、族裔和性别刻板印象	Racial, Ethnic and Gender Stereotypes

138 / 群体内部偏见：指导、后援、人际关系网和工作分配	In-group Bias: Coaching, Support, Networking, and Job Assignments
143 / 工作场所结构和性别角色	Workplace Structure and Gender Roles
148 / 抵触情绪	Resistance
149 / 法律的界限	Limits of Law
154 / 支持多样性的商业理由	The Case for Diversity
160 / 个人战略	Personal Strategy
164 / 组织战略	Organizational Strategy
第五章 法律职业的规制	**Chapter 5 Regulation of the Legal Profession**
175 / 规制结构	Governance Structure
178 / 跨司法辖区执业	Practice Across Jurisdictions
186 / 多行业执业	Multi-industry Practice
191 / 非律师人员投资	Non-lawyer Investment
199 / 继续法律教育	Continuing Legal Education
209 / 惩戒	Disciplinary
225 / 可选的规制模式：国外经验	Alternative Modes of Regulation: Foreign Experience
232 / 对规制结构的反思	Reflection on the Regulatory Structure
第六章 法律教育	**Chapter 6 Legal Education**
238 / 财务	Financial
250 / 结构	Structure
252 / 课程	Course

257 / 价值观	Values
265 / 法律评论	Law Review
268 / 战略	Strategic
第七章　结论	**Chapter 7　Conclusion**
291 / 重要译名对照表	**Important Translation Table**

01
Chapter

第一章
导　言

这可不是美国律师最美好的时光。关于法律职业的书籍的标题,充分说明了这一点:《律师的泡沫》《衰落的前景》《美国法律职业的危机》《失败的法学院》《律师的终结》《美国律师的消亡》《年轻律师的毁灭》《被背叛的职业》《迷失的律师》。[1] 不到1/5的美国人将律师的诚实和伦理标准评为很高或者高,仅仅将他们排在保险销售代理人前面。[2] 2010年皮尤(Pew)研究中心进行的一项调查中的一个问题是哪个行业对社会福祉贡献最大,在10个行业中,法律行业排名最低。[3] 自相矛盾的是,困扰这个国家的,一方面是律师供给过多,另一方面则是为贫穷或者中等收入的人员提供的法律服务不足。

这是全面说明美国律师业所面临的挑战的适当时刻,所

---

[1] Steven J. Harper, *The Lawyer Bubble* (2013); Michael Trotter, *Declining Prospects* (2012); James E. Moliterno, *The American Legal Profession in Crisis: Resistance and Responses to Change* (2012); Richard Susskind, *The End of Lawyers* (2010); Thomas Morgan, *The Vanishing American Lawyer* (2010); Douglas Litowitz, *The Destruction of Young Lawyers: Beyond One L* (2006); Sol M. Linowitz with Martin Mayer, *The Betrayed Profession: Lawyering at the End of the Twentieth Century* (1994); Anthony Kronman, *The Lost Lawyer: Failing Ideals of the Legal Profession* (1993).

[2] Gallup Opinion Poll, Honesty/Ethics in Professions, Nov. 26–29, 2012.

[3] Sheldon Kranz, *The Legal Profession: What Is Wrong and How to Fix It* 1 (2013).

有这些挑战,都有代表人物:

● 阿什利·纽霍尔(Ashley Newhall)拥有法律学位,并取得了在宾夕法尼亚州和新泽西州执业的执照。她正在为一些极其苛刻的委托人工作,但是他们中的大部分人都不到3岁。在过去3年中,她的主要收入来自于当保姆。考虑到在法学院学习期间欠下的6位数的债务,她需要3份兼职工作才能在经济上应付自如。①

● 比利·杰罗姆·普雷斯利(Billy Jerome Presley)因拖欠子女抚养费而在看守所里关了17个月。他没有前科,也没有律师。如果他能够付得起法律援助费用,他的律师就可以保释他,把他从监狱里捞出来,并制定一个还款计划。②

● 一名在高伟绅律师事务所工作的非合伙律师记载了这样的一天:从凌晨4点45分婴儿的哭闹开始,到第二天凌晨1点30分结束,以妄图达到计费时数的要求。③

---

① Samantha Melamed, For College Grads, Nannying Is Not Such a Bad Deal, Philly. com, Apr. 24, 2014, available at http://articles. philly. com/2014-04-24/entertainment/49351220_1_college-grads-labormarket-rough-job-market.

② Ethan Bronner, Right to Lawyer Can Be Empty Promise for Poor, *N. Y. Times*, Mar. 16, 2013, available at http://www. nytimes. com/2013/03/16/us/16gideon. html? pagewanted=all&_r=0. 普雷斯利最终从人权南方中心找到了一名提供该种帮助的律师。

③ Ellie Mystal, Departure Memo of the Day: Parenting Gets the Best of One Big Law Associate, Above the Law, Nov. 8, 2012, available at http://abovethelaw. com/2012/11/departure-memo-of-the-dayparenting-gets-the-best-of-one-big-law-associate/.

第一章
导 言

这些人为下面的章节所描述的失灵付出了代价,这样的人数以千计。这些章节探讨了法律市场的趋势,这些趋势给法律职业和依靠其服务的公众带来了越来越多的问题。本书的中心前提是,律师行业在法律实务活动的条件、近用司法、法律职业多样性、律师规制、法律教育等方面,没有处理好基本问题。有些问题是市场驱动的,其他的则是法律职业自己造成的。本章对这些挑战进行了概述。

第二章探讨了法律实务活动的条件,特别关注的是律师事务所。本章讨论了当代法律实务活动的体量、规模、竞争、技术变革,以及是如何加剧了经济压力的。经济衰退加剧了这种压力,因为委托人的要求越来越多,而付费却越来越少。即使在经济复苏之后,困难依然存在,大多数律师认为,其结果是法律市场的永久性变化。

因对驱动律师事务所决策的短期利润的不懈关注,这些压力被放大。利润的优先性是导致过去几十年来可计费时数上升的原因,并且这是以生活质量为代价的。大多数律师报告说,他们没有足够的时间留给自己和他们的家人,大多数人每周甚至无法投入1个小时到公益服务中。这些趋势对律师对工作场所的满意度造成了负面影响。法律不在排名前十二个最令人满意的职业之列,如果他们可以再作一次选择的话,大多数律师会选择不同的职业。律师罹患抑郁症、药物滥用和相关疾病的比率也高得不成比例。只有当律师更多地了解职业满足感的来源,并更积极主动地塑造工作场所以满足他们的需要时，才可能对这些问题作出反应。

第三章讨论的是近用司法。这是一个可耻的讽刺，即超过 1/3 的法学院毕业生无法找到全职的法律工作，而超过 4/5 的穷人的法律需要和中等收入美国人的大部分法律需要，仍然没有得到满足。贫困者的刑事辩护情况尤其成问题。政客们通过承诺强力打击犯罪而不是资助刑事辩护，来赢得选票。因此，该系统长期资金不足。公共辩护人经常会有让人难以承受的工作量。一些律师每年处理超过 1000 件轻罪或者 500 件重罪案件，这几乎是全国平均水平的 3 倍。为贫困委托人进行辩护的私人律师得到的补偿低得令人感到荒唐。在一些司法辖区，水管工每小时挣得更多。结果是律师接办了过多的案件，而不能花时间进行足够的辩护。90%的刑事案件未经审判就解决掉了，通常没有进行任何事实调查。在进入审判的案件中，律师有效代理的标准之宽松是众所周知的。在律师没有进行任何调查、提出任何证据甚至在审判中无法保持清醒和冷静的情况下，定罪都被维持了。

类似的资金不足问题也困扰着民事司法系统。美国人并不认为正义应当被出售，但是他们也不愿意为替代品买单。最近对法律援助的预算削减，使得糟糕的情况变得雪上加霜。联邦政府每年在这类援助上的支出，人均每天不足 1 美元。数以百万计的美国人因法律服务价高而退出市场，在由律师设计的和为律师设计的系统中自行代理。因全面禁止合格的非律师人员提供的帮助，他们的问题变得更加复杂。尽管律师协会长期以来以通过公益服务填补司法制度的缺口而感到自豪,但是参与率却低得很不体面。只有大约1/4的律师达到了美国律师协会《职业行为示范规则》规定的每年50小时服务的建议性标准。

第四章探讨了关于多样性的挑战。原则上,律师协会致力于种族平等和两性平等。在实践中,律师职业在保持公平竞争环境方面落后于其他职业。只有两种职业的多样性少于法律,许多职业做得更好。问题的部分原因在于对问题究竟是什么以及如何解决缺乏共识。毫无疑问,在律师事务所合伙人和总法律顾问等领导人中,女性和少数群体的人数严重不足。然而,律师协会的领导人往往将这些成就上的差异,归因于能力和投入上的差异。

这种解释低估了无意识偏见的影响。大量证据表明,女性和少数群体缺少白人男子被赋予的能力推定。许多女性和少数群体也仍然在指导、后援和业务发展的网络之外,而这些网络往往是职业晋升的关键。由于计费工时的要求不断增加和工作场所结构僵化,这些问题变得更加复杂。这些成本被女性过度承担了,因为她们还承担了过度的家庭责任。

当代的反歧视法尽管提供了针对公然的蓄意偏见的救济措施,但已经被证明不足以对抗无意识的刻板印象、老同学关系网络和妨碍机会均等的工作场所结构。就歧视提起诉讼的高昂成本,以及举证的巨大困难,使许多受害者无法勇敢地站出来。

然而，雇主和个人都在这种法律背景下面临着不平等的竞争环境。相当多的研究支持多样化的商业理由。多样性观点鼓励批判性思维和创造性的问题解决；其扩大了考虑的替代选项的范围，并抵消了"群体思维"。许多改善女性和有色人种律师条件的做法，服务于更广泛的组织利益。更好的指导计划、更公平的薪酬和工作任务，以及监督律师负起更多的责任，从长远来看都可能产生回报。在这个大部分人才由女性和有色人种律师构成的世界里，如果律师事务所不能有效地留住并使这些群体得到晋升，那么就有理由认为他们会遭遇一些竞争上的劣势。

第五章关注的是律师规制程序。法律职业在某种程度上是其自身成功的受害者。没有一个国家的律师协会能够像美国的律师协会这样，在保护其规制独立性的权利方面更具影响力和效力。然而，这种成功和确保这种成功的结构性力量，使得该职业与最有利于社会利益的问责制和创新隔绝开来。律师规制面临两个结构性问题：法律职业对自己的治理的不受制约的控制，以及以州为基础的监督制度。这两种情况，都源于州法院宣称对规制法律实务活动有固有和专属的权力，以及它们在行使该权力时倾向于服从有组织的律师协会。

在律师协会对跨司法辖区执业和多行业执业的处理上，以及禁止非律师人员投资律师事务所方面，问题是显而易见的。一个以州为基础的准入制度，不适合当代的实践。许多法律事务和律师之间的交流并不在律师取得执业执照的司法辖区内。委托人也不需要尊重行业间的界限。律师协会禁止与非律师分享报酬,阻碍了许多委托人认为符合费效比的合作。禁令也阻止了非律师的资本注入,以及可以改善法律服务的创新营销策略。在反对多行业执业和非律师人员投资时,律师协会已经声明,律师将要对来自不同传统的监督者负责,而这些其他行业在保密、利益冲突和公益服务的标准上不太严格。但是,在其他允许这种非律师参与的国家,这些问题却没有出现。对反对者提出的问题,规制是明显的解决方案,而不是禁止。

在继续法律教育方面,律师协会的规制工作同样存在缺陷。全国只有5个州要求律师每年完成一定数量的继续法律教育,通常是每年10到12个小时。虽然持续的教育在原则上是有意义的,但是在实践中,这个制度还有许多不足之处。没有证据表明,消极、被动地参加课程有助于改善律师的执业表现,或者找到了大多数委托人对律师进行投诉的原因并加以解决。此外,缺乏质量控制或者监督,也导致了对该制度的滥用。律师可以通过放松减压和"自学"获得学分,但是这不能确保继续法律教育的"磁带"在运转的时候,参与者在参与,且保持着清醒。

惩戒是规制程序不足的另一个所在,目前的系统既做得太少,也做得太多。对于保护委托人和第三方免受伦理不端行为的侵害,它做得太少;对于不涉及委托人的不端行为而惩戒律师，它又做得太多。许多惩戒机构甚至根本就不处理"轻微的"不端行为，例如疏忽和过度收费，理由是存在其他民事责任救济手段。因此，这也是结构上的基本问题。州最高法院已经声称有权对律师进行规制，但是却没有足够的时间、兴趣或者能力来有效地行使这种权力。它们已经将规制权下放给了律师协会或者与之紧密结合的机构。这些机构也缺乏足够的资源对不端行为作出回应。对于委托人投诉，该制度几乎是被动反应性的，而当委托人受益于不端行为——例如滥用诉讼——或者当委托人缺乏进行投诉的信息或者动因时，该制度没有作出回应。许多人怀疑投诉的实效，他们在很大程度上是正确的。只有大约3%的投诉导致了公开惩戒。

法律职业所面临的最后一系列挑战，涉及法律教育。第六章探讨了法学院在财务、结构、课程和价值观等方面存在的问题。法律服务市场的变化，给长期存在的问题带来了新的紧迫性。市场对应届毕业生的需求在下降，加上学费上涨，债务负担加重，导致许多新律师陷入了财务困境。只有大约2/3的人获得了全职法律工作，他们的工资中位数往往达不到平均债务水平。

造成高学费的部分原因，是由美国律师协会法律教育与律师准入部门委员会设定的严格的认可标准。它规定了一大堆花钱的要求。其结果是造成了法律教育一刀切的框架，阻碍了创新。它也未能承认与法律实务活动的职业化存在的巨大差异，以及法学院教育对这种多样性作出相应变革的需要。

法律教育成本高昂的另一个原因是《美国新闻和世界报道》排名的影响,这鼓励了排名公式所奖赏的开支方面的军备竞赛。一个例子是自从排名生效以来,每个学生的开支急剧上升。另一个例子是旨在提高声望的支出,包括对教员学术活动和令人瞩目的出版物补贴。然而,影响每个法学院的排名的40%的声望调查尤其不足以代表教育质量。被调查者中,很少有人有足够的知识作出准确的比较判断。

课程存在许多不足:实践技能训练不足,缺少互动学习、团队合作、反馈和跨学科教学的机会。90%的律师报告说,法学院没有传授在当今经济社会中取得成功所必需的实践技能,随着法律雇主减少了对应届毕业生的培训,这一缺陷变得更为严重。

法律教育的最后一个困难是,它所培养或未能培养的有关职业责任的价值观。法律伦理往往被归入单一的课程——职业行为规则。在整个课程中未能整合职业责任的问题,边缘化了其重要性。一个相关的弱点涉及公益服务。只有约10%的学校要求参与公益服务,大多数学生毕业时没有参与其中,尽管这是他们教育的一部分。在对最近的法律毕业生进行的一项调查中,参加者将公益活动列在执业者认为对其实务有帮助的教育体验清单的最后。如果法律教育的一部分使命是奠定职业认同的基础,那么,未能培养对公共服务的忠实信念,是一项重大的失误。

最后一章总结了关于改革的建议和横亘在道路上的阻

碍。至关重要的是，减少律师协会对规制结构的控制，以及扩大公众参与的机会和建立问责制。更重要的是促使大量律师去解决执业条件、职业多样性、近用司法和法律教育等方面的基本问题。我们并不缺乏改革战略。剩下的挑战就是让律师们确信，在这一过程中，他们利害攸关。

02
Chapter

第二章
执业条件

- 变革的驱动力
- 利润优先
- 对实务活动的满意度
- 错位的优先事项
- 改革战略

"美国律师事务所的'钱'景不妙",这是《经济学人》的一个鲜明标题。① 这种悲观情绪反映了论者们的普遍看法,律师们的情绪则常常是渴望辞职。许多人哀叹,更为幸福的时代已经逝去,那个时候与商业相比,法律更像是职业。② 在当前的法律市场中,竞争和商业化在上升,而文明礼貌和共治则反向而行。③ 然而,尽管执业的压力似乎有可能增加,但是律师协会并没有表现出能够改变这些动因或者重塑其未来的迹象。

本章探讨了美国法律职业近期趋势的原因和后果。它特别关注律师在中型和大型律师事务所的实务活动,因为这些律师事务所是律师行业的领先者,在其工作场所的条件上发挥着最大的影响力。然而,本章所描述的许多动因适用于更广泛的领域,并对整个职业构成了挑战。法律实务活动中的

---

① *The Economist*, May 7, 2011, at 73.

② 关于对这些主题的探讨,see Anthony Kronman, The Lost Lawyer: Failing Ideals of the Legal Profession (1992).

③ 在美国律师协会的一项研究中,69%的律师认为文明礼貌程度在下降,大型律师事务所的 90%的律师发现律师事务所之间的竞争在加剧。Stephanie Francis Ward, Pulse of the Legal Profession, *ABA J.*, Oct. 2007, at 31-32. See also Jeffrey A. Parness, Civility Initiatives: The 2009 Allerton House Conference, *96 Ill. B. J*, at 636, 637 (Dec. 2008) (法官和律师一致认为,在过去 10 年中,民事诉讼的不礼貌行为数量激增)。

所有这些趋势对于法律而言并非独一无二的。一些是由更广泛的市场和社会力量共同作用的。但是不管是什么原因,律师需要对影响他们职业生活的条件有更多的控制,这对于律师而言,有着利害关系。

/ 变革的驱动力 /

- 规模

当代法律职业中最重要的变化之一,就是业务体量和规模的扩大。在 1960 年,最大的律师事务所有 169 名律师。今天最大的律师事务所律师已经超过 4000 人。[①] 从 1978 年到 2008 年,全国 250 家最大的律师事务所的平均规模增加了 4 倍多,从 102 名律师发展到 535 名律师。[②] 在过去的四十年中,律师的数量大约翻了两番。[③] 结果是竞争的加剧,共治关系的紧张,以及供求之间的不匹配。应届法律毕业生的数量

---

① NLJ 350: Our Annual Survey of the Nation's Largest Law Firms, *Nat'l L. J.*, Jun. 10, 2013 (它给出的数字是 4036 人). See Steven J. Harper, *The Lawyer Bubble* 69 (2013) (在 2012 年超过了 4200 人).

② William Henderson, From Big Law to Lean Law, *3 Int'l Rev. L. & Econ.* 1 (2013).

③ Thomas Morgan, *The Vanishing American Lawyer* 81 (2010). 1950 年,每 687 个美国人中有 1 名律师,今天,每 254 个美国人中有 1 名律师。Benjamin Barton, *Glass Half Full: America's Lawyer Crisis and Its Upside* (forthcoming, 2015).

远远超过了市场可提供的入门级职位。① 但是,正如第三章所指出的那样,与律师的供过于求并存的是,中产阶级和低收入美国人的法律服务供给不足。在低端市场,律师不能以许多消费者支付得起的价格提供帮助。② 在高端市场,对于法律服务的需求与律师的供应不匹配。正如一位论者所指出的那样,"今天高价律师比高价法律工作要多得多……事实上,你们与主要律师事务所的合伙人和非合伙律师谈得越多,你就越能感觉到,这就像是一个庞大的心理实验:老鼠们被关在一个笼子里,而里面的面包屑太少了。"③

● **竞争**

规模的增加并不是导致竞争加剧的唯一力量。联邦最高法院关于广告的判决,减少了反竞争的限制。④ 消费者的需求,限制了律师协会在某些涉法服务方面制止非律师人员竞争的能力。会计师事务所对法律职业的传统地盘形成了特别的威胁。全球化给美国金融中心带来了更多的外国竞争者。它还鼓励委托人将业务外包给离岸法律服务提供者。

其他的动因也减少了对律师的需求,加剧了对剩下的法

---

① 参见第六章。
② Paul Campos, *Don't Go to Law School* (*Unless*) 5-6 (2013).
③ Norm Scheiber, The Last Days of Big Law, *New Republic*, Jul. 21, 2013.
④ *Bates v. Arizona State Bar*, 433 U.S. 350 (1977); *Zauderer v. Office of Disciplinary Counsel*, 471 U.S. 626 (1985); *Shapiro v. Kentucky Bar Association*, 486 U.S. 466 (1988).

律工作的竞争。技术正在取代对许多律师服务的需求。① 对于为自然人委托人提供服务的律师,文件制作服务(例如 LegalZoom)正在获得越来越多的法律市场份额。理查德·萨斯坎德(Richard Susskind)曾认为,对于几乎所有法律实务领域的律师而言,传统的"工匠"律师模式正在被商品化的法律工作所取代,而更广泛的经济带来的"物美价廉"的无情压力,将强化这一趋势。② 技术驱动的法律服务提供者"不只是吃着大型律师事务所的午餐;他们还盯着早餐和晚餐"③。同样,在自己的市场上面临越来越大压力的公司委托人,也在通过削减法律成本作出回应。企业已经把更多的例行工作放在了内部,外包项目更多是基于短期竞争的考虑,而不是基于长期的律师—委托人关系的考虑。尽管很少有领导人会像 Finley Kumble 律师事务所的管理合伙人那样把它说得那么粗鲁,但"从其他律师事务所窃取律师和委托人",已经成为"进步的基石"。④

随着律师事务所内部竞争的加剧,窃取其他合伙人的委托人的行为也变得更加普遍。"自食其力"的薪酬结构加剧了

---

① Richard Susskind, *The End of Lawyers* (2010); Henderson, From Big Law to Lean Law.

② Richard Susskind, *Tomorrow's Lawyers: An Introduction to Your Future* 3 (2013); Susskind, *From The End of Lawyers*.

③ Rachel M. Zahorsky & William D. Henderson, Who's Eating Law Firms' Lunch? *ABA J.*, Oct. 2013, at 34.

④ Kim Isaac Eisler, *Shark Tank: Greed, Politics, and the Collapse of Finley Kumble, One of America's Largest Law Firms* 84 (1990).

紧张关系,因为这种结构对拉来业务实施奖励,从而鼓励积聚和争夺那些能拉来业务的人。在大型律师事务所中,只有一半的受访合伙人感到能得到其他合伙人的支持。①

经济衰退加剧了所有这些竞争压力。委托人越来越多地采取削减成本的措施,例如,拒绝支付培训初级非合伙律师的费用。律师事务所的反应则是冻结雇用、裁员和取消收益不佳的合伙人的股权。一些论者乐观地认为,随着经济回升、婴儿潮一代退休、人口增长,形势将会有所好转。② 然而,即使经济复苏了,压力依然存在,大多数律师认为,法律市场的这些变化将是永久性的。③

/ 利润优先 /

● 制度性的优先事项的起因和后果

许多问题的根源是利润的优先地位。因为金钱是几乎每

---

① Chris Klein, Big Firm Partners: Profession Sinking, Nat'l L. J., May 26, 1997.

② René Reich-Graefe, Keep Calm and Carry On, 27 Geo. J. Legal Ethics, 55, 63-66 (2014). 就几十年来大型律师事务所的死亡被过分夸大的观点,see Mark Obbie, The Fascinating Vampire Squids of Law, Slate, Jul. 24, 2013, http://www.slate.com/articles/news_and_politics/jurisprudence/2013/07/death_of_big_law_new_republic_s_claim_is_grossly_exaggerated.html.

③ LexisNexis, State of the Legal Industry Survey: Complete Survey Findings 10 (2009).

个人都最关心的问题,所以在经济回报上达成共识比在其他价值上达成共识更容易,比如更短的工作时间、非合伙律师培训或者重大公益投入。那些为其他工作满意度而牺牲薪酬的律师事务所会有这样的风险,即失去那些喜欢更高收入并且拥有可以带走的委托人的优秀员工。一旦建立了高工资标准,他们就很容易变得自我延续;向下流动的前景令人感到痛苦。即使是在进入法学院时有着其他追求的律师,也常常会被困在这些报酬循环中。如果他们没有经济能力做他们真正喜欢的公益工作,他们希望至少他们所做的事情可以得到很好的报酬。对律师事务所按照每个合伙人的利润进行评级的媒体排名制度,加上律师薪酬的透明化,也导致了律师事务所牺牲其他价值来追求短期利润。

律师事务所规模越大,地理分布越分散,横向人员流动量越高,它就越难以维系共同的文化,就越难以确定与短期利润相抗衡的优先事项。[1] 2000年以来,大型律师事务所之间的合伙人的流动率也增长了50%。[2] 在这种文化中,制度上的忠诚、信任和共治的纽带变得更加脆弱。律师将注意力集中在拉业务和计费工时上,扭曲了激励结构,因而这一问题变得更加复杂,这是以诸如牺牲促进集体利益的指导性活动为

---

[1] See Larry E. Ribstein, The Death of Big Law, 2010 *Wisc. L. Rev.* 749, 775.

[2] See William D. Henderson, More Complex than Greed, *Am. Law. Daily*, May 29, 2012.

第二章
执业条件

代价的。① 合伙人将花费更多的时间来营销他们的服务,更少有机会和动机来培训下级同事,这些下级同事中的大多数有可能离职。

追求每个合伙人的利润率,还有其他不良后果。特别是在大型律师事务所,它使得合伙关系更不容易达成,在某些方面也不那么吸引人。许多律师事务所降低了股权合伙人的比例,延长了进入合伙的路径,并创设了其他身份,例如收入合伙人、特邀律师或者永久非合伙律师。越来越少的律师可以获得股权合伙人身份,它不再承诺终身保障,或者进行更为理智的日常安排。② 随着晋升机会的减少,更多的非合伙律师体验到了拉·罗什富科(La Rochefoucauld)的洞察力:仅仅成功是不够的,其他人必须失败。任何成功都只是暂时的。缺乏足够业务的合伙人,可能会失去他们的地位。对许多律师来说,争取晋升的努力,看起来越来越像是"吃馅饼比赛,奖品是

---

① Ribstein, The Death of Big Law, at 755-756; Barton, *Glass Half Full*; William D. Henderson & Leonard Beirman, An Empirical Analysis of Lateral Lawyer Trends from 2000 to 2007: The Emerging Equilibrium for Corporate Law Firms, *22 Geo. J. Legal Ethics* 1395 (2009); Harper, *The Lawyer Bubble*, at 70; Ben W. Heineman, Jr., William F. Lee & David B. Wilkins, Lawyers as Professionals and Citizens: Key Roles and Responsibilities in the 21st Century 35 (2014).

② Deborah L. Rhode, *In the Interests of Justice: Reforming the Legal Profession* 35 (2000); Ashby Jones, Law-Firm Life Doesn't Suit Some Associates, *Wall St. J.*, May 23, 2006, at B6.

更多的馅饼"①。

- **计费工时**

利润的优先地位也助长了计费工时的暴政。三十年前,大多数合伙人每年的计费时数是在1200个小时和1400个小时之间,大多数非合伙律师的计费时数在1400个小时和1600个小时之间。如今,许多律师事务所都认为,只有对那些在年中去世的律师来说,这些值域才是可以接受的。② 平均而言,非合伙律师每年收费时数接近1900个小时,而大型事务所的数据则显然更高。③ 在这个水平上诚实地开具账单,需要每周工作50个至60个小时。从某种程度上说,技术通过加快实务活动的步伐和让律师没完没了地打电话,使情况变得更为糟糕。法律服务的截止期限没完没了,律师仍然被电子邮件和手机拴在工作场所。尽管这些技术的好的一面,是使律师更有可能在家里工作,但是他们也使得在家不工作的可能性降低了。个人生活在匆匆忙忙中迷失了方向。④ 在新年前夕收到一位委托人发来的电子邮件,因为律师事务所在周日早

---

① Marie Beaudette, Associates Leave Firm in Droves, *Nat'l L. J.*, Oct. 6, 2003, at A1 (quoting Mark Plotkin).

② Patrick J. Schlitz, On Being a Happy, Healthy, and Ethical Member of an Unhappy, Unhealthy, and Unethical Profession, *52 Vand. L. Rev.* 871 (1999).

③ Nancy Levit & Douglas O. Linder, *The Happy Lawyer: Making a Good Life in the Law* 54 (2010); Harper, The Lawyer Bubble, at 78.

④ Harper, The Lawyer Bubble, at 97.

第二章
执业条件

上的回应不够迅速而解雇了律师事务所,这并不少见。某律师事务所的一名非合伙律师叙述了一个常见的经历:一名合伙人"走进办公室,问你周末是否有任何计划。正确的回答是'没有'"。第一次被问及这个问题的时候,该非合伙律师犯了一个错误,他实事求是回答了这个问题,咕哝着说希望去佛蒙特州办事。"那个合伙人'又是怀疑又是同情地看着他'……'这是一个很讲究艺术的问题'"[①]。

律师事务所经常把令人心碎的日程安排归咎于委托人的需求。但是有理由相信,还有其他因素也在起着作用。委托人不会从睡眼惺忪、疲惫不堪的律师那里得到高效的服务。主要的问题是,计费工时制度将利润与花费的时间联系在了一起,而不是与时间使用效率联系在一起,利润已成为主要关注点。高计费工时量也筛选出了具有竞争价值的人。愿意长时间工作代表着愿意投入。那些最常被排除在外的,是承担着繁重家庭责任的律师,通常是女性。但是这一结果被认为是竞争性执业文化的一个虽然令人遗憾但必要的副产品,而不值一提。其结果是民间的军备竞赛,个人成本不断攀升。尽管律师作为一个群体,会受益于一个更为正常的日程安排,但是大多数执业者不愿去冒单方面退出竞争的风险。

[①] Jonathan Foreman, My Life as an Associate, *City J.*, Winter 1997.

/ 对实务活动的满意度 /

● **满意率**

在回顾法律实务活动的最新趋势后,斯坦福大学法学院院长拉里·克雷默(Larry Kramer)问道:"有人真的想要这个吗?"①同样重要的是,律师在多大程度上对其职业生涯感到快乐呢?

事实证明,这是一个复杂得令人惊讶的问题,答案取决于你问的是谁和你怎么问。问的是短期满意度还是长期成就感?这项调查是否只包括当前的执业者,这当然会排除那些最可能不满意的人:那些已经完全离开了法律的人士。不满的个人也可能不太会对调查问卷作出反应,从而使满意率上升。② 专家还指出,有关工作满意度的直接问题,往往会产生过于积极的结果;人们不愿意向陌生人,甚至对自己承认,他们不快乐,也没有采取措施来纠正这种情况。更能透露真情的满意度测量,往往来自不太直接的问题,例如律师是否打算离职,或者他们是否会为自己或者子女作出同样的

---

① Marc S. Galanter & William D. Henderson, The Change Agenda: Tournament Without End, *Am. Law.*, Dec. 2008 (quoting Kramer).

② David L. Chambers, Overstating the Satisfaction of Lawyers, *39 Law & Soc. Inq.* 1, 18 (2013).

职业选择。

　　承认存在这些困难的最有效的数据来自对 25 年以来进行的调查的整合分析。它发现,大约 80% 的律师表示,他们非常满意、有些满意、或者对自己的工作感到满意。① 在美国律师协会的大规模纵向研究中,76% 的年轻律师对自己成为律师的决定相当或者极其满意。② 全国意见研究中心的职业比较研究发现,大约一半的律师(52%)非常满意,这个数字略高于美国人总体水平(47%)。③ 但是情况可能会更好。法律未能跻身于满意度排名前十二的行业。④ 在工作特点的评级上,如可预测的工作增长、中位数工资、就业率、压力水平和工作—生活平衡,法律排名第 51。⑤ 律师对其工作的评级,与会计师、民用工程师和汽车销售人员相同,并且显著低于牙医、工程师、医生、警察和房地产中介。⑥ 在《美国律师协会期刊》

---

　　① Jerome M. Organ, What Do We Know About the Satisfaction/Dissatisfaction of Lawyers? A Meta-Analysis of Research on Lawyer Satisfaction and Well-Being, 8 U. St. Thomas L. J. 225, 262 (2011).

　　② Bryant Garth & Ronit Dinovitzer, Satisfaction, in After the JD III 50 (Gabriele Plickert, ed., 2014); Ronit Dinovitzer et al., After the JD II: Second Results From a National Study of Legal Careers (2009).

　　③ National Opinion Research Center, Job Satisfaction in the United States (2007).

　　④ Alan B. Krueger, Job Satisfaction Is Not Just a Matter of Dollars, N. Y. Times, Dec. 8, 2005, at C3.

　　⑤ Debra Cassnes Weiss, "Lawyer" Ranks 51st in US News List of Best Jobs in America, Down from 35th, ABA J., Jan. 27, 2014.

　　⑥ On the Job, Time, Oct. 30, 2006.

的一项调查中,虽然4/5的法律执业者为成为律师而自豪,但是只有大约一半的人会向年轻人推荐他们的职业。① 在其他调查中,60%到70%的律师表示将会选择其他职业。② 对那些对自己的工作感到满意的律师进行的一项深入调查发现,他们对自己的工作的某些方面,包括其社会价值和工作与生活的平衡,有了很大的疑虑;一半的人不会选择再上法学院。③

律师的不满情绪反映在其他量度上,如高离职率和心理困难。近半数的非合伙律师在3年内离开了律师事务所;3/4的在5年内离开。④ 估计有1/3的律师患有抑郁症、酗酒或者药物成瘾。他们的抑郁症患病率大约是其他美国人的3倍,药物滥用率几乎是其他美国人的2倍,在所有职业群体中律师的抑郁症患病率最高。⑤ 大约一半的律师报告说他

---

① Stephanie Ward, The Pulse of the Profession, at 34(发现80%的人感到自豪,但是仅有44%的人会向他人推荐)。

② 关于调查,see Levit & Linder, *The Happy Lawyer*, at 4; Becky Beaupre Gillespie & Hollee Schwartz Temple, Hunting Happy, *ABA J.*, Feb. 2011, at 41.

③ Chambers, Overstating the Satisfaction of Lawyers, at 7.

④ National Association for Law Placement (NALP), Update on Associate Attrition 11 (2006). See Kristin K. Stark & Blane Prescott, Why Associates Leave, *Legal Times*, May 7, 2007; National Association for Law Placement (NALP), Toward Effective Management of Associate Mobility 26 (2005) (40%在3年内离职,78%在5年内离职)。

⑤ See studies reviewed in Levit & Linder, *The Happy Lawyer*, at 6; Fred C. Zacharias, A Word of Caution for Lawyer Assistance Programs, *18 Geo. J. Legal Ethics* 237, 237 n1, 241 n15 (2004)(回顾了有关研究); Sue(转下页)

们很疲劳,压力很大。① 其后果对所有有关的人来说都代价高昂。虽然大多数律师事务所的经济模型都预示会有大量的离职,但是目前的非合伙律师的流失是有费效比问题的。大多数初级律师在产生可观利润之前离开了。② 每次离职都会带来用于招募和培训一个替补人员的 20 万美元到 50 万美元的费用,并在中断委托人和共治关系方面造成更难以量化的损失。③ 此外,离开的律师不一定是律师事务所想要失去的人;那些拥有最好的资质的人的不满意率最高。④ 通过药物和酒精来解决不满问题的律师,还会带来更多的成本;他们在这个职

(接上页)Shellenbarger, Even Lawyers Get the Blues: Opening Up About Depression, *Wall St. J.*, Dec. 13, 2007, at D1(指出大约 19% 的律师患有抑郁症,而总人口的抑郁发病率是 7%,20% 的人有药物滥用,而总人口的药物滥用率是 10%)。See Debra Cassins Weiss, Lawyer Depression Comes Out of the Closet, *ABA J.*, Dec. 2007; Jean Guiccione, Attorneys Find Defense Against Dependence, *L. A. Times*, Aug. 30, 2002, at B2.

① Mark B. Schenker et al., Self-Reported Stress and Reproductive Health of Female Lawyers, *39 J. Occup. & Envt'l Med*. 556 (1997); Susan Saab Fortney, The Billable Hours Derby: Empirical Data on the Problems and Pressure Points, *33 Fordham Urb. L. J.* 171, 183 (2005).

② See Deborah L. Rhode, Balanced Lives: Changing the Culture of Workplace Practices 20 (2002).

③ Rhode, *Balanced Lives*, at 21; Patti Giglio, Rethinking the Hours, *Legal Times*, Nov. 8, 2004, at 33; Stark & Prescott, Why Associates Leave, at 45; Cynthia Thomas Calvert, Linda Bray Chanow, & Linda Marks, Reduced Hours, Full Success: Part-Time Partners in U. S. Law Firms, *21 Hastings Women's L. J.* 223, 225 (2010).

④ Ronit Dinovitzer & Bryant Garth, Lawyer Satisfaction in the Process of Structuring Legal Careers, *41 Law & Soc'y Rev.* 1 (2007).

业的惩戒和业绩问题上,占据了非常不成比例的高份额。① 高度疲劳也会损害判断和决策。②

各实务领域的满意度各不相同。一般而言,在公共部门执业的律师比私人执业者更快乐,而大中型律师事务所的律师则最不满意。③ 在美国律师协会基金会的一项追踪年轻律师的职业生涯的研究中,最不满意的是那些在大型律师事务所工作的精英法学院的毕业生。这些律师只有 1/4 对自己成为律师的决定感到非常满意,60%的人说他们希望在未来 2 年内离职。来自排名较低的法学院的毕业生在所有的领域中都有较高的满意度。43%的对其职业选择是感到非常愉快的,仅有 40%的人计划在 2 年内换工作。④ 研究人员从期望值角度解释了这些变量:来自排名较高的法学院的毕业生拥有更大的应得权利感,当他们的工作没有达到期望标准时,他们的不

---

① Zacharias, A Word of Caution, at 241 n15; Nick Badgerow, Apocalypse at Law: The Four Horsemen of the Modern Bar—Drugs, Alcohol, Gambling, and Depression, 18 Prof. Law. 1 (2007).

② Martin Moore-Ede, *The Twenty-Four-Hour Society: Understanding Human Limits in a World That Never Stops* 133 (1993); Yvonne Harrison & James Horne, The Impact of Sleep Deprivation on Decision Making: A Review, 6 J. Exp. Psych. Applied 236 (2000); Susan Saab Fortney, Soul for Sale: An Empirical Study of Associate Satisfaction, Law Firm Culture, and the Effects of Billable Hour Requirements 58 UMKCI 238, 273 (2000) (2/3 的受访者认为长时间工作,会对其进行批判性和创造性思维的能力造成不利影响).

③ Ward, The Pulse of the Legal Profession; Organ, What Do We Know About the Satisfaction/Dissatisfaction of Lawyers, at 265; Garth &Dinovitzer, Satisfaction.

④ Dinovitzer & Garth, *After the JD*.

第二章
执业条件

满就会不成比例地高。

种族、性别、族裔和年龄也发挥着作用。总的来说,女性和少数族裔对自己的职业决定满意度并不低,尽管他们对执业的某些方面更不满意。① 在美国律师协会基金会对应届毕业生的研究中,非洲裔美国人最满意于他们成为律师的决定和他们的工作内容,但是最不满意的是社会条件、职业发展机会和影响力。② 与男性相比,女性更满意她们所做的事情内容,对其工作场所和机会不太满意;特别是如果是在一家大型律师事务所的话,她们也更有可能离职。③ 在《美国律师》最近的一项针对中层非合伙律师的调查中,与男性相比,女性在执业的所有方面都不满意,她们更有可能离职以实现工作和生活的更好平衡。④ 在其他研究中,有色人种女性是所有群体中对包括工作场所在内的几乎所有方面中感到最不满意的。⑤ 女

---

① Organ, What Do We Know About the Satisfaction/Dissatisfaction of Lawyers, at 265-266.

② Ronit Dinovitzer et al., After the JD: First Results of a National Study of Legal Careers 64 (2004).

③ Dinovitzer et al., *After the JD*, at 58; ABA Commission on Women in the Profession, A Current Glance at Women in the Law 2 (2006); studies cited in Theresa Beiner, Not All Lawyers Are Equal: Difficulties That Plague Women and Women of Color, *58 Syr. L. Rev.* 317, 321 n21 (2008).

④ Vivia Chen, He Said, She Said, *Am. Law.*, Sept. 2013, at 44.

⑤ 如果将其平均评定"表达为分数的话……有色女性将给其[职业生涯]打分为 B-或者 C+;白人男性将给其体验打分为 A;白人女性和有色男性将给其体验打分为 B。" Beiner, Not All Lawyers Are Equal, at 329. See also ABA Commission on Women in the Profession, Invisible Visibility:(转下页)

性和少数族裔的流动率也较高,这表明工作不满意率也比较高。① 总的来说,经验丰富的律师比年轻的律师更满意,部分原因是他们最终找到了最符合他们偏好的工作,而那些最不满意的人则退出了这个职业。②

• **满意度的来源**

什么能让律师感到更快乐?职业满意度是对遗传特征、工作条件和人际努力的综合反映。专家们普遍认为,就幸福而言,人们有一个基因决定的设定值,而至少50%的满意度变量反映了这一生理基线。③ 环境的变化,例如健康、财务和人际关系,使人们在幸福水平上上下移动,但是随着时间的推移,人们通常会回到他们的设定值。一些研究还表明,法律吸引了过多的具有较低设定值和不容易满足的人格特质的人。带来的职业回报往往是悲观、好斗和竞争,而不是培养关于满

(接上页) Women of Color in Law Firms and Minority Experience Study, discussed in D. M. Osborne, The Woman Question, *Am. Law.*, Nov. 2007, at 106 (指出少数族裔女性对工作质量、对工作的满意度和职业发展作出更低的评价).

① Dinovitzer & Garth, Lawyer Satisfaction, at 8.

② Organ, What Do We Know About the Satisfaction/Dissatisfaction of Lawyers, at 264.

③ David T. Lykken & Auke Tellegen, Happiness Is a Stochastic Phenomenon, 7 *Psych. Sci.* 186 (1996); Edward Diener et al., Subjective Well-Being: Three Decades of Progress, *125 Psych. Bull.* 276 (1999); Kennon M. Sheldon & Sonja Lyubomirsky, Achieving Sustainable Gains in Happiness: Change Your Actions, Not Your Circumstances, 7 *J. Happiness Stud.* 55, 56 (2006); Levit & Linder, *The Happy Lawyer*, at 42.

第二章
执业条件

足感的看法和共治关系。① 然而,律师的特征不能解释不同的实务领域在满意度水平上的差异。即使是强调遗传倾向的重要性的研究人员,也会注意到个体改善的可能性。人们不需要让他们的"基因舵手为所欲为……他们可以在相当大的自由度内控制他们的目的地……"②工作的性质和条件也很重要。工作满意度取决于职位在多大程度上满足自尊、控制、称职性、安全感和与他人的关系等基本心理需求。③

---

① Martin E. P. Seligman, Why Lawyers Are Unhappy, 23 Cardozo L. Rev. 1, 34 (2001); Levit & Linder, The Happy Lawyer, at 75. 就关于律师个性类型的概述, see Susan Daicoff, Lawyer, Know Thyself: A Psychological Analysis of Personality Strengths and Weaknesses (2004); Susan Daicoff, Lawyer, Know Thyself: A Review of Empirical Research on Attorney Attributes Bearing on Professionalism, 46 Am. U. L. Rev. 1337 (1997). 就乐观主义的重要性, see Edward Diener et al. Subjective Well Being: Three Decades of Progress, 125 Psych. Bull. 276 (1999).

② David T. Lykken, Happiness: The Nature and Nurture of Joy and Contentment 60 (2000); Sheldon & Lyubomirsky, Achieving Sustainable Gains in Happiness 55, 57-58, 60 (2006). Levit & Linder, The Happy Lawyer, at 44; William C. Compton, Introduction to Positive Psychology 48-49, 53-54 (2004); Kennon Sheldon, What Is Satisfying About Satisfying Events? Testing 10 Candidate Psychological Needs, 80 J. Personality & Soc. Psych. 325, 325-327 (2001); Diener et al., Subjective Well-Being, at 276.

③ David G. Myers, The Pursuit of Happiness 32-38 (1992); David G. Myers & Edward Diener, Who is Happy? 6 Psych. Sci. 13 (1995); surveys reviewed in Deborah L. Rhode, In the Interests of Justice 26 (1999). 就关于力量与美德的讨论, see Compton, Introduction to Positive Psychology, at 170-172; C. Peterson & Martin P. Seligman, Character Strengths and Virtues: A Handbook and Classification (2004).

总的来说，当人们觉得自己能达到预期效果，发挥了自己的长处和优点，能迎接生活的挑战，并为具有意义和目的的社会价值目标作出贡献时，他们是最快乐的。① 对高度成功的个人的研究，发现了成功的四个结构域："快乐（快乐或者知足的感觉）；成就（与其他人努力追求的类似目标相比的成就感）；意义（正面影响的感觉）；遗产（帮助他人找到未来成功的路径）"②。持久的成功包括在所有四个领域中找到平衡点，并且在每个领域中实现"刚刚好"③。正如研究表明的那样，个人受益于造福他人。志愿工作不仅与更大的满意度有关，而且与更多的身心健康和自尊相关。④ 对于律师而言，公益活动能促进职业发展；它们是建立技能、声誉和关系的一种方式，同时

---

① Laura Nash & Howard Stevenson, Success That Lasts, *Harv. Bus. Rev. Rev.*, Feb. 2004, at 104. See also Laura Nash & Howard Stevenson, *Just Enough: Tools for Creating Success in Your Work and Life* (2004).

② Nash & Stevenson, *Just Enough*.

③ See research summarized in Alan Luks with Peggy Payne, *The Healing Power of Doing Good* xi-xii, 17-18, 45-54, 60 (2d ed., 2001); John Wilson & Marc Musick, The Effects of Volunteering, *62 Law & Contemp. Probs.* 141, 142-143 (1999); Marc A. Musick, A. Regula Herzog, & James S. House, Volunteering and Mortality Among Older Adults: Findings From a National Sample, *548 J. Gerontol*. S173, S178 (1999); John M. Darley, Altruism and Prosocial Behavior Research: Reflections and Prospects, in *Prosocial Behavior* 312-327 (Margaret S. Clark, ed., 1991).

④ Deborah L. Rhode, *Pro Bono in Principle and in Practice* 29-30 (2005); Deborah L. Rhode, Profits and Professionalism, *33 Fordham Urb. L. J.* 49, 58 (2005).

也促进了这些人所致力的事业。①

● **不满意的原因**

当代律师执业工作的结构在太多方面是不利于满意度的。一系列问题涉及法律实务活动的实质和期望与现实之间的差距。人们通常选择法律作为职业,但对律师的实际工作知之甚少。出现在媒体的黄金时段的法律,常常展现的是财富、权力、戏剧和英雄机遇的组合。在现实生活中,法律则是其他的东西,特别是对于那些在社会底层的人而言。没有人会去制作名为"文件制作大冒险"或者叫做"进行尽职调查的人"的影片。② 某些法律事务纯粹是苦差事,要求付出很大的代价。最有声望的学校的应届毕业生虽然在最具声望的律师事务所工作,但是对自己的职业表达了最大的不满,这并不奇怪。他们对其资质有着更多的期望。③

心理学家马丁·塞利格曼(Martin Seligman)就法律工作的

---

① Allen K. Roston, Lawyers, Law and the Movies: The Hitchock Cases, 86 Cal. L. Rev. 211, 214 (1998).

② Dinovitzer & Garth, Lawyer Satisfaction; see also K. Charles Cannon, *The Ultimate Guide to Your Legal Career* 4, 9 (2007)(指出那些陷于单调乏味的文件审查的非合伙律师的幻灭,他们感到"这并不是他们去哈佛法学院读书所想要干的事")。

③ Seligman, Why Lawyers Are Unhappy, at 47-48(讨论了实务活动的对抗性); Ward, Pulse of the Profession, at 31(指出69%的律师认为,法律职业已经变得不那么温文尔雅了); Walt Bachman, *Law vs. Life*: *What Lawyers Are Afraid to Say About the Legal Profession* 117 (1995)(描述了法律职业的刻薄性)。

实质,指出了进一步问题。他强调了实务活动中的对抗性、零和性、不文明的方面,以及作为下级非合伙律师的主要生活特点,即无法控制的压力。① 事实证明,自愿性文明守则在遏制滥权方面是无效的,而且律师行业规模的扩大已经削弱了非正式制裁的威力。在实务活动中,执业者经常看到的是粗暴无礼所带来的回报。在诉讼中以使用污言秽语和进行人身侮辱而闻名的乔·贾麦尔(Jo Jamail),在他的母校得克萨斯大学,却获得了两尊雕像,甚至不是一尊。②

其他研究人员指出,律师经常会在委托人处于压力之下与其会面,并且会传达法律程序的不受欢迎的讯息。当律师扮演"苦难的商人"的角色,成为不是他们自己制造的用来争吵的替罪羊时,他们肯定会感到不满。③

执业律师还强调了其他因素。在他们的说法中,职业发展问题以及工作与生活的平衡,比法律实务活动的实质或者对抗性发挥着更重要的作用。④ 在美国律师协会一项全国性调查中,超过4/5 的律师发现他们的工作在智力上是令人兴奋的。⑤ 根据美国

---

① Douglas O. Linder & Nancy Levit, *The Good Lawyer: Seeking Quality in the Practice of Law*, 108 (2014).

② Levit & Linder, *The Happy Lawyer*, at 65.

③ National Association for Law Placement [NALP], Toward Effective Management of Associate Mobility: A Status Report on Attrition 35 – 36, 39, 42 (2005); NALP, Update on Associate Attrition 25 (2006).

④ Ward, The Pulse of the Profession, at 32.

⑤ ABA Young Lawyers Division, Career Satisfaction Survey 20 (2000); ABA Young Lawyers Division, Career Satisfaction Survey 11 (1995).

第二章
执业条件

律师协会的其他研究,律师对实务活动感到失望的最主要的原因,是"缺乏与社会福祉之间的联系"。① 只有16%的律师报告说,他们为社会福祉作出贡献的能力与他们开始执业时的期望相符。② 正如一份职业指南所说的那样,委托人追求的结果一般"不会让世界变得更美好"。③ 在一定程度上是出于对社会正义的关注而选择法律职业的人,经常像阿奇博尔德·麦柯勒斯(Archibald MacLeish)④那样,不太关心90万美元的归属问题。⑤

对这种不满的一个明显的回应是公益工作。然而,许多法律雇主在原则上更赞同这种参与,在实践中则不太支持。当全国法律就业协会和美国律师协会基金会最近进行的一项联合研究要求入行相对较晚的律师对16个方面的工作满意度进行评定时,他们把公益机会排在倒数第二位。⑥ 在我自己的调查中,大约半数的律师对公益活动的数量和质量表示不满。⑦ 就

---

① ABA Young Lawyers Division, Career Satisfaction Survey 17 (2000).
② Cannon, The Ultimate Guide, at 13.
③ Richard Delgado & Jean Stefancic, *How Lawyers Lose Their Way* 15 (2005).
④ 美国诗人,曾就读于耶鲁大学和哈佛大学法学院,在波士顿担任过律师。他发现法律很肮脏,大多数案件都是关于90万美元的归属问题,对社会不是特别有用。——译者注
⑤ Dinovitzer et al., *After the JD*, at 49.
⑥ Rhode, *Pro Bono*, at 147-148.
⑦ Rhode, *Pro Bono*, at 20, 148; ABA Standing Committee on Pro Bono and Public Service, Supporting Justice II: A Report on the Pro Bono Work of America's Lawyers (2013). 美国律师协会根据《示范规则》第6.1条,就公益的定义使用了一个极其宽泛的定义,包括参与律师协会的活动。

像第三章所指出的那样,只有大约 1/3 的律师平均每周有至少 1 小时的慈善工作,而所谓的慈善工作包括律师协会的工作,给其他律师、委托人和家庭帮忙,监督律师的"宠物组织"。① 仅有 1/4 的律师所在的律所将公益工作完全计算在计费工时内,几乎 2/3 的律师认为,这类工作在晋升和薪酬决策中是一个消极或者不重要的因素。②

然而,高回报意味着要接受加班加点和不灵活的时间安排。《纽约客》上的一幅漫画反映了流行的观点:一个富有的专业人士在为年轻的同事提供建议,"全身心扑在工作上,没有娱乐,这能使你成为一个有价值的雇员。"③然而,这是造成不满和离职的主要原因,特别是女性,她们承担着过多的家庭责任。④ 只有 1/5 全职工作的母亲对她们照顾孩子的时间感

---

① Rhode, *Pro Bono*, at 138-140.

② Lee Collum, *The New Yorker*, Oct. 30, 1998, available at http://www.Cartoonbank.com.

③ Joan Williams, *Unbending Gender* 71-73 (2000); Boston Bar Association Task Force on Work-Family Challenges, Facing the Grail: Confronting the Course of Work Family Imbalance 39 (1999); Catalyst, A New Approach to Flexibility: Managing the Work Time Equation 20-21 (1997). 她们照看孩子的时间是男性的 2 倍,做家务的时间是男性的 3 倍。U.S. Department of Labor, Bureau of Labor Statistics, American Time Use Survey, 2012; Ruth Davis Konigsberg, Chore Wars, *Time*, Aug. 8, 2011, at 47.

④ Jean E. Wallace, Juggling It All: Exploring Lawyers' Work, Home, and Family Demands and Coping Strategies 15 (Law School Admission Council Research Report, RR-00-02, Sept. 2002).

第二章
执业条件

到满意。① 那些临时离职以解决这一问题的女性,在准备回来时,往往找不到令人满意的职位。② 大多数受调查的律师表示,他们没有给自己和他们的家人留足够时间。③ 只有 1/3 到一半的律师相信他们的雇主会支持平衡生活和工作的灵活安排。④ 据一位非合伙律师说,她所在的律师事务所解决这个问题的办法是举办研讨会,就如何"外包你的生活"提供建议。⑤ 但是过长

---

① Sylvia Ann Hewlett & Carolyn Buck Luce, Off Ramps and On Ramps: Keeping Talented Women on the Road to Success, *Harv. Bus. Rev.*, Mar. 2005, at 43, 45(被调查的选择离职的职业女性中,1/4 未能找到可以接受的工作,半数未能找到全职岗位)。

② ABA Young Lawyers Division Survey, Career Satisfaction, Table 20 (2000).

③ Gregory J. Mazores, Association Retention for Law Firms: What Are Your Lawyers Saying About You? 29 *Cap. U. L. Rev.* 903, 904 (2002)(发现仅有1/3 的非合伙律师认为,他们所在的律师事务所的律师被鼓励在工作与工作之外的生活之间保持平衡); Martha Neil, Lawyers Shun Firms' Offers of Part-Time Work, *Chi. L. Bull.*, Dec. 18, 2000, at 1(提出大约半数的被调查执业者怀疑其雇主是否真心支持灵活的工作场所安排)。

④ Noam Scheiber, The Last Days of Big Law, *New Republic*, Jul. 21, 2013.

⑤ 几乎半数的女性律师和几乎 2/3 的每周工作超过 45 小时的人,认为工作压力对其生殖健康造成不利影响。Schenker et al., Self-Reported Stress and Reproductive Health of Female Lawyers. See also Mary Beth Grover, Daddy Stress, *Forbes*, Sept. 6, 1999, at 202(指出了男性魅力的问题)。压力也会对幸福感产生不利影响。Gregg Easterbrook, *The Progress Paradox: How Life Gets Better While People Feel Worse* 191 (2003). 就过度工作压力的成本的讨论,see Sylvia Ann Hewlett & Carolyn Buck Luce, Extreme Jobs: The Dangerous Allure of the 70-Hour Workweek, *Harv. Bus. Rev.*, Dec. 2006; Jill Andresky Fraser, *White-Collar Sweatshop* 36-37 (2001); Families and Work Institute, Feeling Overworked: When Work Becomes Too Much 5-8 (2001).

的工时会带来巨大成本。过度劳累是导致律师的压力、药物滥用、生殖机能障碍和心理健康等问题高比例发生的主要原因。[1]

/ 错位的优先事项 /

为什么这么多的律师忍受了实务活动这些不利的方面,为什么这么多的法律雇主未能作出调整,以提高满意度,改进招聘、留用和绩效? 解释是相互关联的。如果有太少的心怀不满的律师用脚投票,雇主们就没有太多的动机作出回应。同样,如果有太少的律所贯彻实施了有效的改革,那么律师很少有别的地方可以投奔。

产生问题的部分原因是,人们对什么会使他们快乐出乎意料地不能作出正确判断,律师也不例外。心理学家发现了许多干扰理性选择的因素。关注高度显著的事件或者其他外在的奖赏,会夸大它们实际带来幸福的重要性。[2] 因此,举例

---

[1] Daniel Kahneman et al., Would You Be Happier if You Were Richer? A Focusing Illusion, *312 Science* 1908 (2006); Christopher K. Hsee & Reid Hastie, Decision and Experience: Why Don't We Choose What Makes Us Happy, *10 Trends Cogn. Sci.* 31 (2006).

[2] Seligman, *Authentic Happiness*, 49; Edward Diener, Richard E. Lucas, & Christie Napa Scollon, Beyond the Hedonic Treadmill: Revising the Adaptation Theory of Well-Being, *61 Am. Psych.* 305 (2006); Kennon M. Sheldon & Sonia Lyubomirsky, Achieving Sustainable Gains in Happiness: Change Your Actions, Not Your Circumstances, *7 J. Happiness Stud.* 55, 60 (2006);(转下页)

来说,律师可能高估了成为合伙人或者取得巨额奖金所能带来的好处。欲望、期望和比较标准,往往会随着它们的实现而迅速增加。人们被困在了"享乐跑步机"上:他们拥有的越多,需要拥有的就越多。① 正如心理学家戴维·迈尔斯(David Myers)所指出的那样,最好是让"我们最好的经历成为我们经常经历的事情,而不是为了追求偶然且难以捉摸的大奖而牺牲每天的快乐"②。满意度与其说是去得到你想要的东西,而不如说是安分知足。③

- 金钱

特别是,与包括律师在内的大多数人通常认为的相比,金钱在提升个人满意度方面的作用要小得多。当被问及什么事情最有可能让他们更加快乐时,大多数美国人回答是"更多的钱"。④ 然

(接上页)Edward Diener & Robert Biswas-Diener, Will Money Increase Subjective Well Being? A Literature Review and Guide to Needed Research, 57 Soc. Ind. Res. 119 (2002).

① Myers, Pursuit of Happiness, at 63.
② Myers, Pursuit of Happiness, at 39.
③ Sonja Lyubomirsky, The How of Happiness: A New Approach to Getting the Life You Want 44 (2007); Eric Weiner, The Geography of Bliss 310 (2008).
④ David G. Myers & Ed Diener, Who Is Happy? 6 Psych. Sci. 12, 13 (1995); Juliet B. Schur, The Overspent American 7 (1998); Robert F. Frank, Luxury Fever 72, 112-113 (1999); Rhode, In the Interests of Justice, at 26; Levit & Linder, The Happy Lawyer, at 38-39; Matthew Herper, Money Won't Buy You Happiness, Forbes, Sept. 21, 2004, http://www.forbes.com/2004/09/21/cx_mh_0921happiness.html; Eric Quinones, Link Between Income and Happiness Is Mainly an Illusion, Jun. 29, 2006, http://www.princeton.edu/main/news/archive/S15/15/09S18/index.xml.

而，大多数研究人员发现，对于在律师这样的收入水平上的人来说，薪酬的差异与满意度的差异关系不大。① 赚取20万美元的人并不比收入仅此一半的人感到更幸福。② 在不同的法律实务领域中，薪酬与成就感之间没有关系。就像前面所指出的那样，在收入相对较低的公共利益和公共部门雇员中，不满情绪最不明显。③

财富与满足感脱节的一个原因是，高收入所能买到的大部分东西并不能产生持久的幸福感。就像丹尼尔·吉尔伯特（Daniel Gilbert）所说的那样，"我们认为金钱会在很长一段时间内带来许多幸福，但它实际上仅仅在短时间内带来一点点快乐。"④新买到的东西或者环境改变所带来的新奇性，很快就会消失，它们带来的短暂快感在促进幸福感方面，不如其他因

---

① Frank, *Luxury Fever*, at 183; Robert E. Lane, Does Money Buy Happiness, 113 *Pub. Int*. 56, 61, 63 (1993). See Daniel Gilbert, *Stumbling on Happiness* 217 (2006)（指出赚500万美元的人并不比赚10万美元的人幸福多少）。

② Dinovitzer, *After the JD*, at 8, 10; Kenneth G. Dau-Schmidt & Kaushik Mukhopadhaya, The Fruits of Our Labors: An Empirical Study of the Distribution of Income and Job Satisfaction Across the Legal Profession, 49 *J. Legal Educ*. 342, 346-347 (1999); Marc Galanter, Old and in the Way: The Coming Demographic Transformation of the Legal Profession and Its Implications for the Provision of Legal Services, 1999 *Wisc. L. Rev.* 1081, 1105-1106.

③ Lyubomirsky, *The How of Happiness*, at 17 (quoting Daniel Gilbert).

④ Seligman, *Authentic Happiness*, at xiii（认为愉悦与持久的幸福关系更少，与参与各种关系和有意义的感觉关系更大，后者涉及运用个人能力作出更广泛的社会贡献）; Herper, Money Won't Buy You Happiness; Jonathan Haidt, *The Happiness Hypothesis: Finding Modern Truth in Ancient Wisdom* 83 (2006)（指出如何适应不断完善的物质环境侵蚀了他们的价值观）。

素那样重要,例如个人与家人、朋友和社区的关系,以及他们为更大的社会目标作出贡献的感觉。① 金钱的影响力有限的第二个原因是,满意度受相对而非绝对收入的影响最大,而财富的增加通常会被参考群体的变化抵消。② 在很大程度上,薪酬是一种"地位利益";个人对工资的满意程度取决于其相对于他人的地位。③ 正如 H.L.门肯(H. L. Mencken)曾经所说的那样,"一个富有的人就是比他妻子的妹夫多赚了 100 美元的人"④。

然而,律师薪酬的日益公开化使得相对收入的竞争更容易进行,也更难取胜。《美国律师》前编辑史蒂文·布里尔(Steven Brill)指出,一旦法律期刊开始比较律师事务所的工资,"突然间,一个赚 25 万美元的快乐的合伙人变得不满,因为他读到在下一个街区的律师事务所的同学们赚的是 30 万美元。"⑤这种军备竞赛几乎没有几个赢家,失败者则很多。事实

---

① Kahneman et al., Would You Be Happier, at 1910. See also Myers, *Pursuit of Happiness*, at 39 (指出满意度是一个功能而不是对实际财富的感知); Compton, *Introduction to Positive Psychology*, at 62 (讨论了对相对福祉的感知).

② Robert H. Frank, How Not to Buy Happiness, *Daedelus*, Spring 2004, at 69–79. See also Compton, *Introduction to Positive Psychology*, at 62 (讨论了社会比较).

③ Levit & Linder, *The Happy Lawyer*, at 87.

④ Steven Brill, "Ruining" the Profession, *Am. Law.*, Jul./Aug. 1996, at 5.

⑤ Robert H. Frank & Philip J. Cook, The Winner Take All Society: How More and More Americans Compete For Ever Fewer and Bigger Prizes, Encouraging Economic Waste, Income Inequality, and an Impoverished Cultural Life 41, 66 (1995); O'Neil, The Paradox of Success 29–30 (1994); William R. (转下页)

上,高处不胜寒。① 当律师将他们的情况与腰缠万贯的委托人进行比较时,问题就更加复杂了。② 那些看起来足够努力的律师,总能发现比自己更富有的人。

其他因素也把律师进一步困在了高估收入的陷阱中。一是经济下行流动的困难。最初选择高薪工作以获得培训和声望或者还清助学贷款的律师,往往习惯于这种职位的生活方式。因此,赚取高收入所需的工作,也创造了刺激经济增长的需要。在血汗工厂工作的律师们觉得自己有权利享受那些能使他们的生活更轻松、更愉快的商品和服务。这种补偿性的消费模式可以成为自我延续的方式。奢侈品很容易成为必需品,许多律师感到无法负担在个人、职业和公共服务追求之间更令人满意的平衡。

对地位的渴望和把金钱等于价值的做法,同样适得其反。对于包括律师在内的许多人来说,收入是衡量成就和自尊的关键指标,也是社会地位的标志。给人留下深刻印象的表现

(接上页) Keates, Proceed With Caution: A Diary of the First Year at One of America's Largest, Most Prestigious Law Firms 144 (1997); Juliet B. Schor, The Overspent American: Upscaling, Downshifting, and the New Consumer 5–12 (1998); Mike Papantonio, Legal Egos on the Loose, ABA J., Sept. 1999, at 108.

① Vivia Chen, Rich Lawyer, Poor Lawyer, Am. Law., Dec. 2007, at 15 (指出在"纽约和硅谷这样的超级地区"的律师,生活在使财富向上偏斜的金融投资者的阴影中).

② See Richard Conniff, The Natural History of the Rich: A Field Guide 145 (2002).

欲,深深植根于人性,而在美国人日益增长的实利主义文化中,自我价值与净资产挂钩。① 然而,律师为这些优先事项付出了高昂的代价。就像帕特里克·施利茨(Patrick Schlitz)总结的那样:

> 金钱几乎是律师不喜欢他们的职业的一切的根源:长时间工作,商业化,吸引和留住委托人的巨大压力,竞争激烈的市场,合伙人之间缺乏共治和忠诚,职业的公众形象不佳,甚至缺少礼义廉耻。②

● **改革的理由**

越来越多的证据表明,律师以及雇用他们的机构如果减少对收入的关注,更多专注于促进个人的幸福和工作满意度的其他条件,则会做得更好。过度劳累会损害健康和绩效,需要更好地平衡工作与生活,是造成非合伙律师离职的主要原因。③ 快乐

---

① Patrick J. Schlitz, On Being a Happy, Healthy, and Ethical Member of an Unhappy, Unhealthy, and Unethical Profession, *52 Vand. L. Rev.* 871, 903 (1999).
② Michel Janati, A Nation Overworked: Abandoning Happiness and Health for Paychecks, *Wash. Times*, Apr. 22, 2012; Stark & Prescott, Why Associates Leave, at 45.
③ Sonja Lyubomirsky et al., The Benefits of Frequent Positive Affect: Does Happiness Lead to Success? *131 Psych. Bull*. 803, 822 (2005); Lyubomirsky, *The How of Happiness*, at 25; Peter Huang & Rick Swedloff, Authentic Happiness and Meaning at Law Firms, *58 Syr. L. Rev*. 335, 337 (2008)(引述了有关研究); John M. Zelensky, Steven A. Murphy, & David A. Jenkins, The Happy-Productive Worker Thesis Revisited, *9 J. Happiness Stud*. 517, 533 (2008).

的人表现得更好,活得更长寿、更健康。① 幸福感与工作满意度有关。② 人性化的时间安排、可选性的工作安排和其他家庭友好型政策,是具有费效比的。这些举措改善了招募,有助于留住人才,有助于减少压力、失眠和其他疾病。一些评估表明,在有关生活质量的政策上投资的每1美元都节省了2美元的其他费用。③ 其他调查发现,非全职员工通常比全职雇员更有效率,特别是对那些在血汗工厂熬钟点的人而言;任何额外的开支都要好于员工离职所产生的成本。④ 总之,平衡的生活

---

① Nathan A. Bowling, Kevin J. Eschleman, & Qiang Wang, A MetaAnalytic Examination of the Relationship Between Job Satisfaction and Subjective Well-Being, 83 J. Occup. & Org. Psych. 915 (2010).

② Richard Ellsberry, The Family Friendly Office, *Off. Sys.*, Mar. 1, 1999, at 42; Mackenzie Carpenter, A Few Ounces of Prevention, *Pittsburgh Post Gazette*, Jun. 5, 1998, at A1; Keith Cunningham, Note, Father Time: Flexible Work Arrangements and Law Firms' Failure of the Family, 53 Stan. L. Rev. 967, 1004 (2001).

③ Joan Williams, *Unbending Gender*, 112 (2001); Joan Williams, Canaries in the Mine: Work/Family Conflicts and the Legal Profession, 70 Fordham L. Rev. 221, 227 (2007); Boston Bar Association Task Force on Work Family Challenges, Facing the Grail: Confronting the Causes of Work-Family Imbalance 25 (1999); Lotte Bailyn, *Breaking the Mold: Men, Women, and Time in the New Corporate World* 80-84 (1993); Linda Bray Chanow, Report for the Women's Bar Association of D. C., Lawyers, Work, and Family: A Study of Alternative Schedules at Law Firms in the District of Columbia 8 (2000); M. Diane Vogt and Lori-Ann Rickard, *Keeping Good Lawyers: Best Practices to Create Career Satisfaction*, 55 (2000).

④ John B. Heinz & Paul S. Schnorr, with Edward O. Laumann & Robert L. Nelson, Lawyers' Roles in Voluntary Associations: Declining Social (转下页)

会提高底线。

公益服务机会也是如此。它们使律师能够发展新的技能、专业领域和潜在的委托人关系,并提高他们的声望和自尊。① 正如一位律师所指出的那样,这种活动可能是"整个律师事务所士气高涨的一个巨大助力。每个人都觉得他们接触了生活,办事处的野餐或者聚会不会给你带来这些"②。公益服务还可以提高整个法律职业的声誉。在一次有代表性的民意调查中,当被问及怎样才能改善律师的形象时,受访者最常选择的反应是向有需要的人士提供免费的法律服务。2/3 的受访者表示,这会改善他们对法律职业的看法。③ 在一个人才

(接上页) Capital? 26 Law & Soc. Inq. 597, 599 (2001); Jill Schachner Chanen, Pro Bono's Pros—and Cons: Rewards Are Great but It Takes a Deft Balance of Time and Effort, ABA J., May 1998, at 80; Donald W. Hoagland, Community Service Makes Better Lawyers, in The Law Firm and the Public Good 104, 109 (1995); Jack W. Londen, The Impact of Pro Bono Work on Law Firm Economics, 9 Geo. J. Legal Ethics 925 (1996); Thomas J. Brannan, Pro Bono: By Choice or By Chance, Ill. B. J., 481 (Sept. 1996); Ronald J. Tabak, Integration of Pro Bono into Law Firm Practice, 9 Geo. J. Legal Ethics 931, 932 (1996).

① Talcott J. Franklin, Practical Pro Bono: How Public Service Can Enhance Your Practice, S. C. L., Feb. 1999, at 14, 19-20.

② Peter D. Hart Research Associates, A Survey of Attitudes Nationwide Toward Lawyers and the Legal System 18 (1993).

③ 关于地位的下降,see Williams, Unbending Gender, at 1, 8-9; Debra Cassans Weiss, Legal Careers Lose Their Allure, Drop to Dentistry Status, ABA J. - L. News, Jan. 11, 2008, available at http://www.abajournal.com/news/legal_careers_lose_their_allure_drop_to_ dentistry_status/. 关于申请的减少,参见第六章。

竞争日益激烈,律师的地位不断降低和法学院申请人数不断减少的世界中,律师业显然可以从更多的公益活动中受益。①

/ 改革战略 /

《我们关心的东西的重要性》是一篇有影响力的文章,在文中,哲学家哈利·法兰克福(Harry Frankfurt)认为,人们在从事他们认为有意义的工作,并且该工作在最深层面上反映了符合这一定义的事物时,他们最有成就感,并最为深刻地反思了什么会符合这个定义。② 其实,重要的是要提醒自己,我们最关心的是什么,至少从长远来看,不应满足于不合乎标准的工作。虽然法律实务活动的消极一面并不容易避免,但是律师可以在个人和集体方面做更多的事情,以减少他们对职业生活的期望与实际体验之间的差距。最需要改变的是变革是不可能的这种观念。

• 个人战略

在个人层面上,律师需要更积极地寻找"他们的价值观、

---

① Harry Frankfurt, The Importance of What We Care About, 53 Synthesis 257 (1982).

② Levit & Linder, The Happy Lawyer, at 105. For similar suggestions, see Martin E. P. Seligman, Authentic Happiness: Using the New Positive Psychology to Realize Your Potential for Lasting Fulfillment (2002); Huang & Swedloff, Authentic Happiness; Seligman & Steen, Positive Psychology Programs, 60 Am. Psych. 410 (2005); Sheldon & Lyubormirsky, Achieving Sustainable Gains, at 82.

快乐和优势的交集"这种工作。① 这反过来又要求个人在职业选择上变得更有见地和自我反省。实现该目的的一个措施是利用排名和数据库,如 BBLP 和《美国律师》A-List 排名,它们根据多样性、工作与生活计划、非合伙律师满意度、公益活动等因素对选定的律师事务所进行评分。② 律师、律师协会和法学院应当要求所有法律工作提供更多的这类信息,包括其政策在实务活动中的运行情况。例如,非全职身份或者大量公益参与会如何影响晋升和薪酬?律师对他们的日程安排、各种任务和公益服务机会有多少控制权?

执业者一旦受雇,也需要被敦促进行这样的考虑。这对女性来说尤为重要,她们在社会化过程中,不能显得咄咄逼人

---

① 由学生运营的 BBLP 考虑了多样性、收费工时和公益活动。See Peter Schmidt, Advocates of Diversity Grasp for Ways to Drive Change in the Legal Profession, *Chronicle of Higher Education*, Nov. 27, 2007; G. M. Filisko, Students Aim for BigLaw Change, *ABA J.*, Dec. 2007, at 28. 美国律所 A-List 排行榜考虑了利润率、非合伙律师满意度、多样性和公益工作。See The A-List, *Am. Law.*, Jul. 2007, at 80.

② Linda Babcock & Sara Laschever, *Women Don't Ask* 1-11 (2003). 关于使女性避免看起来咄咄逼人或者好斗的社会化力量的其他研究, see Sheryl Sandberg, *Lean In: Women, Work, and the Will to Lead* (2013); Deborah L. Rhode & Barbara Kellerman, Women and Leadership: The State of Play, in *Women and Leadership: The State of Play and Strategies for Change* 7, 101 (Barbara Kellerman & Deborah L. Rhode, eds., 2007); Alice Eagly & Steven Karau, Role Congruity Theory of Prejudice toward Female Leaders, 109 *Psych. Rev.* 573 (2002); Todd L. Pittinsky, Laura M. Bacon, & Brian Welle, The Great Women Theory of Leadership: Perils of Positive Stereotypes and Precarious Pedestals, in Kellerman & Rhode, *Women and Leadership*, at 101.

或者好斗。一本关于谈判行为的开创性著作的书名直接提出了这个问题:《女人不找麻烦》(Women Don't Ask)①。但是,当涉及职业发展和工作与家庭的权衡时,男女律师都需要考虑;他们必须积极追求获得成就感所必需的事情。一项关于职业晋升的研究显示,实现晋升最有效的策略是不满于现状;人们要抓住每一个机会并从中获益,在发现更有前途的机会时离开岗位。② 因此,致力于改善其当前状况的职业人员也常常会发现人数众多会带来更大的力量。在工作场所内外把同事们组织起来,可以显著改善多样性和平衡工作与家庭的政策。③

- 制度战略

在太多的工作中,律师面临着不受欢迎的权衡。在《快乐的律师(The Happy Lawyer)》中,南希·列维特(Nancy Levit)和道格拉斯·林德(Douglas Linder)指出,幸福既需要工作保障,也需要为家庭、朋友和其他活动留下时间,正是这些方面给日常生活带来了意义和快乐。他们建议律师通过满足或者超过雇主的期望来使他们的工作更安全,并找到一个"舒适的

---

① Kimberly A. Eddleston, David C. Baldridge, & John F. Veiga, Toward Modeling the Predictors of Managerial Career Success: Does Gender Matter? *19 Manage. Psychol.* 360 (2004).

② 这方面的例子包括女性在律师事务所内的人际关系网,取得在雇用、晋升目标和时间表方面作出承诺的法律雇主的支持建立律师协会工作小组。See Rhode & Kellerman, *Women and Leadership*, at 1, 30, 34.

③ Levit & Linder, *The Happy Lawyer*, at 110.

第二章
执业条件

工作与生活的平衡点"。① 对于许多律师来说,这些目标似乎不相容。这种情况必须改变。

法律雇主必须做更多的事情来解决不满的根源,并评估他们的回应是否足够。对生活质量的承诺需要反映在工作场所的优先事项、政策和奖励结构中。这反过来又需要对律师的满意度和影响满意度的实务活动进行系统评价。雇主应当进行匿名调查,询问他们的律师就实务活动的方方面面的满意度,以及他们最希望看到什么样的变革。决策者必须追踪女性和少数族裔等代表人数不足的群体在数量上是否与白人男性对等,以及所有群体在职业发展中是否都感到得到了同样的支持。对于工作时间减少的律师,他们的时间安排是否得到了尊重,他们的薪资和福利与他们的绩效是否相称,他们是否仍然有机会晋升、完成理想的工作任务?律师如何评估他们的培训和指导?参加正式指导计划的学员是否认为他们分配的导师有足够的时间、兴趣、动机和知识来提供必要的支持?律师是否定期、建设性和坦率地反馈他们的表现?是否可以让律师对他们的日程安排、任务和工作环境有更多的控制权?现在有太多的雇主缺乏对这些问题的回答,而依赖于

---

① 有关多样性政策存在的问题,see Kimberly Krawiec, Cosmetic Compliance and the Failure of Negotiated Governance, *81 Wash. L. Q.* 487 (2005). 关于指导政策的不足, see Katherine Giscombe & M. G. Mattis, Leveling the Playing Field for Women of Color in Corporate Management: Is the Business Case Enough? *37 J. Bus. Ethics* 103 (2002).

某些政策,可是这些政策对其预期受益者的服务效果不佳。①

有太多的法律组织也没有充分支持公益工作。第三章指出了参与公共服务的社会重要性。本章的讨论说明了公益工作在满足律师自身对职业满意度的需要方面的价值。为了满足这一需要,雇主必须对公共服务作出有形的承诺,这要反映在资源分配和奖励结构中。律所至少应当为公益工作提供充分的条件,要接近计费工时的要求,在晋升和薪酬上要体现公益工作的价值,确保对其进行充分的培训和监督,并制定一个有效的系统,使参与者与他们认为有意义的工作相匹配。②

实务活动的结构也必须进行改革。一个大有希望的措施是律师事务所的分轨制,即权衡不同的时间和薪酬,而不是割裂的状态。③ 另一个选项是将律师与符合其实质偏好和日程偏好的项目进行匹配;这项工作常常是在家里或者委托人办公室完成的,以最大限度地提高灵活性并减少开销。④ Axiom公司是法律雇主成功使用这一模型的范例。⑤ 这种替代收费

---

① Rhode, *Pro Bono in Principle*, at 138–140. For the ABA's rule, see ABA Model Rules of Professional Conduct, Rule 6.1.

② 创新安排的例子,see Natasha Sarkisian, Who Says Being a Lawyer Has to Suck?, *San Francisco Mag.*, Oct. 2007; Lisa Belkin, Who's Cuddly Now? Law Firms, *N.Y. Times*, Jan. 24, 2008, at G1, G8.

③ Leigh Jones, The Rise of the New Model Firm, *Nat'l L. J.*, May 21, 2007.

④ See http:www//.axiom.legal.com.

⑤ ABA Commission on Billable Hours, Report to the House of Delegates (2002).

第二章
执业条件

办法减少了对计费工时制度的依赖,也有助于奖励效率,减少加班加点的经济压力。①

同样重要的是解决过度离职的改革,包括缺乏指导和与合伙人的关系存在问题。② 一项研究发现,43%的员工对他们接受的指导质量感到不满,而其他研究发现,女性和少数族裔的不满率更高。③ 部分原因是,3/4 的律师事务所并不把用于指导的时间计算在计费工时内。④ 带教律师需要就指导和对待下属方面得到充分的培训、评估和奖励。⑤ 初级律师应当有机会对上司进行评价,并将此反映在律所的薪酬结构中。⑥

同样,更多的律师可以尝试减少经常伴随着对抗性程序的冲突。一个例子是合作性律师实务活动,在这种情况下,各方当事人合作解决问题;如果他们不能通过谈判达成和解,他

---

① Stark & Prescott, Why Associates Leave; NALP Foundation for Research and Education: Keeping the Keepers: Strategies for Associate Retention in a Time of Attrition 14 (1998).

② Susan Saab Fortney, Soul for Sale, at 283; American Bar Association Commission on Women in the Profession, Visible Invisibility 18-19 (2012).

③ ABA Commission on Billable Hours Report 48 (2002).

④ 关于培训和评估那些进行监督的人员的重要性,see Stark & Prescott, Why Associates Leave; NALP, Effective Management, at 58-59.

⑤ 关于全方位绩效评估的价值, see Elizabeth Goldberg, Playing Nice, *Am. Law.*, Aug. 2007, at 100.

⑥ Sheila M. Gutterman, Collaborative Law: A New Model for Dispute Resolution (2004); Sherrie R. Abney, Avoiding Litigation: A Guide to Civil Collaborative Law (2006); Pauline H. Tessler, Collaborative Law: *Achieving Effective Resolution in Divorce Without Litigation* (2001); Principles and Guidelines for the Practice of Collaborative Law, available at http://www.mediate.com/articles/coallabpg.cfm.

们的律师将不会在以后的诉讼中提供代理。① 通过消除律师延长诉讼程序的经济动机,这项安排能够在最小化冲突方面,给所有参与者带来好处。

委托人还应向法律雇主施加压力,要求他们解决长期不满的根源。委托人很少能从拥有繁重的日程安排和高离职率的律师那里得到有效的服务,高离职率往往带来委托人事务中断。给委托人带来不便和额外的培训费用。此外,正如第四章所指出的那样,越来越多的公司律师认为,多样性既是经济上的也是道义上的当务之急。他们需要的是能够充分利用现有人才的律师事务所,以及具有不同背景和视角的团队。为此,许多大公司承诺在分配法律工作时考虑多样性。② 更多的委托人需要照做,并且认真履行他们的承诺;这种压力可能促使律师事务所改善影响女性和少数族裔的政策。除了多样性,委托人还应当考虑其他问题,例如公益项目的数量是否充足,这是现在一些政府机构在分配外部工作时所考虑的因素之一。③

---

① 关于委托人的多样性努力,see Deborah L. Rhode & Lucy Ricca, Diversity in the Legal Profession: Perspectives from Managing Partners and General Counsel, *Fordham L. Rev.* (forthcoming, 2015); Karen Donovan, Pushed By Clients, Law Firms Step Up Diversity Efforts, *N. Y. Times*, Jul. 21, 2006, at C1; Diversity Calls, *Cal. Law.*, Nov. 2005.

② See Rhode, *Pro Bono*, at 168.

③ Laura Stiller Rickleen, *Ending the Gauntlet: Removing the Barriers to Women's Success in Law* 372-374 (2006)(讨论了旧金山的"玻璃顶行动计划"和"芝加哥律师协会女性联盟行动号召"); Rhode & Kellerman, *Women and Leadership*, at 34.

律师协会和州法院可以做更多的工作来支持多样性、公益服务和生活质量改革。例如,一些地方性律师协会团体已经取得了律师事务所的支持来拥护其种族和性别平等的目标和时间表。① 其他律师协会已采取了措施,以提高公益活动的参与度,还有一些州法院要求律师报告公益工作。② 通过提高此类工作的知名度,律师协会能够向雇主施加压力,让他们支持公益活动。

● **法律教育**

法学院在回应职业满意度的问题上,发挥着显著的作用,但大多数法学院都不想承担这一作用。部分问题在于缺乏这样的共识:它们有责任解决这个严重问题。正如第六章所指出的那样,相对来说,教员与不满的根源和症状是有距离的。在法律职业中,他们的满意度是最高的,部分原因是他们对于工作是否契合其需要、日程表是否合适、工作是否有意义等方面,有很大的控制权。③ 尽管法学院学生存在压力、药物

---

① 9个州要求进行报告,具体内容参见第三章。关于该等规则的价值,see Rhode, *Pro Bono*, at 167-169. 有关律师协会的举措,see ABA Commission on the Renaissance of Idealism in the Legal Profession, Final Report (Aug. 2006).

② See Kenneth G. Dau-Schmidt & Kaushik Mukhopadhaya, The Fruits of Our Labors: An Empirical Study of the Distribution of Income and Job Satisfaction Across the Legal Profession, *49 J. Legal Educ.* 342 (1999).

③ Robert P. Schwerk, The Law Professor as Fiduciary: What Duties Do We Owe to Our Students, *45 S. Tex. L. Rev*. 753, 764-766 (2004) (指出大多数法学教授不熟悉其学生的心理障碍,或者将其归于不受法学院控(转下页)

滥用和其他心理健康问题的概率出奇的高,但是症状并不总是显而易见的,法律教育也未能充分解决该问题。① 在法学院课程设置中存在明显问题,即缺少有关执业条件的课程。超过90%的法学院没有开设能够解决律师满意度问题的课程。② 只有一半的学生报告说,他们的学校非常重视培养他们,使他们能够应对法律实务活动所带来的压力。③

法学院未能确保学生参与公益服务,也未能明确其与职业成就感的联系。就像第六章所指出的那样,1/3的毕业生并不参加作为其教育体验一部分的公益活动,许多参加者只是在象征性地参与。④ 公益活动通常也不是核心课程、定向课程或者专业责任课程的一部分。⑤

然而,法律教育也是法律职业的分支,在某些方面最适合

(接上页)制的原因); Accord, Lawrence S. Krieger, Institutional Denial About the Dark Side of Law School and Fresh Empirical Guidance for Constructively Breaking the Silence, 52 J. Legal Educ. 112 (2002). 关于一般性问题, see Thomas Adcock, Despite '93 Report, Substance Abuse Persists at Law Schools, N. Y. L. J., Jun. 30, 2003; Kenneth Sheldon & Lawrence S. Krieger, Understanding the Negative Effects of Legal Education on Law Students: A Longitudinal Test of Self-Determination Theory, 33 Personality & Soc. Psych. 853 (2007).

① Levit & Linder, The Happy Lawyers, at 123.
② Law School Survey of Student Engagement, Student Engagement in Law School: Enhancing Student Learning 7 (2009).
③ Law School Survey of Student Engagement, Student Engagement, at 8.
④ William Sullivan et al., Educating Lawyers 187 (2007); Rhode, Pro Bono, at 162.
⑤ Harlan F. Stone, The Public Influence of the Bar, 48 Harv. L. Rev. 1, 11 (1934).

解决法律职业的问题。有了这个机会,也就有了相应的义务。美国最高法院大法官哈兰·斯通(Harlan Stone)在他1934年发表的关于"律师业的公共影响力"的演讲中指出,法律学者是法律职业的成员,他们"最脱离于那些深刻影响着其从事实务活动的同胞的新经济秩序的压力。"① 这种独立赋予他们独一无二的能力,即公正地分析律师协会这个机构,并"充分了解其问题……"② 大约65年后,哈佛法学教授戴维·威尔金斯(David Wilkins)在美国法学院协会作演讲时,呼应了类似的主题。正如他所指出的那样,职业教育的责任之一,是就法律职业进行研究和教育:

> 当美国法律职业几乎在每一个维度上都在彻底地进行变革时……法学院必须成为发展的积极参与者……关于法律实务活动的知识,将使我们能够构建一个与21世纪相契合的法律职业主义的愿景。

学术界的部分责任,是准确描述执业条件和可能改善它的战略。更多的法学教授应当就律师实务活动进行讲授、研究和写作。法律教育也可以做更多的工作,使后代能够通过个人和集体解决职业不满的根源问题。例如,法学院可以通过课程覆盖、课外小组和活动,使学生接触到不同的实务环境

---

① Stone, The Public Influence, at 11.
② David B. Wilkins, The Professional Responsibility of Professional Schools to Study and Teach About the Profession, *49 J. Legal Educ.* 76 (1999).

和关于满意度的文献。学校也可以要求雇主进行校园面试,以披露有关行业生活质量的信息。更多的法律教员也应当从事能够促进职业成就感的研究。我们需要更多地了解世界上有哪些做法行之有效。例如,哪些法学院和雇主的举措在长期改善健康和满意度方面最为有效?什么样的激励措施和压力最有可能确保这些举措?

法律学者为在社会变革的前沿而感到自豪。我们愿意相信,我们的教学和研究有助于构建更公正、更有效的治理制度。我们现在需要将更多的精力转向我们自己的职业,并促进各种形式的实务活动,以满足律师们最深切的需要和愿望。

03
Chapter

第三章
近用司法

- 刑事辩护
- 民事司法制度中的障碍

令人感到可耻的讽刺是,作为世界上律师最为集中的国家之一,我们在保障法律服务的可近用性方面做得很少。① 根据世界正义项目,美国在近用司法和法律服务的可负担性方面,在97个国家中名列第67(与乌干达并列)。② "法律上的公平正义"是美国最骄傲的宣告,却也是经常违反的法律原则之一。它装点着法院的大门,但是绝不会说明在它们背后发生了什么。数以百万计的美国人没有任何近用司法的机会,更不用说平等近用的机会了。超过4/5的穷人的法律需求和大多数的中等收入者的需求仍未得到满足。③ 贫困者刑事辩护制度是国家的耻辱。下面的讨论探讨了造成正义的差

---

① 本章是基于:Deborah L. Rhode, Access to Justice: A Roadmap for Reform, 41 *Fordham Urb. L. J.* 1227 (2014). 就表明美国在经济发达国家中排名第一或者第二的研究,see Charles Keckler, Lawyered Up: A Book Review Essay, 27 *T. M. Cooley L. Rev.* 57 (2010); America Lawyers: Guilty as Charged, *The Economist*, Feb. 2, 2013.

② World Justice Project Rule of Law Index 175 (2013).

③ 关于低收入人员的法律需求的讨论,see Legal Services Corporation, Documenting the Justice Gap in America: The Current Unmet Civil Needs of Low-Income Americans 1-13 (2009), available at http://www.lsc.gov/pdfs/dcoumenting_the_justice_gap_in_america_2009.pdf. 调查发现,中等收入人员中2/5到3/4的人的需求没有得到解决,大多数的研究结果至少是一般性的。See Deborah L. Rhode, Access to Justice 3, 79 (2004); Luz E. Herrera, Rethinking Private Attorney Involvement in the Delivery of Civil Legal Services for Low- and Moderate-Income Clients, 42 *Loy. L. Rev.* 1 (2009).

距的原因,并指出了最有希望的对策。

/ 刑事辩护 /

- 制度化的不公正:对代理不足的回应不足

自从美国最高法院判决吉迪恩诉温赖特案以来,五十年已经过去了。这是一项具有里程碑意义的判决,它承认付不起律师费的刑事被告有权获得律师帮助。[1] 然而,正如总检察长埃里克·霍尔德(Eric Holder)所指出的那样,这一权利"尚未完全实现"。"在全国范围内,公共辩护人和为贫困者提供辩护的资金不足,人手不足。在为穷人提供法律代理时,由于资源不足、工作量过大、监督不力等原因,这种代理效果往往很差。"[2]乔治亚州的一名被告的母亲说得很对:"除非你能花钱买一个,否则就没有公平的审判。"[3]在许多司法辖区,有罪的富人比贫穷的无辜者更安全;获得最糟糕的量刑的,是那些请

---

[1] Gideon v. Wainwright, 372 U. S. 335 (1963).

[2] Debra Cassens Weiss, Would Decriminalizing Minor Offenses Help Indigent Defense Crisis? ABA Committee Weighs In, *ABA J.*, Jan. 8, 2013, http://www.abajournal.com/news/article/decriminalizing_minor_offenses_could_help_indigent_defense_crisis_aba_commi/.

[3] No Fair Trial unless You Can Buy One, *Atlanta J. -Const.*, Sept. 9, 2001, at 8D (quoting Paula McMichen).

第三章
近用司法

了最差劲的律师的人,而不是犯了最恶劣的罪行的人。①

许多问题涉及资源和法院不愿意要求为贫困者辩护须有足够的预算或者执行适当的代理标准。全国每年在刑事执法方面花费超过1000亿美元,但是只有约2%至3%用于支持律师为贫困被告进行辩护。② 每年因重罪被捕的约有100万人,其中约3/4的人是穷人,足以达到法院指定律师的资格标准,800万因轻罪被捕的人中大部分也是如此。足够的辩护律师对刑事司法系统的公正性和正当性至关重要。在死刑案件中尤其如此,在这种情况下,人的生命和自由的利害关系最大。然而,专家们普遍认为,决定被告是否会被判处死刑的最重要因素不是犯罪情节,而是被告律师是否称职。③

虽然法院已经解释说,美国宪法第六修正案要求律师提供有效帮助,但是现行的有效性标准却是对宪法保障的嘲弄。④ 当律师在刑事案件审判方面缺乏经验或者专门知识时,当他们没有进行任何调查、没有对任何证人进行交叉询

---

① Stephen Bright, Counsel for the Poor: The Death Sentence Not for the Worst Crime but for the Worst Lawyer, *103 Yale L. J.* 1835, 1850-1854 (1994).

② David Cole, *No Equal Justice: Race and Class in the American Criminal Justice System* 64, 84 (1999); Douglas McCollum, *The Ghost of Gideon*, Am. Law., Mar. 2003, at 63, 67.

③ Rhode, Access to Justice, at 140.

④ 关于宪法保障,see *Strickland v. Washington*, 466 U.S. 668 (1984). 最近的判例表明对无效表现更不能容忍。参见下文所回顾的判例:Deborah L. Rhode, David Luban, & Scott Cummings, *Legal Ethics* 211-212 (6th ed., 2013).

问、没有咨询任何专家或者提供任何证据时,法院都维持了有罪判决。① 在许多美国刑事法院伸张正义是一种耻辱,尤其是对于一个把自己标榜为在人权领域处于领导地位的国家来说。

问题不是大多数穷人的辩护律师都缺乏能力或者投入。绝大多数的人在富有挑战性的情况下尽了最大的努力。然而,主要的问题在于结构层面:对少数不称职的律师来说,资源太少,救济办法也太少。

在过去半个世纪的大部分时期,贫困者辩护制度一直处于财政危机之中。此外,近年来由于刑事定罪和监禁的急剧升级,这个问题变得更加复杂。自吉迪恩案判决后,美国的监禁率已经增加了3倍多,现在是世界上最高的。② 为贫困者辩护的资金没有跟上这一增长的步伐,最近的预算削减把情况变得更糟。③ 正如一位专家所指出的那样,"你把飞镖投到美

---

① Rhode, Access to Justice, at 122; Laurence Hurley, Second Guesses, *Cal. Law.*, Jan. 2012, at 29, 31 (描述了就无效帮助获得救济所存在的障碍).

② Michelle Alexander, *The New Jim Crow: Mass Incarceration in the Age of Color Blindness* 6-9 (2010); William Stuntz, *The Collapse of American Criminal Justice* 247 (2011).

③ Roger A. Fairfax, Jr., Searching for Solutions to the Indigent Defense Crisis in the Broader Criminal Justice Reform Agenda, *122 Yale L. J.* 2316, 2319, 2321 (2013); Joe Davidson, Budget Cuts "Threaten" Justice for the Poor; Defenders Furloughed but not Prosecutors, *Wash. Post*, Aug. 20, 2013; ABA Standing Committee on Legal Aid and Indigent Defendants, *Gideon's Broken Promise: America's Continuing Quest for Equal Justice* 7-14 (2004).

国的地图上,就可以击中一个失灵的贫困者辩护制度。"①超过90%的贫困刑事被告在没有审判的情况下认罪,而法院通常并没有对他们的案件进行任何重大调查。②

司法辖区有3种提供贫困者辩护的方法。一个是公共辩护律师服务。虽然少数司法辖区有可以与检控资源相媲美的示范项目,但是它们是例外;贫困者的辩护制度匮乏是个常态。公共辩护人办公室不得不应对裁员、无薪休假和难以承受的案件负荷。③ 美国律师协会标准建议每个律师每年最多办理150个重罪或者400个轻罪案件,但是许多司法辖区都远远超过了这些限制。④ 只有9个州限制了公共辩护人的最大工作量。⑤ 辩护律师每年不得不竭力对付多达2000件轻罪和

---

① Accessing Counsel and Courts, *Liman Cent. Newslet.*, Fall 2003, at 19 (quoting Brandon Buskey, ACLU Criminal Justice Reform Project).

② 关于辩诉交易的数量,see George Fisher, *Plea Bargaining's Triumph: A History of Plea Bargains in the United States* 134, 222, 223 (2003).

③ Ron Nixon, Public Defenders Are Tightening Belts Because of Steep Federal Budget Cuts, *N. Y. Times*, Aug. 24, 2013, at A14; Karen Houppert, *Chasing Gideon: The Elusive Quest for Poor People's Justice* 154 (2013).

④ See James C. McKinley, Jr., Cuomo Pledges More Aid for Indigents in Court, *N. Y. Times*, Oct. 22, 2014, at A22; Robert C. Boruchowitz et al., Minor Crimes, MassiveWaste: The Terrible Toll of America's BrokenMisdemeanor Courts 22-27 (2009) (提供了诸如芝加哥、亚特兰大、迈阿密等大都市地区的平均轻罪案件量数据), available at http://www.nacdl.org/WorkArea/DownloadAsset.aspx?id=20808.

⑤ David Rudovsky, *Gideon* and the Effective Assistance of Counsel: The Rhetoric and the Reality, *32 J. L. & Inequality* 372, 379 n43 (2014).

500件重罪案件。① 新奥尔良的律师在每个轻罪案件上花费的时间,平均只有7分钟;纽约的一些律师从未亲自会见过他们的委托人。②

在依赖于第二种方法施行贫困者辩护制度的司法辖区,问题可能更严重:竞标。在这一制度中,在固定费用基础上,律师出价为法院总案件量的特定百分比提供代理,而不论案件的数目或者复杂程度如何。在司法辖区往往没有一个有意义的质量控制体系的情况下,这一过程鼓励的是逐底竞争。胜出者是能够处理大量案件的律师,他们往往在走廊与委托人简短交谈后就把案件办了。③

在采用第三种方法的司法辖区,被告也不一定过得会更好,这种方法按小时支付律师的费用,但是封顶收费往往低到荒谬的程度。2013年的一项调查发现,30个州的平均薪酬仅为每小时65美元,有些州甚至每小时只支付

---

① Jenna Greene, A Muted Trumpet, *Nat'l L. J.*, Mar. 18, 2013, at A4; Eve Brensike Primus, Not Much to Celebrate, *Nat'l L. J.*, Mar. 18, 2013, at 26; Rudofsky, *Gideon*, 379; Carol S. Steiker, *Gideon*'s Problematic Promises, *Daedalus*, Summer 2014, at 53.

② Federal Oversight on Public Defense, *N. Y. Times*, Sept. 8, 2013, at SR10; Matt Apuzzo, Holder Backing New York Suit Over Legal Service for the Poor, *N. Y. Times*, Sept. 25, 2014, at A24.

③ Amy Bach, Justice on the Cheap, *The Nation*, May 21, 2001, at 25; Contract Lawyer Can't Get the Job Done, *Atlanta J.-Const.*, May 5, 2001, at F10; Martin Lasden, For a Fistful of Dollars, *Cal. Law.*, Nov. 2001, at 28.

第三章
近用司法

40美元。① 许多司法辖区还将特定案件的总支出限制在不切实际的水平,这意味着在某一临界点之后,律师在作为志愿者为其委托人工作。如果司法辖区对收费规定了不切实际的上限,那么认真详尽的准备工作肯定会给律师带来经济上的损失。

这些方法都缺乏资金促使律师"会见"当事人,"打个招呼",然后"为他们进行辩护"。② 很少有律师提出动议,咨询专家,会见证人,或者调查事实。③ 在为其敷衍的做法进行辩护时,一位律师向记者解释说,他根本无法把"太多的时间或者金钱投入到这些案件中"。他接着补充说,如果他的委托人"想要克拉伦斯·丹诺(Clarence Darrow)辩护的效果,④他们就应当雇用克拉伦斯·丹诺。"⑤代理艾迪·乔·劳埃德(Eddie Joe Lloyd)上诉案件的律师从未见过他,甚至也不曾接过他的任何

---

① National Association of Criminal Defense Lawyers, Rationing Justice: The Underfunding of Assigned Counsel Systems 8 (2013); Greene, A Muted Trumpet.

② Alan Berlow, Requiem for a Public Defender, *Am. Prospect*, Jun. 5, 2000, at 28; ABA, *Gideon*'s Broken Promise, at 16.

③ Benjamin H. Barton, Against Civil *Gideon* (and for Pro Se Court Reform), *62 Fla. L. Rev.* 1227, 1253 (2010); Rhode, Access to Justice, at 124.

④ 克拉伦斯·丹诺(1857年-1938年),美国律师,因参与李奥波德与勒伯案(LeopoldandLoeb)谋杀案、斯科普斯(Scopes)"猴子"案件审判等的辩护工作而闻名。——译者注

⑤ Adam Liptak, County Says It's Too Poor to Defend the Poor, *N. Y. Times*, Apr. 15, 2003, at A1, A13 (quoting Thomas Pearson).

电话。这位律师解释说:"没有人就其从杰克逊监狱打来的长途电话向我付钱。我已经尽我所能做得最好了。"①上诉失败后,劳埃德在监狱服刑 17 年,后来一个全国性的诉辩小组接手了他的案子,并用 DNA 证据证明他是清白的。

在一些司法辖区,被告在看守所困窘数月后才能与律师取得一点联系。对于那些被控犯有轻罪的人来说,他们等待律师的时间甚至可能比最长刑期还要长,这并不少见。② 密西西比州一名女性被指控在商场行窃,在法院指定律师之前,已经在看守所关押了 11 个月。③ 那些被认定无罪的被告,可能因这种拖延失去工作或者家庭。④ 在一些公共辩护律师办公室,案件积压意味着,在他们的上诉提交并得到解决之前,几乎半数的委托人将服刑完毕。⑤

即使在死刑案件中,代理不足也太常见了。一项名为"致命冷漠"的调查发现,在得克萨斯州被判处死刑的人,有"1/3

---

① Jonathan Oosting, NPR: Want to Know What's Wrong with the Nation's Public Defender System? Just Look at Detroit, MLive, Aug. 18, 2009, available at http://www.mlive.com/news/detroit/index.ssf/2009/08/npr_want_to_know_whats_wrong_w.html (quoting Bob Slameka).

② Primus, Not Much to Celebrate, at 26.

③ Primus, Not Much to Celebrate, at 26. 就其他拖延案例, see Houppert, *Chasing* Gideon, at 153 (描述了 16 个月的等待)。

④ Mary Sue Backus & Paul Marcus, The Right to Counsel in Criminal Cases, A National Crisis, *57 Hastings L. J.* 1031, 1032 (2006); Stephen Bright, Fifty Years of Defiance and Resistance After *Gideon v. Wainwright*, *Liman Cent. Newslet.*, Fall 2003, at 3.

⑤ Rhode, Access to Justice, at 129.

第三章
近用司法

的概率在其案件没有得到称职律师的适当调查,任何无罪或者不公平的主张也在没有被听审的情况下被判决。① 在许多司法辖区,各州也不愿意为必要的专家提供报酬。②

鉴于目前的贫困者辩护结构,无效代理是导致错误定罪和上诉推翻原判的主要原因,这一点不足为奇。③ 然而,令人震惊的是,在法官、立法机关和律师惩戒机构中,对这一点严重缺乏关注。从理论上讲,得不到充分代理的刑事被告有三种救济手段:惩戒投诉、民事不当执业索赔以及推翻定罪。事实上,前两个几乎从来都做不到,第三种也很少发生。律师惩戒机构一般不会考虑"仅仅是疏忽"的主张,甚至严重的疏忽和不称职在很大程度上也不会受到惩处。④ 此外,通常可以在律师惩戒程序中实现的补救措施,如不公开谴责、公开申诫或者停止执业,对提出投诉的被告没有任何帮助。不当执业救济同样无益,因为现行的原则拒绝赔偿,除非被告可以证

---

① Texas Defender Service, *Lethal Indifference* (2002), available at http://www.texasdefender.org.

② No Fair Trial Unless You Can Buy One.

③ 就可发回重审的错误, see James S. Liebman, Jeffrey Fagan, & Valerie West, *A Broken System*: *Error Rates in Capital Cases*, 1973-1995 (2000) (发现有律师不进行调查、不提出异议、放弃交叉询问或者终局辩论); Death Penalty Information Center, Innocence and the Crisis in the American Death Penalty (2004), available at http://www.deathpenaltyinfo.org/innocence-and-crisis-american-death-penalty (指出不足代理是造成错误定罪的一个原因).

④ See Backus & Marcus, The Right to Counsel, at 1083i; Dennis E. Curtis & Judith Resnik, Grieving Criminal Defense Lawyers, *70 Fordham L. Rev.* 1615, 1617-1621 (2002).

明,如果不是他们的律师不称职,他们实际上已经被宣告无罪。实际上,他们必须证明自己的清白。① 因为被定罪的罪犯是无人同情的索赔者,而且很难达到这个标准,他们很少能找到律师来提起索赔。

从被告个人的角度来看,对无效代理的最可取的补救办法是推翻定罪或者宣告认罪无效。然而,在这方面,通常情况下有着不可逾越的障碍。被告必须证明,律师的表现没有达到社群内的职业称职性帮助的程度,并且要不是律师不称职,结果会有所不同。② 这项任务特别困难,因为被告必须根据无效律师所作的记录来证明这一点。因此,对无效帮助索赔的调查发现,只有不到5%的人能够成功。③ 问题在一定程度上是社群的代理标准通常极低。还有一个困难是,绝大多数案件涉及辩诉交易,这种交易缺乏律师所作的记录,或者更多的情况下根本没有这样的记录。

即使律师的表现存在毫无争议的不足,也不可能证明结果受到了影响。即使律师缺乏先前的审判经验,或者在案件

---

① See Meredith J. Duncan, The (So-Called) Liability of Criminal Defense Attorneys: A System in Need of Reform, *Brigham Young U. L. Rev.* 1, 30-43 (2002); John Leubsdorf, Legal Malpractice and Professional Responsibility, *48 Rut. L. Rev.* 101, 111-119 (1995); Backus & Marcus, The Right to Counsel, at 1084.

② Strickland v. Washington, 466 U.S. 668 (1984).

③ Cole, *No Equal Justice*, 80; Victor E. Flango & Patricia McKenna, Federal Habeas Corpus Review of State Court Convictions, *31 Cal. W. L. Rev.* 237, 259-260 (1995).

第三章
近用司法

进行的关键时候醉酒、打瞌睡、吸毒或者停车,死刑判决也将被维持。① 即使是死刑案件的辩护律师,他此前从未参加过死刑案件的审理也不会有下次,死刑判决也可能被维持。② 审判中辩护律师已经睡得太多了,以至于形成了一整套判例来确定睡多少算是宪法所允许的。在这些案件中,法院采用了三步标准。那位律师睡了很长时间吗?律师真的睡得不省人事了吗?在律师在打瞌睡的时候,关键的辩护利益是否在危急关头?③ 在一个驳回了辩护不足的主张的案件中,得克萨斯州上诉法院认为,决定去睡觉可能是一个"战略性"的策略,以获得陪审团的同情。审查该案件的法官坚持认为,"宪法规定每个人都有权选择自己的律师。但是宪法并没有说律师必须保持清醒。"④ 在另一个案件中,一名休斯敦律师错过了为三名被判处死刑的被告提交复核请愿书的法定时限,但是尚未被追究责任。根据最新统计,他当时正在努力处理超过 350 宗重罪

---

① Stephen B. Bright & Sia M. Sanneh, *Gideon v. Wainwright*, Fifty Years Later, *The Nation*, Mar. 20, 2013; Rhode, Access to Justice, 136; Stephen B. Bright, Sleeping on the Job, *Nat'l L. J.*, Dec. 4, 2000, at A26.

② See Stephen B. Bright, Keep the Dream of Equal Justice Alive, Address at Yale Law School, May 24, 1999. http://www.schr.org/files/resources/commence.pdf.

③ *Tippins v. Walker*, 77 F. 2d 682 (2d Cir. 1996); *Burdine v. Texas*, 66 F. Supp. 2d 854 (S.D, Tex. 1999), aff'd sub nom. *Burdine v. Johnson*, 362 F. 2d 386 (5th Cir.) cert. den. sub nom;. *Cockrell v. Burdine*, 535 U.S. 1120 (2002); *McFarland v. State*, 928 S.W. 2d 482, 506 (1996).

④ Bruce Shapiro, Sleeping Lawyer Syndrome, *The Nation*, Apr. 7, 1997, at 29 (quoting Judge Doug Shaver).

案件。① 然而,正如得克萨斯州的一位法官所指出的那样,"一位称职的律师应当不仅仅是一个拥有法律执照的活蹦乱跳的人"。②

- **改革战略**

这种状况令人感到惭愧。最重要的是,该系统需要注入大量的资源,但是缺乏政治动力来使之成为可能。贫穷的被告是一个非常无力且不受欢迎的群体。例如,大约3/4的美国人认为,太多的罪犯因为技术问题而逃脱了处罚。③ 因此,法院需要对立法机关施加压力,即承认受困于资金不足和案件过多的制度中存在宪法性问题。④ 法院还需要维护在这种情况下公共辩护人拒绝办理案件的权利,因为如果不这么做将会导致无效辩护。例如,密苏里州最高法院的一项裁决判定,不应违反限制案件负荷的行政规则指定辩护人,佛罗里达州最高法院裁决,如果公共辩护人的工作量使他们无法提供足够的代理,他们可以拒绝接办新的案件。⑤ 司法机构还应

---

① Bright &Sanneh, Gideon v. Wainwright.
② Texas Defender Service, *Lethal Indifference*, at xii.
③ ABA, Perceptions of the U. S. Justice System 59 (2000).
④ 就该等诉讼的能力和局限性,see Cara H. Drinan, Getting Real about *Gideon*: The Next Fifty Years of Enforcing the Right to Counsel, 70 Wash. & Lee L. Rev.1309, 1331 (2013); Backus & Marcus, The Right to Counsel, at 1116-1117.
⑤ State ex. rel. Missouri Public Defender Commission v. Waters, 370 S. W. 3d 592 (2012); Public Defender, Eleventh Judicial Circuit of Florida v. State of Florida, discussed in Richard Bust, When the Defenders Are the Plaintiffs, ABA J. , Oct. 2013, at 14-15.

当重新审查律师无效帮助的标准,代之以更切合实际的标准,新标准侧重于充分代理的具体职责,并在律师不符合标准时推定有害。①

因此,州立法机关也应当通过将轻微的犯罪行为重新分类而"在犯罪上聪明起来"。正如一些专家所指出的那样,

> 解决美国贫困者辩护危机的办法,必须同时关注制度的前端和后端。有太多的案件涉及了贫困者辩护制度。罪犯很少被判监禁的轻微的、非暴力的罪行,也过度依赖于刑事检控,使得辩护人的工作负荷达到了难以承受的极端程度,损害了所有被告,并给公众带来了巨大的成本。②

通过重新分类所节省的成本可能相当可观。得克萨斯州的一项法律规定,对持有少量某些药物的人要判处缓刑,在2年内为该州节约了约5100万美元的成本。③

"在犯罪上聪明起来"的倡导者所认可的一项有关战略,是将未成年罪犯从刑事法院分流出去。更多的司法辖区

---

① Donald A. Dripps, Why *Gideon* Failed; Politics and Feedback Loops in the Reform of Criminal Justice, 70 Wash. & Lee L. Rev. 883, 903 (2013).

② Joel M. Schumm, Standing Committee on Legal Aid and Indigent Defendants, National Indigent Defense Reform, The Solution Is Multifaceted 37 (2012), available at http://www.nacdl.org/reports/indigentdefensereform/; Fairfax, Searching for Solutions, at 2331.

③ Debra Cassens Weiss, Would Decriminalizing Minor Offenses Help Indigent Defense Crisis? ABA Committee Weighs In, *ABA J.*, Jan. 2013.

应当仿效那些实施专业化的"整体性""治疗性"或者"社区"法院的国家,来处理诸如家庭暴力、无家可归、持有毒品和少年犯罪等问题。这些系统的法官得到了特别培训、资源和近用社会服务提供者的机会。其目标是解决问题的根源,而不仅仅是症状。① 通过将低级别的罪犯从刑事司法系统中分流出去,也能把律师解放出来,使其专注于更严重的问题。② 鉴于费效比,分流和重新分类可以作为解决双方当事人的财政问题的办法而推出。③

通过绩效标准、指引方针和对贫困被告的律师的监督,我们可以取得进一步的指引。这些指引可以包括工作量限制和经验要求。对于有效代理而言,它们还可以澄清,哪些事实调查、与委托人的沟通和相关事宜是必要的。④ 对于一贯疏怠基本责任的律师,应当有程序将其从有资格被指定的律师名单

---

① Greg Berman & John Feinblatt, Problem Solving Courts: A Brief Primer (2001); Julia Weber, Domestic Violence Courts, 2 J. Cent. Fam. Children & Cts. 23 (2000); Anthony C. Thomson, Courting Disorder: Some Thoughts on Community Courts, 10 Wash. U. J. L. & Pol'y 63(2002).

② Fairfax, Searching For Solutions, at 2332; Backus & Marcus, The Right to Counsel, at 1125-1126; Peter Joy, Rationing Justice by Rationing Lawyers, 37 Wash. U. J. L. &Pol'y 205 (2011); Norman Lefstein, ABA Standing Committee on Legal Aid & Indigent Defendants, Securing Reasonable Caseloads: Ethics and Law in Public Defense 19-24 (2011).

③ Drinan, Getting Real about Gideon, at 1330.

④ Schumm, National Indigent Defense Reform, at 10.

中除名。① 律师协会惩戒机构还应对那些因缺乏必要的时间或者专门知识而接受诉讼的律师实施重大惩处。应当有一个独立的机构来监督律师的绩效,以确保他们具备适当的资格,并使他们的代理达到最低的有效标准。在必要时,法官可以任命监督员监督遵守情况。②

另一个值得尝试的策略,是使用训练有素的非律师人员承担某些辩护职能,例如在保释听证会上代表被告。正如下面的讨论所表明的那样,在广泛的民事案件中,外行诉辩者已被证明是有效的,没有理由认为在轻微的刑事案件中他们的表现是不够的。③

最后,法官和律师协会需要做更多的事情来教育公众,让他们了解在贫困者辩护方面存在的问题,以及公众与解决这些问题利益相关。很少有美国人意识到流水线式的答辩和无效的律师辩护已经成为例行事件。大众的观念是由广为宣扬的案件和虚构的剧本塑造的,其中热忱的诉辩是常态。但是在黄金时段出现的法律与现实中的法律之间,仍然存在巨大的差距。公民不但需要了解贫穷的被告所面对的情况,也要了解改革对其本身的利益。辩护律师进行有力辩护的可

---

① See ABA Standards for Criminal Justice: Providing Defense Services Standard 44-45 (3d ed., 1992).

② Adam Liptak, Need-Blind Justice, *N.Y. Times*, Jan. 5, 2014, at wk. 4 (描述了西雅图法院的裁决).

③ Drinan, Getting Real about *Gideon*, at 1343.

能，为执法人员有效地工作和尊重个人权利创造了动力。为那些看似有罪的被告提供足够的代理，也是保护那些没有犯罪的人的最好方法。

当然，无效代理只是困扰美国刑事司法制度的问题之一。其他问题包括种族和族裔偏见、大规模监禁、草率或者暗示性的调查手段、警察和检察官不当行为、过度量刑、政治化的司法选举和应付不过来的法院案件负荷。一些论者认为，把注意力放在更好的律师辩护上，会使人们转移对这些更广泛的问题的注意力。① 但是无效代理是一个会使其他问题进一步恶化的问题，因为它排除了在法律上对这些问题提出挑战的可能性。拒绝为那些负担不起律师费用的被告给予足够的辩护，会损害我们在法律上对平等正义的最基本承诺。

/ 民事司法制度中的障碍 /

类似的问题困扰着民事司法制度。原则上，美国深深地忠信个人权利。实践中，很少有美国人能负担得起执行它们的费用。这些障碍体现在经济、系统、教义和政治等方面。

- 经济上的障碍

金钱可能不是万恶之源，但是它确实要对当前法律援助

---

① Paul D. Butler, Poor People Lose: *Gideon* and the Critique of Rights, *122 Yale L. J.* 2176 (2013).

第三章
近用司法

体系的许多问题负责。美国人不认为正义应当被出售,但是他们也不愿意为其他选项买单。即使在最近的预算削减之前,每6415个低收入人员也只有1名法律援助律师。① 在某些司法辖区,穷人必须等待2年,才能就未被视为紧急事件的事务见到法律援助律师,而其他司法辖区则完全排除此类案件。② 美国联邦政府用于法律援助的资金,每人每年只有大约1美元。③ 在这样的资金水平上,没有多少正当程序可用。与其他发达经济体相比,美国在法律援助方面的人均支出较少,而且满足常规需求的咨询机构和监察专员等机构也较少。④ 因此,与其他类似国家相比,更多的人因为价格问题而被排除出了法律体系。例如,一项调查报告说,在美国,38%的穷人和26%的中等收入者没有采取任何行动来应对法律

---

① Legal Services Corporation, Documenting the Justice Gap in America 19 (2009).

② Rhode, Access to Justice, at 14.

③ 2013年联邦法律援助拨款是3,408万美元。See Legal Services Corporation, http://www.lsc.gov/congress/lsc-funding.

④ 关于支出,see Gillian K. Hadfield, Higher Demand, Lower Supply? A Comparative Assessment of the Legal Resource Landscape for Ordinary Americans, *37 Fordham Urb. L. J.* 129, 139 (2010); Earl Johnson, Jr., Justice for America's Poor in the Year 2020: Some Possibilities Based on Experiences Here and Abroad, *58 DePaul L. Rev.* 393, 397-398 (2009); Raven Lidman, Civil *Gideon* as a Human Right: Is the U.S. Going to Join Step with the Rest of the Developed World? *15 Temp. Pol. & Civ. Rts. L. Rev.* 769, 780 (2006). 关于中间人制度,see Rebecca Sandefur, The Fulcrum Point of Access to Justice: Legal and Nonlegal Institutions of Remedy, *42 Loy. L. A. L. Rev.* 949, 957-962 (2009).

问题,而与此相比,在英格兰是5%,在荷兰则是10%。① 根据最新的全国性研究,只有1/4的美国民事司法问题由律师处理,只有14%的问题是由法院或者其他听证机构处理的。②

此外,最近的经济下行,使情况进一步恶化。高失业率、破产、丧失抵押品赎回权以及社会服务的减少,创造了更多的法律代理需求,与此同时,许多代理服务提供者都面临着预算的削减问题。③ 联邦法律援助预算自2010年以来已减少了近1/5,而在有资格获得这种代理的委托人人数增加的同时,私

---

① Hadfield, Higher Demand, at 139.

② Rebecca L. Sandefur, The Impact of Counsel: An Analysis of Empirical Evidence, 9 Seattle J. Soc. Just. 56, 60 (2010).

③ Robert J. Derocher, The IOLTA Crash: Fallout for Foundations, B. Leader, Sept./Oct. 2012 [报告了以律师信托基金账户利息(IOLTA)进行的资助的下降]; Lonnie A. Powers, As Fiftieth Anniversary Approaches, Public Funding of Civil Legal Aid Remains Vital to Justice, Huffington Post, Dec. 19, 2013 (指出2014年IOLTA资金比5年前少了85%); Emily Savner, Expand Legal Services Now, Nat'l L. J., Jun. 28, 2010 (报告说需求在上升,而在2007年和2009年期间,IOLTA资金下降了75%); Need a Lawyer, Good Luck, N. Y. Times, Oct. 14, 2010; Karen Sloan, Perfect Storm Hits Legal Aid, Nat'l L. J., Jan. 2011, at 1, 4 (指出来自政府的IOLTA资金在下降,私人筹款风潮在收紧,而服务需求在上升); Erik Eckholm, Interest Rate Drop Has Dire Results for Legal Aid Groups, N. Y. Times, Jan. 19, 2009, at A12 (报告说法律服务需求上升了30%); Richard Zorza, Access to Justice: Economic Crisis Challenges, Impacts, and Responses 8-9 (Self-Represented Network, 2009), available at http://www.Selfhelpsupport.org (发现大多数法官报告说,自行代理案件在增长,但是39%的法官也报告说资助服务预算在削减)。

人基金会的资助也在减少。① 实际上,缺少人手和过度扩张的法律援助计划常常被要求用更少的钱去做更多的事。因此,数以百万计的美国人发现,原则上可获得的法律保护在实践中是得不到的。例如,家庭暴力受害者无法获得保护令,老年医疗病人无法领取健康福利,残疾儿童缺少教育服务,被欺诈的消费者缺乏承受得起的救济办法。名单很长,并且成本是无法计算的。

- **系统障碍**

第二组问题是结构性的,即缺乏一个连贯的系统来分配帮助,并使委托人与最具费效比的服务提供者相匹配。美国律师基金会的研究人员最近首次对可用于民事法律服务的资金情况逐州进行了研究。他们发现,在州内部和各州之间,存在相当大的不平等:"地理就是命运:那些面临民事司法问题的人所能得到的服务,不是由他们的问题或者他们可能需要的服务所决定的,而是由他们碰巧住在哪里所决定的。"② 乔治

---

① See Legal Services Corporation, Temporary Operating Budget and Special Circumstance Operating Authority for Fiscal Year 2014; Erik Eckholm & Ian Lovett, A Push for Legal Aid in Civil Cases Finds Its Advocates, *N. Y. Times*, Nov. 22, 2014. 关于基金会的削减,see Sara K. Gould, Foundation Center, *Diminishing Dollars: The Impact of the 2008 Financial Crisis on the Field of Social Justice Philanthropy* (2011).

② Rebecca Sandefur & Aaron C. Smyth, Access Across America: First Report of the Civil Justice Infrastructure Mapping Project, American Bar. Foundation at v (Oct. 7, 2011).

亚州提供了一个供需不匹配的典型例子,这种不匹配往往是不平等的来源。该州大约70%的律师在亚特兰大地区,而70%的穷人住在亚特兰大地区以外。① 6个县没有律师,还有许多县只有2个或者3个律师。② 此外,正如美国律师基金会的研究人员所发现的那样,"民事法律援助几乎没有什么协作,现有的协作机制往往只有劝诫和磋商的权利。"③有关谁获得服务以及他们能获得哪些类型的服务的优先事项,通常由当地法律援助项目确定。其结果不仅是各司法辖区的资源差距,而且在推广大有可为的方案方面,资源也不足。④ 一个相关问题是,缺乏可靠的"经验证据……来说明什么[形式的]帮助最能满足[提出要求者]的需要,以及……什么样的协调和规划能确保那些有需要的人随时容易得到正确的帮助"⑤。

该制度也过度地以律师为中心。在近用司法的争论中,律师协会一直发出最有力的声音,它们认为对这一问题的解决办法是有"更多的律师"。2006年,美国律师协会一致通过一项决议,敦促"在涉及人的基本需要的对抗制程序中,以公共费用支出的方式向低收入者提供法律顾问,这应当是他

---

① Ethan Bronner, Right to Lawyer Can Be Empty Promise for Poor, *N. Y. Times*, Mar. 16, 2013, at A1, A6.
② Bronner, Right to Lawyer, at A6.
③ Sandefur & Smyth, Access Across America.
④ Jeanne Charn, Celebrating the "Null" Finding: Evidence-Based Strategies for Improving Access to Justice, *122 Yale L. J.* 2206, 2216 (2013).
⑤ Charn, Celebrating the "Null" Finding, at 2212.

们的权利。"① 许多州和地方律师协会都通过了类似的决议。② 这些组织并没有同样热衷于法庭程序的简化和非律师人员帮助,而是积极地与自助刊物和非律师人员进行斗争。③ 正如纽约大学法学教授史蒂芬·吉勒斯(Stephen Gillers)所指出的那样,这不是"律师行业最美好的时光"。④ 从行业的角度来看,注重保障有更多的律师,显然是说得通的。但是从公众的角度来看,其目标是更多地近用法律,而不一定要近用律师。

在处理住房、破产、小额诉讼和家庭事务的法院,没有律师的当事人现在往往不是少数。⑤ 但是他们必须遵守由律师

---

① American Bar Association Resolution 112A(2006), available at http://www.americanbar.org/content/dam/aba/administrative/legal_aid_indigent_defendants/ls_sclaid_06A112A.authcheckdam.pdf.

② 这些数据来源于获得律师帮助的民事权利联盟的网站:http://civilrighttocounsel.org/.

③ 关于历史上的反对的例子,see Deborah L. Rhode, Professionalism in Perspective: Alternative Approaches to Nonlawyer Practice, 22 N.Y.U. Rev. L. & Soc. Change 701, 705 (1996). 关于律师协会当前的反对意见和执行活动,see Richard Zorza & David Udell, New Roles for Non-Lawyers to Increase Access to Justice, 41 Fordham Urb. L. J. 1259, 1278 (2014); Deborah L. Rhode & Lucy Ricca, Unauthorized Practice Enforcement: Protection of the Public or the Profession, 82 Fordham L. Rev. 2588, 2588 (2014).

④ Steven Gillers, A Profession, If You Can Keep It, 63 Hastings L. J. 953, 979 (2012).

⑤ See, e.g., Russell Engler, Connecting Self-Representation to Civil Gideon: What Existing Data Reveal About When Counsel Is Most Needed, 37 Fordham Urb. L. J. 37, 41-43 (2010)(总结了在住房、小额诉讼和家庭法案件中代理率).

设计且为律师设计的程序。尽管法院已越来越多地试图迎接这些无人代理的诉讼当事人,但是一项全国性调查发现只有11个州有综合性计划来帮助自行代理的当事人。① 大多数可用的服务都无法被最需要帮助的人使用,因为低收入的当事人计算机能力和英语能力有限。② 通常情况下,当事人都面临着过度复杂和令人迷惑的程序,以及充斥着古老的行话的表单。与其他国家相比,美国在通过低成本方法而不是律师代理来近用司法方面,已经落后了。③ 例如,在英国,训练有素的非律师志愿者在3400个公民咨询局提供例行帮助。④ 法律援助还可以通过服务台、在线服务、保险公司、银行、工会、消费者组织甚至杂货店等政府网络得到。⑤ 在美国,数以百万计的人缺乏这种帮助,只有约半数的美国人对自己的法律问题的

---

① Alan W. Houseman, Civil Legal Aid in the United States: An Update for 2007 20-21 (2007), available at http://www.clasp.org/publications/civil_legal_aid_2007.pdf.

② 问题存在已久。See Jona Goldschmidt, How Are Courts Handling Pro Se Litigants? 82 *Judicature* 13, 20-22 (1998) (描述了可得的服务).

③ Charn, Celebrating the "Null" Finding, at 2225, 2226.

④ See the website for Citizens Advice Bureaus, at http://www.citizensadvice.org.uk/index/aboutus/ourhistory.htm.

⑤ Gillian K. Hadfield & Jamie Heine, Life in the Law-Thick World: The Legal Resource Landscape for Ordinary Americans, in *Beyond Elite Law: Access to Civil Justice for Americans of Average Means* (Samuel Estreicher & Joy Radice, eds., forthcoming).

解决表示满意。① 没有律师的诉讼当事人的经历太普遍了。当审判法庭告诉一个人,他缺少一份命令草案来授权转介咨询时,这个人开始询问有关如何准备该命令的问题。法官回答说:"我不是你的秘书",并把那个人赶出了法庭。②

此外,在某些情况下,如在无争议的离婚案件中,律师对问题的贡献可能大于对解决办法的贡献。在一项对由律师代理的离婚案件的调查中,71%的人认为,法律程序加剧了敌意。③ 这些当事人还认为,律师将直接交流替换为只通过律师沟通,这样一来就加剧了冲突。④ 其他研究发现,离婚当事人更青睐于更简单、更少的对抗性程序,而且许多人因为担心激化冲突而不会聘请律师。⑤

• 教义障碍

在教义层面上,一个根本性的问题源于法院规制法律实务活动的固有权力,以及为行使这一权力而禁止非律师人员

---

① ABA Consortium on Legal Services and the Public, Legal Needs and Civil Justice: A Survey of Americans; Major Findings from the Comprehensive Legal Needs Study 7-19 (1994).

② Amanda Ripley, Who Needs Lawyers? *Time* Jun. 12, 2000, at 62.

③ Marsha Kline Pruett & Tamara D. Jackson, The Lawyer's Role During the Divorce Process: Perceptions of Parents, Their Young Children, and Their Attorneys, *33 Fam. L. Q.* 283, 298 (1999).

④ Pruett & Jackson, The Lawyer's Role, at 298.

⑤ See research summarized in Rebecca Aviel, Why Civil *Gideon* Won't Fix Family Law, *122 Yale L. J.* 2106, 2117-2118 (2013).

的非法执业,而不顾及其质量或者费效比。第二个问题涉及法院确定当事人什么时候可以获得法院指定的律师的限制性标准。其结果是让无律师的诉讼当事人承担了不现实的负担,证明如果没有律师,法律程序将存在根本性的不公平。

成文法和普通法关于禁止非法执业的一个共同特点是其广泛而模糊的范围。许多司法辖区在没有进行界定的情况下径行对非律师人员执业加以禁止。① 其他司法辖区采取了一种循环方法:法律执业活动就是律师所开展的活动。② 用文字罗列出一些行为,如法律咨询、法律代理和法律文件的制作,然后以一些含糊的"无所不包"的条款结束,如"在与法律关联的事务中为他人采取行动"。③ 从表面看,这些禁令包括广泛的常见商业活动。许多人,包括会计师、金融顾问、房地产经纪人、保险代理人甚至报纸的咨询专栏作家在内,都不能在不考虑法律问题的情况下提供明智的建议。此外,禁止个性化帮助是对称职的低成本服务提供者的一个强有力的障碍。因此,例如,表单处理可以提供文秘帮助服务,但是禁止

---

① 例如,see Deborah L. Rhode, Policing the Professional Monopoly: A Constitutional and Empirical Analysis of Unauthorized Practice Prohibitions, *34 Stan. L. Rev.* 1, 45, n135 (1981). 关于州法院不愿意做出定义的问题,see cases cited in Susan D. Hoppock, Enforcing Unauthorized Practice of law Prohibitions: The Emergence of the Private Cause of Action and its Impact on Effective Enforcement, *20 Geo. J. Legal Ethics* 719, 722 n35 (2007).

② Rhode, Policing, at n136.

③ Rhode, Policing, at n140-n142; Ga. Code Ann. Section 9-401.

纠正明显的错误或者回答有关何时何地提交文件的简单问题。① 一些判决甚至判定,在线文档帮助构成非法执业,因为这些服务超出了文秘辅助的范围。② 法院书记员也被禁止为无人代理的当事人提供咨询。③ 一些法院有这样的告示,即书记员"不能回答法律性质的问题"④。然而,正如一位加利福尼亚法官所指出的那样,除了"洗手间在哪里",那些都是书记员通常遇到的问题。⑤

这种宽泛性的禁止不利于为公众利益服务。虽然法院一再坚称,广泛禁止非法执业有助于保护公众,但是这一主张往往得不到支持。⑥ 在我最近对近十年以来公布的非法执业

---

① *Fifteenth Judicial District Unified Bar Association v. Glasgow*, 1999 WL 1128847 (Tennessee Appellate 1999); Florida Bar v. Brumbaugh, 355 So. 2d 1186 (Fla. 1978).

② *In re Reynoso*, 477 F. 3d 1117 (9th Cir. 2007); *Committee v. Parsons Technology*, 179 F. 3d 956 (5th Cir. 1999); *Janson v. LegalZoom*, 802 F. Supp. 1053 (W. D. Mo. 2011). 得克萨斯州的一项裁决被一项立法豁免推翻了,密苏里州的案件随后和解了,没有完全禁止该等服务。See Tom McNichol, Is LegalZoom's Gain Your Loss? *Cal. Law.*, Sept. 2010, at 20. 2014 年,LegalZoom 在 4 个州迎战诉讼。See also Susan Beck, The Future of Law, *Am. Law.*, Aug. 2014, at 36.

③ John M. Greacen, No Legal Advice from Court Personnel: What Does That Mean? *10 Judges J.* 10, 10-12 (Winter 1995).

④ Rhode, Access to Justice, at 83.

⑤ Rhode, Access to Justice, at 83.

⑥ *Kentucky Bar Ass'n v. Tarpinian*, 337 S. W. 3d 627 (Ky. S. Ct. 2011) (通过了特别专员的报告); *Louisiana State Bar Ass'n v. Carr and Assocs., Inc.*, 15 So. 3d 158, 167 (Louisiana Ct. App. 2009).

案例进行的回顾中,只有 1/4 的案例分析了非法执业是否造成或者可能造成实际损害的发生。① 在我对参与非法执业执法的官员进行的全国性调查中,2/3 的人想不起来过去一年中造成伤害的具体案件。② 同样,其他研究也对给委托人造成伤害的频度产生了怀疑。绝大多数针对在线服务的非法执业诉讼,都不是由消费者提起的,而是由律师或者非法执业委员会提出的,一般在没有损害的情况下就和解了。③

其他国家允许非律师人员提供法律咨询和协助制作例行文件,现有证据并未表明他们的表现不合格。④ 在一项比较双方在英国低收入委托人在福利、住房和就业等问题上取得的结果的研究中,在具体结果和委托人满意度方面,非律师人员的表现通常优于律师。⑤ 在回顾了他们自己和其他的实证研

---

① Rhode &Ricca, Protecting the Public or the Profession, at 2604.

② Rhode &Ricca, Protecting the Public or the Profession, at 2595.

③ Mathew Rotenberg, Stifled Justice: The Unauthorized Practice of Law and Internet Legal Resources, *97 Minn. L. Rev.* 709, 722 (2012).

④ Rhode, Access to Justice, at 89; Julian Lonbay, Assessing the European Market for Legal Services: Developments in the Free Movement of Lawyers in the European Union, *33 Fordham Int'l L. J.* 1629, 1636 (2010) (讨论了瑞典的法律咨询提供者); Herbert Kritzer, Rethinking Barriers to Legal Practice, *81 Judicature* 100, 101 (1997) (讨论了有训练有素的非律师志愿者的英国公民咨询局).

⑤ Richard Moorhead, Alan Paterson, &Avrom Sherr, Contesting Professionalism: Legal Aid and Nonlawyers in England and Wales, *37 Law & Soc. Rev.* 765, 785-787 (2003). 有关讨论, see Deborah J. Cantrell, The Obligation of Legal Aid Lawyers to Champion Practice by Nonlawyers, *73 Fordham L. Rev.* 883, 888-890 (2004).

究后,该研究的作者得出结论:"质量的最佳预测因素,似乎是专业化,而不是职业的地位。"①安大略省允许持照律师助理在法院轻微案件和行政法裁判庭诉讼中代理自然人,为期5年的审查报告说,"公众对所得到的服务非常满意"②。

在美国,对在破产和行政机关听证中提供法律代理的外行专家进行的研究发现,他们的表现一般都和律师一样,甚至要比律师更好。③ 与有效辩护的日常经验相比,广泛的正式培训不太重要。④ 然而,现有的非法执业学说只关注非律师人员是否在提供法律帮助,而不是帮助的质量或者公共损害的证据。

法院为确定民事诉讼中获得律师帮助的权利而确立的限制性标准,引起了进一步的教义问题。最新的权威案例是最高法院在特纳诉罗杰斯案中的判决。此案中,迈克尔·特纳（Michael Turner）,因未能向其子女的母亲丽贝卡·罗杰斯（Rebecca Rogers）支付子女抚养费而多次被判民事藐视法庭,并被关进了看守所。在民事藐视法庭案听证会上,特纳无人代理,在服刑一年后,他找到一位公益律师对南卡罗来纳州法院未能为他指定律师而提出异议。最高法院一致裁定,正当程

---

① Moorhead, Paterson, &Sherr, Contesting Professionalism, at 795.

② David B. Morris, Report to the Attorney General of Ontario 12 (Nov. 2012).

③ Herbert Kritzer, *Legal Advocacy: Lawyers and Nonlawyers at Work* 76, 108, 148, 190, 201 (1998).

④ Kritzer, *Legal Advocacy*.

序条款没有赋予特纳获得律师帮助的权利。法院采用了马修斯诉埃尔德里奇案件中阐明的权衡标准,这需要考虑"(1)'将受影响的私人利益'的性质;(2)在有无'额外或者替代性程序保障的情况下错误剥夺该利益'的相对'风险';以及(3)不提供'额外或者替代性要求'的任何抵消性利益的性质和大小。"①经过权衡,法院得出结论说,尽管被告有强烈的自由利益,但是案件事实不支持为他指定律师。在这样判决时,法院强调,被告是否有能力支付抚养费这一关键问题是"足够明了"的,在没有律师的情况下解决起来也不复杂。此外,由于罗杰斯没有代理律师,只为特纳指定律师可能造成不对等,可能会导致其支付抚养费过慢,并使诉讼"在整体上不公平"。② 多数意见还认为,在没有指定律师的情况下,有一种可供选择的保护措施,可以"大大减少错误剥夺自由的风险"。③ 这些保护措施包括:发出通知,说明支付子女抚养费的能力是一个关键问题;要求被告人填写财务披露表;允许被告对其财务问题作出答复;并对支付能力作出明确的认定。由于特纳既没有得到指定律师的帮助,也没有得到这些替代性保障的保护,法院推翻了对他的定罪。

这项判决有几个理由是有问题的。一是缺乏经验证据来支

---

① Turner v. Rogers, 131 S. Ct. 2507, 2517 - 2518 (2011) [quoting Mathews v. Eldridge, 424 U.S. 3.19, 335 (1976)].

② Turner v. Rogers, at 2519.

③ Turner v. Rogers, at 2519.

持法院关于程序的复杂性和替代性措施的公正性的断言。一些论者认为,法院的分析"与现实世界的惊人脱节"①。"我认为法院并不理解没有律师出庭是什么感觉",乔治敦大学法学教授彼得·埃德尔曼(Peter Edelman)指出。"最好让他们都在房东—租户法庭待上一天,看看他们是否还有同样的看法。"②一个无律师代理的诉讼当事人如何能够证明替代性程序将缺乏根本的公平性,或者存在不可接受的错误风险?③ 论者还指出,与被判刑事藐视法院相比,被判民事藐视法院的特纳面临着更长时间的牢狱之灾,这要求为其任命律师。④

耶鲁大学法学教授朱迪斯·雷斯尼克(Judith Resnik)发现,特纳案件所应用的马修斯案件的权衡标准存在根本性问题。"无论是法官还是诉讼当事人,都不能严谨地确定各种程序的实际成本,更不用说从[错误]角度[衡量]影响了……"⑤另一个问

---

① Norman Reimer, *Turner v. Rogers*: The Right to Counsel Haunted by the Ghost of Gagnon, *Concurring Opinions*, Jun. 27, 2011. See also Peter B. Edelman, Does the Supreme Court Get It in *Turner*? *Concurring Opinions*, Jun. 27, 2011; Russell Engler, *Turner v. Rogers* and the Essential Role of the Courts in Delivering Access to Justice, 7 *Harv. Law &Pol'y Rev.* 31, 41 (2013).

② Mark Walsh, A Sour Note from Gideon's Trumpet: Playing the Blues for the Right of Counsel in Civil Cases, *ABA J.*, Sept. 2011, at 14 (quoting Peter Edelman).

③ Engler, *Turner v. Rogers*, at 56.

④ Walsh, A Sour Note (quoting Russell Engler).

⑤ Judith Resnik, Comment, Fairness in Numbers: A Comment on *AT&T v. Concepcion*, *Wal-Mart v. Dukes*, and *Turner v. Rogers*, 125 *Harv. L. Rev.* 78, 158 (2012).

题是无律师代理的诉讼当事人如何可以确定法院实际上提供了必要的替代性保障。① 就像雷斯尼克所指出的那样,特纳案件中的审判法官"花了不到 5 分钟的时间……没有将认定结果记录在案……就将特纳送进了看守所关了 12 个月",这表明负责确保这些替代性保护措施的法院存在不足。② 在没有"公共问责和律师的参与的情况下,很少有机制来监督特纳所要求的公平性……"③

此外,特纳案件所支持的权衡标准不仅在理论上有缺陷,在实践中也被证明是行不通的。需要帮助的弱势诉讼当事人几乎从未成功地说服联邦法院提供这些帮助。④ 州法院和立法机关只在极其有限的案件类别中指定律师,通常涉及某些家庭、医疗和民事强制医疗问题。⑤ 从民事法律援助项目的案件负荷来看,约 98% 的案件直接涉及无权获得律师帮助的低收入当事人。⑥ 因此,选择保证提供律师的案件,有时似乎

---

① Resnik, Comment, at 158.
② Resnik, Comment, at 160.
③ Resnik, Comment, at 160.
④ Houseman, Civil Legal Aid in the United States, at 16. 公民吉迪恩的诉讼历史,汇总在民事权利联盟的网站上:http://www.civilrightocounsel.org/advances/litigation/.
⑤ Clare Pastore, Life After *Lassiter*: An Overview of State-Court Right to Counsel Decisions, 40 Clearinghouse Rev. 186, 189-191 (2006); Laura K. Abel & Max Rettig, State Statutes Providing for a Right to Counsel in Civil Cases, 40 Clearinghouse Rev. 245 (2006).
⑥ Houseman, Civil Legal Aid in the United States, at 16.

是很特别的。为什么那些挑战自愿接种疫苗命令或者接受学校教育的人能得到律师的帮助,而那些面临如食物、住房、医疗福利或者家庭暴力等生存问题的人,却得不到律师的帮助?① 即使在有律师在场的情况下,对律师有足够的经验、培训和律师获得薪酬的要求,通常既不是强加的,也是不能满足的。②

拒绝向无证移民提供帮助,带来了特别大的困难。他们经常缺乏语言技能和对美国法律程序的理解,这使得他们很难在没有法律援助的情况下开展程序。然而,只有约 1/3 的外国人和 10% 的在押者在移民程序中有法律代理。③ 由联邦法律服务公司资助的项目被禁止代理无证外国人。④ 虽然大部分联邦判决授权指定律师以防止发生错误的判决,但是调查发现,30 年来,没有一宗移民案件的非美国公民得到了法院指定律师的帮助。⑤

---

① Abel & Rettig, State Statutes, at 246-247.
② Abel & Rettig, State Statutes, at 248.
③ Robert A. Katzman, The Legal Profession and the Unmet Needs of the Immigrant Poor, 21 Geo. J. Legal Ethics 3, 7-8 (2008). 超过 40% 的非公民在驱逐出境听证会上缺少律师。Robert A. Katzmann, When Legal Representation Is Deficient: The Challenge of Immigration Cases for the Courts, *Daedalus*, Summer 2014, at 37.
④ 45 C. F. R. Section 1626 (2009).
⑤ See *Aguilera-Enriquez v. INS*, 516 F. 2d 565, 568 (6th Cir. 1075); Thomas Alexander Alienikoff, David A. Martin, & Hiroshi Motomura, *Immigration and Citizenship* 645 (5th ed. , 2003).

- 政治障碍

司法系统的最后一组障碍是政治性的。公众对近用司法的问题并不知情,毫无组织,更喜欢律师协会给出的有反对理由的选项。① 虽然绝大多数美国人支持向那些负担不起律师费用的人提供法律服务,但 4/5 的人也错误地认为穷人有权在民事案件中获得律师的帮助。② 2/3 的人认为,低收入的个人在寻求法律帮助方面不存在困难,这一看法完全与现实脱节。③ 在罕见的情况下,当征求意见时,4/5 的公众也同意"律师处理的许多事情,非律师人员也可以做好,而且更为便宜。"④然而,普通公民缺乏足够的动机来推进允许近用这些服务的改革。与作为关键和持续需求的医疗保障不同的是,大多数美国人的对法律帮助的需求是偶发性的,很少威胁到生命。

---

① 关于律师在诸如反竞争许可限制等事项上与消费者相比的优势,see Larry E. Ribstein, Lawyers as Lawmakers: A Theory of Lawyer Licensing, *69 Mo. L. Rev.*, 299, 314 (2004).

② 在美国律师协会发起的一次调查中,55%的人强烈同意获得法律服务至关重要,33%的人一定程度上同意。ABA Survey Summary, Economic Downturn and Access to Legal Resources (Apr. 2009), available at http://www.abanow.org/wordpress/wp-content/files/flutter1268261059_20_7_upload_file.pdf. 关于公众对于获得律师帮助的权利的信念,see Johnson, Justice For America's Poor, at 393; ABA, Perceptions of the U.S. Justice System 63 (1999), available at http://www.abanet.org/media/perceptions/pdf.

③ ABA, Perceptions of the U.S. Justice System.

④ Barbara Curran & F. Spaulding, *The Legal Needs of the Public* 231 (1977). 律师业最近没有再提出该问题。

第三章
近用司法

　　鉴于律师协会的动机和抵制能力,改革的障碍尤其巨大。在政府的三个部门中,没有其他职业享有如此突出的地位。因此,律师业在传统上的优势地位可以阻止那些可能会使公众受益但是会让法律职业付出代价的变革。律师协会多次与自助出版进行斗争,反对近用非律师人员的帮助。① 美国律师协会支持加强打击非法执业的做法是有案可查的,超过4/5的被调查律师赞成起诉独立律师助理。② 律师协会还担心,"有关自行代理的法院的改革,将从穷人扩大到中产阶级和其他阶层"③。强制执行非法执业禁令以及控制程序简化和自行代理案件的法院,在影响律师行业生计的事务上,过分服从于

---

① See Beck, Future of Law; Benjamin H. Barton, The Lawyer's Monopoly—What Goes and What Stays, 82 Fordham L. Rev. 3067-3090 (2014); Deborah L. Rhode, Professionalism in Perspective, at 701, 705. 关于得克萨斯州律师协会禁止自助计算机软件程序的努力被得克萨斯州立法机关推翻,see Unauthorized Practice of Law Committee v. Parsons Technology, 1999 WL 47235 (N. D. Tex), vacated and remanded 179 F. 3d 956 (1999); Randall Samborn, So What Is a Lawyer Anyway? Nat'l L. J., Jun. 21, 1993, at 1, 12. 关于律师协会对LegalZoom提起诉讼,不在乎该公司有很高的顾客满意度,see Rhode & Ricca, Protecting the Profession or the Public, at 2605; Terry Carter, LegalZoom Hits a Legal Hurdle in North Carolina, ABA J., May 2013, http://www.abajournal.com/news/article/legalzoom_hits_a_hurdle_in_north_Carolina.

② Rhode, Access to Justice, at 88; ABA Select Committee Report on the 2000 Midyear Meeting, available at http://www.abanet.org/leadership/2000house.html; James Podgers, Legal Profession Faces Rising Tide of Nonlawyer Practice, ABA J., Dec. 1993, at 51, 56.

③ Benjamin H. Barton & Stephanos Bibas, Triaging Appointed Counsel Funding and Pro Se Access to Justice, 160 U. Pa. L. Rev. 967, 994 (2012).

律师业。①

来自律师的政治反对派,也破坏了将公益服务强制化的努力。虽然律师协会领导人和伦理守则一直认为,所有律师都负有向那些负担不起律师费的人提供法律援助的职业责任,但是为强制执行这一义务而提出的建议已经被粗鲁地埋没了。② 在没有要求的情况下,只有大约 1/4 的美国律师符合美国律师协会《职业行为示范规则》所规定的每年 50 小时公益服务的标准。③ 在全国最大的律师事务所中,甚至只有少数律师每年公益服务时长可以达到 20 小时。④ 考虑到参与程度,大多数律师拒绝将公益服务强制化也许不足为奇。甚至只有 9 个州要求律师报告他们的无偿工作时间。⑤

---

① Benjamin Barton, *The Lawyer-Judge Bias in the American Legal Profession* (2011); Benjamin Barton, Do Judges Systematically Favor the Interests of the Legal Profession?, 59 Ala. L. Rev. 453 (2007).

② 这篇文章按照时间顺序说明了律师职业伦理守则和要求公益服务的举措:Deborah L. Rhode, *Pro Bono in Principle and in Practice* 15-17 (2005). 纽约州要求 50 个小时的公益工作,作为准入的条件,但是并没有就已经持照的律师设定该要求。Mosi Secret, Judge Details a Rule Requiring Pro Bono Work by Aspiring Lawyers, *N. Y. Times*, Sept. 19, 2012, at A25.

③ ABA Standing Committee on Pro Bono and Public Service, Supporting Justice II: A Report on the Pro Bono Work of America's Lawyers vi (2009); Model Rules of Professional Conduct, Rule 6.1.

④ 仅有 44%完成了至少 20 个小时的服务。Where the Recession Lingers, *Am. Law.*, Jun. 2013, at 47.

⑤ ABA State by State Pro Bono Service Rules, available at http://apps.americanbar.org/legalservices/probono/pbreporting.html.

律师业的参与不足,说明该职业和公众都错失了良机。律师个人和集体都能从参与公益服务中受益。公益服务可以提高他们的技能、关系、声望和心理健康,以及法律职业的公众形象。①

- 民事司法改革

尽管存在这些障碍,但是有理由期盼在近用司法方面会取得一些进展。首先,越来越多的公众对自助出版和服务感兴趣,自行代理诉讼当事人也越来越多,都给改革带来了相应的压力。正如法学教授罗素·恩格勒(Russell Engler)所指出的那样,对法官和法庭书记员在无律师代理的当事人方面的作用的态度,"在过去15年中发生了翻天覆地的变化……"②大约半数的州有近用司法委员会,最近成立了一个法学教授联盟,以支持关于近用司法问题的研究和教学行动。③ 华盛顿州已建立了一个针对独立的律师助理的颁照制度,允许他们提供某些例行服务,纽约批准了一个关于训练有素的非律师人员的"导航者"制度,他们可以在某些法院帮助自行代理的诉讼当

---

① See Rhode, *Pro Bono in Principle*, at 13–14.

② Russell Engler, *Turner v. Rogers* and the Essential Role of the Courts in Delivering Access to Justice, 7 *Harv. Law &Pol'y Rev.* 31, 45 (2013).

③ 关于近用司法委员会,see Richard Zorza, *Turner v. Rogers*: The Implications for Access to Justice Strategies, 95 *Judicature* 255, 264 (2012). 关于该联盟,see Deborah L. Rhode, Access to Justice: An Agenda for Legal Education and Research, 62 *J. Legal Educ.* 531 (2013).

事人,加利福尼亚州也正在考虑进行类似的改革。① 律师协会打击自助软件的做法,已经引发了州立法机关的抵触情绪,市场对此类产品的需求,已经压倒了律师协会对此加以应对的能力。② 在司法部、联邦贸易委员会和美国律师协会自己的反托拉斯部门提出这么修改是反竞争做法后,美国律师协会放弃对非法执业进行限制性定义的尝试。③ 加利福尼亚州和马萨诸塞州已启动试点项目,以评估在特定情况下保障获得律师帮助的权利的费效比。④ 根据对马萨诸塞州项目的一项研究,在法律援助上花费的每1美元,将为该州在诸如紧急避难所、寄养和执法等其他服务上节省2.69美元。⑤ 美国律师协会"法律教育的未来"工作组建议,针对提供例行法律服务的律师助理,建立一个颁照制度。⑥ 美国律师协会另一个"法律

---

① Elizabeth Chambliss, Law School Training for Licensed "Legal Technicians"? Implications for the Consumer Market, 65 *S. C. L. Rev.* 579 (2014); Don J. DeBenedictis, State Bar to Weigh Licensing Nonlawyers, *San Francisco Daily J.*, Apr. 11, 2013, at 1; Joyce E. Cutler, California State Bar Group Approves Report to Spur Support for Nonlawyer Practitioners, 29 *ABA/BNA Law. Man. Prof. Conduct*, Jul. 3, 2013, at 416; Jonathan Lippman, The State of the Judiciary 2014 8 (2014).

② Barton, The Lawyer's Monopoly, at 3067–3090.

③ See Rhode, Access to Justice, at 88.

④ Sargent Shriver Civil Counsel Act, A. B. 590 (Cal. 2009); Engler, *Turner v. Rogers*, at 49 (描述了马萨诸塞州的建议).

⑤ Eckholm & Lovett, A Push for Legal Aid.

⑥ American Bar Association Task Force on the Future of Legal Education, Report and Recommendations (2014), available at http://www.americanbar.org/content/dam/aba/administrative/professional_responsibility/report_and_recommendations_of_aba_task_force.authcheckdam.pdf.

近用工作组"正在考虑如何帮助律师业的新入行者向服务不足的人群提供援助。① 在近用司法问题上,从来就没有过这样一种喜闻乐见的气氛。

取得进一步的进展将需要四个层面的战略。首先,我们需要为自助和从律师之外的成本较低的服务供应者那里获得法律帮助提供最大的机会。第二项战略应当关注如何将案件与最具费效比的法律服务提供者相匹配,并确保在涉及根本利益且不能以其他方式有效解决的案件中,有获得律师帮助的机会。第三项战略应当是评估不同的援助方法,更好地了解哪些方法在哪些情况下最适合于谁。② 最后的战略应当是确保对公众和专业人员进行更多的有关改革的必要性的教育。

- 自助和非律师人员服务提供者

第一个战略已经很好地实施了。全国各地的法院都在贯彻改革措施,以接纳无律师的自行代理的诉讼当事人。③ 这些诉讼当事人往往特别容易受到伤害。他们特别贫穷,不熟悉法律程序,许多人面临着语言和使用计算机能力的障碍。④ 他

---

① James R. Silkenat, Connecting Supply and Demand, *ABA J.*, Oct. 2013, at 8; Sarah Parvini, ABA Seeks Match of Lawyers, People Needing Services, *San Francisco Daily J.*, Apr. 11, 2004, at 4.

② Charn, Celebrating the "Null Finding," at 2232.

③ See Barton & Bibas, Triaging Appointed-Counsel, at 987-990.

④ Russell Engler, Connecting Self-Representation to Civil *Gideon*: What Existing Data Reveal About When Counsel Is Most Needed, *27 Fordham Urb. L. J.* 37, 79 (2010).

们需要理查德·佐尔扎(Richard Zorza)所称的"自助友好型法院"。① 这种法院将设法减少复杂性,利用技术,并培训法官和工作人员协助诉讼当事人。② 这样的模式越来越多。美国司法协会和全国州法院中心发表了指南,使法律诉讼程序更加公平,并让没有律师的当事人能够近用。③ 自我代理诉讼网还汇编出版了最佳做法和创新方法方面的材料。④ 一些法院系统为自行代理的案件设立了特别治安法庭,或者雇用了律师员工协助自行代理的诉讼当事人。⑤ 其他的法院有热线电话、自行代理文员办公室、"每日值班律师项目"和自助中心。⑥ 但是,所有这些策略都承诺让法院更易近用,说明我们对法院的

---

① Richard Zorza, National Center for State Courts, *The Self-Help Friendly Court: Designed From the Ground Up to Work for People Without Lawyers* (2002).
② Engler, *Turner v. Rogers*, at 58.
③ Cynthia Gray, American Judicature Society and State Justice Institute, *Reaching Out or Overreaching: Judicial Ethics and Self-Represented Litigants* 51-57 (2005).
④ The Self-Represented Litigation Network, Core Materials on Self-Represented Litigation Innovation (2006).
⑤ 关于纽约治安法院, see Lois Bloom & Helen Hershkoff, Federal Courts, Magistrate Judges and the Pro Se Plaintiff, *16 Notre Dame J. L. Ethics & Pub. Pol'y* 475, 493-497 (2002). 关于圣安东尼奥市员工律师项目, see Anita Davis, A Pro Se Program That Is Also "Pro" Judges, Lawyers, and the Public, *63 Tex. B. J.* 896 (2000).
⑥ Engler, Turner v. Rogers, at 42. See also Sheldon Krantz, *The Legal Profession: What Is Wrong and How to Fix It* 97-98 (2013).

第三章
近用司法

近用往往太滞后了。① 在许多司法辖区,严重的财政限制和最近的预算削减,加剧了为自行代理服务提供资金所面临的挑战。② 克服这些障碍,将需要更多地暴露司法制度的难以近用性、更多的创新资源以及让法院承担责任的更多的方法。

美国人也将受益于更有效的非正式争端解决渠道,不仅是在法院,还可以是在社区、工作场所、商业和在线环境。大量证据表明,配置良好的雇员和设计良好的消费者投诉程序有利于商业和个人参与者,而且大多数人更愿意通过非正式的庭外程序解决争端。③ 此类程序通常比司法干预更具费效比,并可能使参与者能够达成更好地解决其背后的问题的结果。可以激励达到某种规模的企业将这种解决争端的程序制

---

① Jona Goldschmidt, The Pro Se Litigant's Struggle for Access to Justice: Meeting the Challenge of Bench and Bar Resistance, *40 Fam. Ct. Rev.* 6, 40 (2002). 关于对自行代理的诉讼当事人及其造成的负担所持的消极看法,see Stephen Landsman, The Growing Challenge of Pro Se Litigation, *13 Lewis & Clark L. Rev.* 439, 449 (2009).

② See Julia Cheever, Deep Cuts to Court Funding Make CA Chief Justice "Afraid to See the Future," *SF Appeal*, Aug. 9, 2013, available at http://sfappeal.com/2013/08/deep-cuts-to-court-funding-makeca-chief-justice-afraid-to-see-the-future/; Sheri Qualters, No Respite: State Courts Face Another Year of Lean Budgets and Tough Cuts, *Nat'l L. J.*, Feb. 20, 2012, at 1.

③ Christine Parker, *Just Lawyers: Regulation and Access to Justice* 184-189 (1990). 关于人们愿意通过该方式解决争端,see Michael Zander, *The State of Justice* 29-32 (2000); and Hazel G. Genn, *Paths to Justice: What People Do and Think about Going to Law* 217-218 (1999). 就在线争端解决,see Ross Todd, Look Ma, No Judge, *Am. Law.*, Aug. 2014, at 34.

度化,应当要求改革现在对较弱的当事人不利的仲裁和调解程序。①

我们也需要改变非法执业的教义和执法。对非法执业的指控,只应在证明消费者受到伤害的情况下提出。法官在决定是否禁止非律师人员的帮助时,应当以已经权衡了公众利益的法院为榜样。例如,科罗拉多州最高法院维持了一个使非律师人员能够在失业诉讼中代理申请人的制度;法院的理由是,50年来,公众已经接受了外行代理,而"这对科罗拉多州人民没有构成威胁。它也没有干扰适当司法。就此也没有提出相反的证据。"②同样,华盛顿州最高法院在考虑诸如成本、服务的可得性和消费者便利等因素后,得出结论,允许持照房地产经纪人填写标准表格协议符合公众利益。③ 这种以消费者为导向的做法,与传统的无论其质量和费效比如何都禁止非律师人员执业的做法相比,将形成一种社会更为拥护的规制结构。

还可以制定颁照制度,使合格的非律师人员能够在例行事项上提供人性化帮助。在资格、免责声明、伦理标准、不当

---

① See Miles B. Farmer, Mandatory and Fair? A Better System of Mandatory Arbitration, *121 Yale L. J.* 2346, 2355 – 2360 (2012); Katherine V. W. Stone, Rustic Justice: Community and Coercion under the Federal Arbitration Act, *77 North Car. L. Rev.* 931, 1015-1017 (1999).

② *Supreme Court of Colorado v. Employers Unity* 716 P. 2d 460, 463 (Col. 1986).

③ *Culum v. Heritage House Realtors*, 694 P. 2d 630 (Wash. 1985).

第三章
近用司法

执业保险和惩戒方面可能需要消费者保护。① 许多行政机构已经有权力管理出庭的非律师人员，没有证据表明这些非律师人员的表现是不够的。② 根据其固有的权力，法院可以监督此种颁照制度的制定，或者批准设立经立法授权与公共利益一致的机构。更多的州应仿效华盛顿州和纽约州的思路，它们已经朝着这个方向迈出了步伐。如果目标是保护委托人免受不称职律师的损害，而不是保护律师免于竞争，则规制外行专业人员是说得通的，而不是加以禁止。

这种规制制度在移民领域尤其有利，这一领域的特点是普遍存在欺诈和未得到满足的需求。③ 一些人宣称自己是公证人和移民顾问，他们利用了那些无法支付律师费用，又不愿

---

① Steven Gillers, How to Make Rules for Lawyers, *40 Pepp. L. Rev.* 365, 417 (2013); Richard Zorza & David Udell, New Roles for Non-Lawyers to Increase Access to Justice, *41 Fordham Urb. L. J.* 1259, 1304-1315 (2014).

② See Kritzer, Rethinking Barriers, at 101; Emily A. Unger, Solving Immigration Consultant Fraud through Expanded Federal Accreditation, *29 Law & Ineq.* 425, 448 (2011). See also Zachery C. Zurek, The Limited Power of the Bar to Protect Its Monopoly, *3 St. Mary's J. Legal Malpractice & Ethics* 242, 265 (2013)（讨论了对非律师专利专家的要求）.

③ 关于欺诈, see Unger, Solving Immigration Consultant Fraud; Careen Shannon, Regulating Immigration Legal Service Providers: Inadequate Representation and Notario Fraud, *78 Fordham L. Rev.* 577, 589 (2009); Jessica Wesberg & Bridget O'Shea, Fake Lawyers and Notaries Prey on Immigrants, *N. Y. Times*, Oct. 23, 2011, at A25. 关于未得到满足的需求, see Erin B. Corcoran, Bypassing Civil *Gideon*: A Legislative Proposal to Address the Rising Costs and Unmet Legal Needs of Unrepresented Immigrants, *115 W. Va. L. Rev.* 643, 654-655 (2012).

向当局投诉欺诈行为的消费者的无知。许多顾问利用了一些拉丁美洲国家的公证人的地位，这些法律专业人员在这些国家有正式的法律培训和提供法律帮助的权利。① 得益于与澳大利亚、加拿大和英国类似的颁照制度，这种制度允许持照非律师人员专家提供与移民有关的帮助。② 虽然美国允许经认可的非律师人员代理个人参加移民上诉，但是只允许作为非营利组织的代表，并且这些人只能就其活动收取微不足道的费用。③ 扩大的颁照制度，允许合格的外行专家收取合理的费用，可以扩大亟需帮助的人对司法的近用。④

总之，目前的状况是这种制度既没有得到执行，禁止事项

---

① Ann E. Langford, What's in a Name? Notarios in the United States and the Exploitation of a Vulnerable Latino Immigrant Population, 7 Harv. Latino L. Rev. 115, 119-120 (2004).

② 关于澳大利亚注册移民代理人的角色，see Information for Consumers, Australian Government Office of the Migration Agents Registration Authority, https://www.mara.gov.au/Consumer-Information/Information-for-Consumers/default.aspx. 关于加拿大授权移民顾问的角色，see Citizenship and Immigration Canada, Use an Authorized Immigration Representative, http://www.cic.gc.ca/english/information/representative/rep-who.asp. 关于英国受规制移民咨询者的角色，see Office of The Immigration Services Commissioner, The Code of Standards: The Commissioner's Rules, available at http://oisc.homeoffice.gov.uk/servefile.aspx?docid=6.

③ See 8 C.F.R. Section 1292.1 (2012); Shannon, Regulating Immigrant Legal Service Providers, at 602-603.

④ See Unger, Solving Immigration Consultant Fraud, at 443-449; Careen Shannon, To License or Not to License? A Look at Differing Approaches to Policing the Activities of Nonlawyer Immigration Service Providers, 33 Cardozo L. Rev. 437 (2001).

也涵盖过宽。律师协会禁止包括一系列称职的、低成本的服务。然而，消费者对这种帮助的强烈需求，使得这些禁令难以执行。因此，大多数的外行执业活动是不受规制的，而且在发生滥权行为时，如在移民情境下，公众的救济措施是不足的。一个更可取的规制结构将提供更少和更多的保护——为律师提供的保护更少，为消费者提供的保护更多。

- 民事案件中获得律师帮助的权利

我们不仅需要增加比律师服务更为便宜的选项，我们还需要建立使委托人与适当的服务提供者匹配的制度，并确保在其他选项不足的情况下提供律师。① 获得律师帮助的权利（"公民吉迪恩"）应取决于其根本利益是否存在争议，以及律师的帮助对于确保基本公平是否至关重要。② 在确定根本利益时，分析的出发点是美国律师协会赞成在"人的基本需要"领域指定律师的决议，这些基本需要被定义为住房、生计、安全、健康和儿童监护。③ 在判定基本公平性时，法院和立法机关应当考虑程序的复杂性和当事人之间的权利关系。

这种获得律师帮助的权利在原则上是令人信服的，但是在实践中具有挑战性。八十多年之前，美国联邦最高法院承

---

① 对这种匹配制度的需要，see Johnson, Justice for America's Poor, at 420-421; Charn, Celebrating the "Null" Finding.

② 其他的教义性标准，see Engler, Self-Representation and Civil *Gideon*, at 81, 85.

③ ABA Report of the House of Delegates 13 (2006).

认,个人"(在法律程序中)被听取意见的权利,在许多情况下,如果不包括在律师代理之下被听取意见的权利,将会无济于事"。① 近用律师,往往对法治和社会正义至关重要。在欧洲理事会中的49个国家和其他国家,如加拿大、日本、印度和澳大利亚,至少在某些民事案件中承认了获得律师帮助的权利,②美国已经落后于这些国家了。

横亘在我们前进道路上的是金钱。美国在刑事案件中试图为获得律师帮助的权利提供资助的经验,并不令人鼓舞。如前所述,在许多司法辖区,令人震惊的案件量和不体面的不足的律师费,使得有效代理成为不可能。③ 鉴于目前国家和地方在预算上的限制,没有理由期望它们会为公民在民事上获得律师帮助的权利提供更多的资金。在目前为儿童抚养案件的被告指定律师的司法辖区中,时间和资源的不足往往妨碍有效的帮助。④ 一个相关的问题是,扩大在民事上获得律师帮

---

① *Powell v. Alabama*, 285 U.S. 45, 68-69 (1932).

② Raven Lidman, Civil *Gideon* as a Human Right: Is the U.S. Going to Join Step with the Rest of the Developed World? *15 Temp. Pol. & Civ. Rights L. Rev.* 769, 771 (2006).

③ See ABA Standing Committee on Legal Aid and Indigent Defendants, *Gideon*'s Broken Promise: America's Continuing Quest for Equal Justice (2004); Barton & Bibas, Triaging AppointedCounsel, at 967, 973-977.

④ Rebecca May & Marguerite Roulet, Center For Family Policy and Practice, A Look at Arrests of Low-Income Fathers For Child Support Nonpayment: Enforcement, Court and Program Practices 45 (2005), available at http://www.cpr-mn.org/Documents/noncompliance.pdf.

助的权利,"将与其他获得律师帮助的权利产生竞争,资金将进一步被摊薄"。①

对此类问题的唯一原则性回应是,法院向州政府和联邦立法机关施加压力,要求其提供足够的法律援助资金,律师协会也必须要求律师提供公益服务。民事法律援助项目现在仅占不到全国法律支出的1%的情况,是国家的耻辱。② 大多数律师每周甚至不能安排一个小时的公益服务,这是法律职业的耻辱。我们可以而且必须做得更好。

- 为穷人提供的法律服务

虽然不充分的近用问题绝不限于穷人,但是低收入群体的特殊需要值得特别注意。与普通美国人相比,穷人和近贫者不仅经历了更多法律上的困难,他们的需求也特别紧迫。在面临被剥夺权利或者福利的情况下,处于经济边缘的个人更不能够"逆来顺受"。在没有帮助的情况下,低收入人员也不太可能具备有效地处理他们的法律问题所需要的教育和技能。

解决这些问题需要政府提供足够的资金,以满足那些需要法律帮助但是实际负担不起的人的需求。当然,"需要"和"负担能力"是什么,是有争议的,但是按照几乎所有标准来

---

① Barton & Bibas, Triaging Appointed-Counsel, at 993-994.
② Access to Justice Working Group, And Justice For All: Report to the State Bar of California 49-50, 58-60 (1996); Talbot "Sandy" D'Alembert, Tributaries of Justice: The Search for Full Access, *25 Fl. St. L. Review* 631 (1998).

说，我们目前的制度都远远不够。大多数欧洲国家为比在美国制度中有权获得法律援助广泛得多的人员提供了法律帮助保障，美国有资格获得法律援助的人限于低于或者刚刚高于官方贫困线的人员。在其他国家，资格标准包括：

- 索赔是否有合理的成功机会？
- 法律帮助会带来什么好处？如果没有法律帮助会有什么危害？
- 如果是一个理性的律师，在为理性的委托人提供咨询时，是否会建议委托人使用自己的钱来继续纠缠这些问题？[1]

在评估经济资格时，这些制度通常以浮动收入的方式运作。与美国当前法律援助办公室所服务的委托人相比，这种办法允许服务于范围更广的委托人。其他国家的更宽松的资格结构，弥补了美国模式排除许多有紧急问题却没有现实财力来解决它们的人员的局限。虽然这样的结构需要更多的资金，但是与目前只惠及穷人的方案相比，它具有更多的政治吸

---

[1] See Mark Richardson & Steven Reynolds, The Shrinking Public Purse: Civil Legal Aid in New South Wales, Australia, *5 Md. J. Contemp. L. Issue* 349, 360 (2004); Jeremy Cooper, English Legal Services: A Tale of Diminishing Returns, *5 Md. J. Contemp. L. Issue* 247, 253 (2004); Sarah Conn Martin, Appointed Counsel in Civil Cases: How California's Pilot Project Compares to Access to Counsel in Other Developed Countries, *37 J. Legal Prof.* 281, 290 (2013); *Quail v. Municipal Court*, 171 Cal App. 3d 572, 590 n13 (1985).

第三章
近用司法

引力。

对扩大的制度的补贴,可以有不同的财政来源,这可能会比一般税收收入得到更多公众的支持。例如,对与法律有关的收入征小额累进税,根据争议金额就法院立案费征收附加费,以及扩大允许向胜诉方支付律师费的范围。[1] 在法律收入总额超过2400亿美元的国家,仅仅是1%的税收就会带来显著的不同。[2]

一个公平和具有费效比的法律援助制度,也将在不限制政府补贴活动的情况下运作。接受联邦基金的法律服务项目可能不得将这笔钱(在某些情况下可能不得将任何其他收入)用于范围广泛的各种事项,包括学校种族隔离、堕胎、政治分区、福利改革、无证的外国委托人或者监狱犯人。这些方案也不能包括从事诸如游说、社区组织、集团诉讼或者在立法和行政规则制定程序中进行代理等活动。[3] 因为这些是最有可

---

[1] 加利福尼亚州的 Civil Gideon 试点项目是通过对不重要的法院服务收取费用的方式进行资助的。Access to Justice—Civil Right to Counsel—California Establishes Pilot Program to Expand Access to Counsel for Low‐Income Persons, *123 Harv. L. Rev.* 1532, 1536 (2010).

[2] Jeffrey D. Koelemay, Public Interest: Individual Pro Bono Not Enough, Judges Say: Pro Se Problem Needs Coordinated Attention, *15 ABA/BNA Law. Man. Prof. Conduct* 32 (2014).

[3] Omnibus Consolidated Rescissions and Appropriations Act of 1996, 110 Stat. 1321; 45 Code of Federal Regulations pt. 1610–1642. See Alan Houseman & Linda E. Perle, What Can and Cannot Be Done: Representation of Clients by LSC-Funded Programs (2001).

能解决法律问题根源的策略,并阻止未来的滥权行为,法律援助计划带来的选择令人难以接受。它们能够在没有联邦资金的情况下运行,以一种更为有效的方式帮助更少的个人委托人。或者,它们也可以处理更多的案件,但是只针对政治上可以接受的委托人,并以不太可能促进真正变革的方式进行。这是我们不应当接受的选择。要求进行这种限制的立法者,试图间接地完成他们无法直接做的事情:剥夺最不受欢迎的穷人的权利和应当享受的社会服务。无论在实践上还是原则上,这与一个致力于法律上的平等正义的国家都是不相称的。

- 公益服务

另外一个明显的增加近用法律顾问的办法,是要求律师作出公益贡献。目前的理想标准是一年 50 个小时,应当是强制性的,同时那些缺乏时间或者服务意向的人员,可以有经济买入的选项,因此买入款项用于支持指定的法律援助提供者。这要求的是 1 周不到 1 小时的援助或者经济上的等价物,使得强制性服务的批判者几乎没有理由提出以下过分渲染的说法:"潜在的法西斯主义""经济奴役"和"非自愿奴役"①。

公益要求的理论基础是显而易见的。由于近用司法往往需要近用律师,因此他们负有使法律服务可获得的特殊责任。

---

① Tigran W. Elred & Thomas Schoenherr, The Lawyer's Duty of Public Service: More than Charity? *96 W. Va. L. Rev.* 367, 391 n. 97 (1993–1994); Michael J. Mazzone, Mandatory Pro Bono: Slavery in Disguise, *Tex. L.*, Oct. 22, 1990, at 22.

第三章
近用司法

就像法院和律师的伦理守则早就指出的那样,州授予律师垄断性特权,也带来了特殊的义务。① 作为法院的职员,律师对确保程序的基本公平性负有一定的责任。由于律师在我们的司法系统中占据了重要的地位,让他们知道法律制度对穷人是如何发挥效用的或者如何无法发挥效用,也具有特别的价值。公益工作为许多律师提供了他们了解穷人的正义是什么样子的唯一的直接渠道。就与贫穷有关的问题和公共利益事业,给律师一些经验,可以为变革作出重要的铺垫。公益项目经常发起社会改革行动计划,加强了对政府资助法律援助的支持。②

要求提供公益服务将既有益于法律职业,也有益于公众。志愿者服务将为律师提供更多的技能、经验和社区联系方式。这种职业发展机会,代表了律师所投身的事业,往往是他们最有益的职业经验。③ 许多律师报告说,他们愿意做更多的公益工作,但是所在机构不支持。④ 美国律师协会的调查发现,年轻律师在实务活动中不满意的最重要的原因,是缺乏与公共福祉之间的联系。⑤ 而公益服务可以提供这种联系。

在没有要求提供公益服务的情况下,可以作出更多努力,以鼓励自愿性贡献。更多的法院和律师协会应当要求律所报告其

---

① See Rhode, *Pro Bono in Principle*, at 28.
② Rhode, *Pro Bono in Principle*, at 29; Robert A. Stein, Champions of Pro Bono, *ABA J.*, Aug. 1997, at 100.
③ Rhode, *Pro Bono in Principle*, at 30.
④ Rhode, *Pro Bono in Principle*, at 138-145.
⑤ ABA Young Lawyers Division, Career Satisfaction Survey 19-20 (2000).

公益帮助活动,更多的委托人在选择律师时应当考虑律师对公益服务的参与。例如,加利福尼亚州立法将公益贡献作为达成超过 5 万美元的州法律服务合同的一个条件。① 诸如美国律师协会公益和公共服务委员会这样的组织,可以发布有关雇主的公益服务政策和贡献的信息名录。它们还可以制定最佳做法,并公布证明它们的律师符合美国律师协会 50 小时公益服务的标准的雇主的名单。最佳做法可包括:

- 通过一项正式的公益政策,将公益工作的点数计入计费工时要求;
- 组织的领导层的明确承诺;
- 将公益服务视为绩效评估、晋升和薪酬决定的有利因素;
- 符合美国律师协会《职业行为示范规则》每年 50 小时的服务或者等值财力的标准的要求;
- 适当的监督和培训;以及
- 对服务的承认和展示。②

它们还可以针对那些服务未得到充分利用的特定律师群体,如退休律师和法律学者,作出更大的努力。③ 律师协会可

---

① Cal. Bus. & Prof. Code § 6072 (West 2013).

② Rhode, Access to Justice, at 180–181.

③ See Deborah L. Rhode, Senior Lawyers Serving Public Interests; Pro Bono and Second Stage Careers, *21 Prof. Law.* 1 (2011).

以提供辅助服务、免费不当执业保险,就公益服务培训提高继续教育学分。其目标应当是确保法律职业关于公共服务的口头承诺与实际投入之间有更紧密的匹配。

● 非捆绑式服务和创新服务结构

另一种扩大中等收入委托人近用律师的途径是非捆绑式法律服务。按照这种方法,律师在独立的法律任务方面提供帮助,如咨询、谈判、文件制作或者法院出庭,而不是全面代理。① 在美国律师协会一项调查中,2/3 的潜在委托人希望有一个关于非捆绑式服务的对话,并表示,律师愿意提供非捆绑式服务对于他们决定雇请谁来说,是很重要的。② 法院可以鼓励这种趋势,允许律师提交代笔诉状,并将其责任限定在特定任务上,只要这种限制是合理的,并且委托人作出了明确同意。③ 为了使此类代理更容易近用,律师可以采用诸如"Chain

---

① See Forrest S. Mosten, Unbundling Legal Services: Servicing Clients within Their Ability to Pay, *Judges J.*, Winter 2001, at 15; Forrest S. Mosten, Unbundled Legal Services Today—and Predictions for the Future, *35 Fam. Advoc.* 14 (2012); ABA Modest Means Task Force, *Handbook on Limited Scope Legal Assistance* (2003), available at http://www.abamet.prg/litigation/taskforces/modest/report.pdf.

② Will Hornsby, Unbundling and the Lawyer's Duty of Care, *35 Fam. Advoc.* 27 (2012).

③ See Model Rules of Professional Conduct, Rule 1.2 (2002) (规定了有限代理); Mosten, Unbundled Legal Services, at 18 (建议为律师提供民事豁免); Margaret Graham Tebo, Loosening Ties: Unbundling of Legal Services Can Open Door to New Clients, *ABA J.*, Aug. 2003, at 35 (指出了各州的规则)。

Legal Grind"（该店提供简短的建议及卡布奇诺和自助材料）以及"LegalForce"（一家提供建议和自助书籍和电脑亭的商店）这样的行动计划思路。① 为了增加对此类服务的需求,更多的州律师协会还可以建立专门的推介项目,将财力有限的委托人与愿意在减少律师费的基础上提供帮助的律师相匹配。②

● 研究

增加近用司法的一个主要障碍是缺乏对关键问题的研究。例如,我们很少知道什么时候需要律师来确保基本的公平。对律师在常规案件中的贡献进行的合理的方法论研究,是稀缺的和相互矛盾的。③ 使用随机对照组的研究人员对

---

① Carol J. Williams, Aid Expands for the Middle Class, *L. A. Times*, Mar. 10, 2009, at 6; Kevin Lee, Company Bets on First Retail Legal Store, *San Francisco Daily J.*, Feb. 8, 2013, at 1.

② Kathryn Alfisi, Low Bono Widens Path to Access to Justice, *Wash. Law.*, Sept. 2013, at 24; Deborah L. Rhode, Whatever Happened to Access to Justice, *42 Loy. L. A. L. Rev.* 868, 898–899 (2009).

③ Barton & Bibas, Triaging Appointed-Counsel, at 991（指出缺少可信的数据,研究结果相互冲突）; research discussed in Laura K. Abel, Evidence-Based Access to Justice, *13 U. Pa. J. L. & Soc. Change* 295 (2010)（描述了相互冲突的结果）; Rhode, Access to Justice: An Agenda, at 538–539（讨论了数据的缺少和相互冲突的结果）; Gillian K. Hadfield, Higher Demand, at 129（指出就评估律师的表现而言,"经验基础极少"）; Charn, Celebrating the "Null" Finding, at 2222（指出我们缺少"经验证据来支持什么样的帮助将最能满足索赔者需要的可信建议"）; Resnik, Fairness in Numbers, at 158（指出法官和诉讼当事人都无法知道"增加了律师是否会提高准确性"）; Engler, Self-Representation and Civil *Gideon*, at 69–73（指出缺少根据案件结果对自行帮助进行的评估,和使用满意度作为热线和自助项目的成功的标准所存在（转下页）

律师是否能改善结果得出了不同的结论。① 此外,短期结果并不是关于影响的唯一或者必然是最重要的量度。我们对指定律师的长期后果几乎一无所知。举例来说,赢得一起业主—租户案件,对稳定一方当事人的生活环境或者改善建筑环境有多少帮助?② 是否能更好地利用律师的时间?他们能否通

(接上页)的问题);D. James Greiner & Cassandra Wolos Pattanayak, Randomized Evaluation in Legal Assistance:What Difference Does Representation (Offer and Actual Use) Make, *121 Yale L. J.* 2118 (2012)(讨论了许多研究和相互冲突的结果在方法论上的不足);Engler, *Turner v. Rogers*, at 53(引用 Laura Abel 的话,指出"就各种类型的诉讼当事人为获得有意义的近用所需要的法律帮助的类型,缺少确实、可靠的数据")。

① Compare D. James Greiner & Cassandra Wolos Pattanayak, Randomized Evaluation in Legal Assistance:What Difference Does Representation (Offer and Actual Use) Make? *121 Yale L. J.* 2118 (2012)(发现获得律师代理与有利的制度之间没有关联性), with Caroll Seron, Martin Frankel, Gregg Van Syzin, & Jean Kovath, The Impact of Legal Counsel on Outcomes for Poor Tenants in New York City's Housing Court:Results of a Randomized Experiment, *35 Law & Soc'y Rev.* 419 (2001)(获得了律师帮助的租户比那些没有律师帮助的租户做得更好)。See also D. James Greiner, Cassandra Wolos Pattanayak, & Jonathan P. Hennessy, The Limits of Unbundled Legal Assistance:A Randomized Study in a Massachusetts District Court and Prospects for the Future, *126 Harv. L. Rev.* 901 (2013)(发现与那些被随机提供信息和自助的租户相比,获得律师帮助的租户进展得更好)。

② See Laura K. Abel & Susan Vignola, Economic and Other Benefits Associated with the Provision of Civil Legal Aid, *9 Seattle J. Soc. Just.* 139, 148-150 (2010)(描述了试图就长期后果进行量化的研究);Gary Blasi, Framing Access to Justice:Beyond Perceived Justice for Individuals, *42 Loy. L. A. L. Rev.* 913, 920-923, 936-939 (2009);Gary Blasi, How Much Access? How Much Justice? *73 Fordham L. Rev.* 865, 871 (2004)(讨论了一个这样的案件,即破旧房屋的屋主即使在一系列诉讼中败诉也拒绝进行必要的改善)。

过更多地关注政策和组织的相关举措,而不是通过个人,来防止无家可归？我们对什么样的案件最适合非捆绑式法律服务知之甚少。① 并且我们对热线、自行代理诊所和诸如 LegalZoom 这样的文件制作服务等各种自助策略缺乏充分数据。② 对于评估特定形式的帮助的相对费效比而言,更多的研究是至关重要的。

我们还需要对公益代理的质量和社会影响进行更多的评估。律师们往往认为,任何公益工作都肯定是无偿的;代理本身被视为是一种善,无论费效比如何。③ 在最近一次对律师事务所公益计划的调查中,没有一个律师事务所采取正式的措施来评估其工作的社会影响,或者是委托人和非营利性合作伙伴的满意度。④ 许多律师事务所都以"遍地开花"的方式运作:他们广泛播撒服务,希望因此结出某些善果。⑤ 有些事情

---

① Molly M. Jennings & D. James Greiner, The Evolution of Unbundling in Litigation: Three Case Studies and a Literature Review, 89 Den. U. L. Rev. 825, 827-828 (2012). 关于这个问题的唯一的随机性研究, see Greiner, Pattanayak, & Hennessy, The Limits of Unbundled Legal Assistance.

② See sources cited in Rhode, Access to Justice, at 121, 228 n. 38; and Milan Markovic, LegalZoom Redux, *Legal Ethics F.*, May 5, 2014, available at http://www.legalethicsforum.com/blog/.

③ 对该问题更为充分的阐述, see Deborah L. Rhode, Rethinking the Public in Lawyers' Public Service: Pro Bono, Strategic Philanthropy, and the Bottom Line, 77 *Fordham L. Rev.* 1435, 1452 (2008).

④ Scott Cummings & Deborah L. Rhode, Managing Pro Bono: Doing Well by Doing Better, 78 *Fordham L. Rev.* 2357, 2401-2403 (2010).

⑤ Rhode, Rethinking the Public, at 1446.

通常是这样,但是这不一定是对资源的最佳利用方式。好的意愿也不能保证好的结果。在一个罕见的场合,当有人问及时,几乎半数的公共利益法律组织都报告了它们从外部律师事务所获得的公益工作的质量问题。①

确保最有效地使用公益资源,将需要进行系统的研究。公益服务提供者应当就提供的服务的数量和类型、获得的结果以及委托人和公共利益伙伴的满意度,收集标准化数据。② 只有通过这样的研究工作,我们才能查明被我们疏忽的法律需求和应当解决的质量问题。

- 法律教育

法律教育可以通过支持研究和将近用司法问题纳入课程和项目活动,来促进近用司法。目前,在传统的核心课程中,这一话题缺失或者被边缘化。③ 即使是专业课程(从逻辑上讲,是涵盖这类问题的论坛)也往往侧重于关于律师实务活动的法律,而忽略了关于法律服务分配的更广泛的问题。④ 在我自

---

① Deborah L. Rhode, Public Interest Law: The Movement at Midlife, *60 Stanford L. Rev.* 2027, 2071 (2008).

② Scott L. Cummings & Rebecca L. Sandefur, Beyond the Numbers: What We Know—and Should Know—About American Pro Bono, *7 Harv. L. & Pol'y Rev.* 83, 105(2013).

③ 关于实质性问题的边缘化,see William M. Sullivan et al., *Educating Lawyers: Preparation for the Practice of Law* 141, 187 (2007).

④ 关于"没有伦理的法律职业伦理"的讨论,see Deborah L. Rhode, *In the Interests of Justice: Reforming the Legal Profession* 200 (2003); Sullivan et al, *Educating Lawyers*, at 149.

已进行的全国调查中,只有1%的法学院毕业生回想起职业责任课程或者迎新计划中涵盖了公益服务问题。① 尽管许多法律诊所提供了一些直接机会,以了解低收入社区的当下的正义现状,但是并非所有的学生都选修这些课程。鉴于需要提供技能培训和有关实体和程序法的知识,并非所有诊所都有时间考虑提供法律服务方面的结构性问题。为了填补这些空白,学校应至少提供一门课程,关注近用司法问题,并鼓励将该专题纳入核心课程。

鉴于法律职业的追求目标是所有律师都提供公益服务,所有法学院都应当为这一忠信打下基础。10年前,美国法学院协会的一个委员会建议每一个学校"为每一个学生提供至少一次受良好监督的公益机会,要么要求参加,要么想办法吸引大多数学生成为志愿者"②。我们与该目标仍然相去甚远。只有少数学校要求有公益工作,更少的学校为教师设定了具体的义务,而且在许多学校中,所要求的公益时数是很少的。③ 尽管

---

① Rhode, *Pro Bono in Principle*, at 162.

② Association of American Law Schools, Commission on Pro Bono and Public Service Opportunities in Law Schools, Learning to Serve: A Summary of the Findings and Recommendations of the AALS Commission on Pro Bono and Public Service in Law Schools 2 (1999).

③ 39所法学院要求学生提供服务,并将此作为毕业的条件。See http://apps.americanbar.org/legalservices/probono/lawschools/pb_programs_chart.html. 在许多这样的法学院中,每年所要求的时数不到10个。ABA Standing Committee on Professionalism, Report of Survey on Law School Professionalism Programs 46-47 (2006).

其他学校也有志愿者项目,但是它们的范围和监督有时还亟待完善,超过1/3的学生在没有进行公益工作的情况下就毕业了。① 法律教育可以做得更好,并且有着可以广泛推广的榜样。一个例子是罗杰·威廉姆斯(Roger Williams)法学院的公益合作项目,其中教师负责监督大约30个行动计划,这些行动计划涉及帮助低收入人员的学生、非营利组织和公益律师。②

美国律师协会的法律教育和律师准入委员会也应当做更多的工作来支持这些举措。其认证标准要求法学院"为学生参与公益活动提供大量机会"③。但是这一标准的执行没有多少强制性。美国律师协会应当规定学校必须要求提供公益服务,并把近用司法问题纳入核心课程。④

法律教育也应当就这些问题更多地教育公众。如前所述,近用司法的许多问题都是由于公众认识不到存在重大问题。大多数美国人不仅不正确地认为穷人已经有权得到指定

---

① Law School Survey on Student Engagement, Student Engagement in Law School: Enhancing Student Learning 8 (2009).

② Laurie Barron et al., Don't Do It Alone: A Community-Based Collaborative Approach to Pro Bono, 23 Geo. J. Legal Ethics 323 (2010).

③ American Bar Association, Standards for Approval of Law Schools 302 (b)(2), http://www.americanbar.org/groups/legal_education/resources/standards.html.

④ 美国律师协会已经要求法学院就法律专业及其成员的规则和责任进行教学。ABA Standards and Rules of Procedure for Approval of Law Schools, Standard 302 (a)(5). 美国律师协会《职业行为示范规则》第6.1条认识到提高近用司法是一种责任。ABA Model Rules of Professional Conduct, Rule 6.1 Comment ("每个律师……都有责任为那些付不起费用的人员提供法律服务……")。

的律师,他们还认为国家有太多的诉讼。① 这种看法,使法律服务预算的增加成为低优先事项。学者们需要为非学术受众撰写更多的文章,以将对法律的需要人性化。

平等正义的理想深深植根于美国的法律传统中,但是在法律实务中经常遭到侵犯。我们的国家以其对法治的忠信而自豪,但是费用却使得绝大多数公民无法获得法律帮助。我们的宪法保障刑事案件中律师的有效帮助,但是我们的法院未能确保这一点。对法律程序的主要控制权,掌握在减少耗费方面利害关系最小的法律职业手中。

30多年前,吉米·卡特(Jimmy Carter)总统指出,美国是"地球上律师最集中的地方,但是与法律技能相比,在人才和培训的资源方面……没有比这更为浪费或者分配不公的了。我们90%的律师为10%的人服务。我们律师过多,但是代理却不足。"②这种情况并没有改善。至少部分问题是法律职业自己造成的。我们的国家并不缺少律师,也不缺少关于如何使法律服务更容易近用的想法。剩下的挑战是更多地了解哪些策略最有效,并使其成为公共和职业的优先事项。如果我们的国家真正致力于法律上的平等正义,我们就必须做更多的事情来把这种口头上的愿望转化为日常的现实。

---

① David G. Savage, The Race to the White House: A Trial Lawyer on Ticket Has Corporate U. S. Seeing Red, *L. A. Times*, Sept. 13, 2004, at 1 (指出80%的美国人认为有太多的诉讼).

② James Carter, Remarks at the 100th Anniversary Luncheon of the Los Angeles County Bar Association, May 4, 1978), printed in *64 ABA J.* 840, 842 (1978).

04
Chapter

第四章
法律职业的多样性

- 原则与实践的差距
- 解释差距
- 种族、族裔和性别刻板印象
- 群体内部偏见：指导、后援、人际关系网和工作分配
- 工作场所结构和性别角色
- 抵触情绪
- 法律的界限
- 支持多样性的商业理由
- 个人战略
- 组织战略

美国正在就业方面继续争取多样性和性别平等,而讽刺的是,领导这一斗争的法律职业未能在自己的工作场所中树立好榜样。① 原则上,律师协会应深深地致力于机会平等和社会公正。在实践中,在营造公平的竞争环境方面它落后于其他职业。根据美国律师协会的数据,只有两个职业(自然科学和牙科)的多样性程度低于法律;医学、会计学、学术界和其他行业做得相当好。② 问题的一部分在于对问题到底是什么缺乏共识。造成律师事务所的性别、种族和族裔不平等的原因是什么? 谁要负责处理这些问题? 哪些解决方案值得付出代价?

这些都不是新问题。但是最近的经济和委托人压力表明,需要有更好的答案。在法律实务活动中,阻碍实现多样化和公平的许多障碍,代表的都是更深层次的结构性问题。本章主要侧重于

---

① 本章基于:Deborah L. Rhode, *Lawyers as Leaders* 129-153 (2013), and Deborah L. Rhode, From Platitudes to Priorities: Diversity and Gender Equity in Law Firms, *21 Geo. J. Legal Ethics* 1041 (2011).

② Elizabeth Chambliss, *Miles to Go: Progress of Minorities in the Legal Profession* ix (2000). 例如,少数族裔占医生的 25%,会计师的 21%,但是只占律师的 11%。Sara Eckel, Seed Money, *Am. Law.*, Sept. 1, 2008, at 20; ABA Legal Profession Statistics, available at http://www.americanbar.org/resources_for_lawyers/profession_statistics.html.

涉及性别、种族和族裔的障碍。虽然这些不是多样性的唯一相关维度,但是它们提供了一个有用的框架,因为它们影响到最多的律师,并且就此有最为系统的研究。然而,本章的大部分分析都有更广泛的应用,也将提高其他职业群体的生活质量。

下文的讨论沿用了"女性和少数族裔"这一传统提法,但是这既不应掩盖有色人种女性的独特经历,也不应掩盖少数族裔内部不同种族之间的差异。更确切地说,关键是要了解不同的身份是如何造就职业经历的。

/ 原则与实践的差距 /

● 性别

从历史上看,美国法律职业在争取两性平等的斗争中取得了重大进展。直到20世纪60年代末,女性在法律职业中所占比例不超过3%,且主要限于低声望实务背景和专业。[1] 现在,近半数的新律师是女性,在实务领域的分布相当均匀。[2] 就像第二章所

---

[1] Deborah L. Rhode, Perspectives on Professional Women, *40 Stan. L. Rev.* 1163 (1988).

[2] 关于新入行者,see Andrew Buck & Andrew Cantor, Supply, Demand, and the Changing Economics of Large Firms, *60 Stan L. Rev.* 2087, 2103 (2008); Margaret Rivera, A New Business and Cultural Paradigm for the Legal Profession, *ACC Docket*, Oct. 2008, at 66, 68. 关于专业领域,see Fiona Kay & Elizabeth Gorman, Women and the Legal Profession, *4 Ann. Rev. Law & Soc. Sci.* 299, 303 (2008).

第四章
法律职业的多样性

指出的那样,女性对实务的满意度与男性大致相同。①

然而,严重的两性不平等现象依然存在。女性占该行业总人数的1/3以上,但是只有大约1/5的律师事务所合伙人、财富500强公司的总法律顾问和法学院院长是女性。② 女性不太可能成为合伙人,甚至在排除了其他因素之后,包括法学院的成绩和非工作时间,或者兼职日程安排。③ 研究发现,男性成为合伙人的概率比女性大2到5倍。④ 即使是那些从不占用工

---

① 参见第二章;Kay & Gorman, Women in the Legal Profession, at 316 (对研究进行了总结); John P. Heinz et al., *Urban Lawyers: The New Social Structure of the Bar* 260 (2006).

② ABA Commission on Women in the Profession, A Current Glance at Women in Law, 2013, available at http://www.americanbar.org/content/dam/aba/uncategorized/2011/cwp_current_glance_statistics_2011. Minority Corporate Counsel Association, MCCA Survey: Women General Counsel at Fortune 500 Companies Reaches New High, Aug. 8, 2012, at 1; Catalyst, Women in Law in the United States: Quick Take, Mar. 11, 2013.

③ Theresa Beiner, Not All Lawyers Are Equal: Difficulties that Plague Women and Women of Color, *58 Syracuse L. Rev.* 317, 328 (2008); Mary C. Noonan, Mary E. Corcoran, & Paul N. Courant, Is the Partnership Gap Closing for Women? Cohort Differences in the Sex Gap in Partnership Chances, *37 Soc. Sci. Res.* 156, 174–175 (2008).

④ 美国律师协会基金会对青年律师的一项研究发现,女性获得股权合伙人地位的概率是男性的一半。See Ronit Dinovitzer et al., National Association for Law Placement [NALP] Foundation for Career Research and Education and the American Bar Foundation, *After the JD II: Second Results from a National Study of Legal Careers*, 63 (2009), available at http://law.du.edu/documents/directory/publications/sterling/AJD2.pdf. See also Joyce Sterling, Rebecca Sandefur, & Gabriele Plickert, Gender, in *After the JD III: Third Results from a National* (转下页)

作时间,而且加班加点的女性,也比同样处境的男性更不可能成为合伙人。① 最高级别职务的情况也是最为冷酷的。女性只占股权合伙人的 17%。② 女性在领导职位(如律师事务所主席、管理和薪酬委员会成员)上的代表人数也不足。③ 全国 100 家最大的律师事务所,只有 7 个由女性担任主席或者管理合伙

(接上页) *Study of Legal Careers* 66 (*Gabriele Plickert*, ed., 2014). 联邦平等雇用机会委员会进行的一项研究发现,男性律师成为合伙人的概率是女性律师的 5 倍。See Equal Employment Opportunity Commission, Diversity in Law Firms 9 (2003), available at http://www.eeoc.gov/eeoc/statistics/reports/index.cfm.

① Mary C. Noonan & Mary Corcoran, The Mommy Track and Partnership: Temporary Delay or Dead End? *596 Annals Am. Acad. Pol. & Soc. Sci.* 130, 142 (2004); Kenneth Gleen Dau-Schmidt, Marc Galanter, Kaushik Mukhopadhaya, & Kathleen E. Hull, Men and Women of the Bar: The Impact of Gender on Legal Careers, *16 Mich. J. Gender & L.* 49, 96-97, 100-102, 107, 111-112 (2009).

② National Association of Women Lawyers and the NALP Foundation, Report of the Eighth Annual NAWL National Survey on Retention and Promotion of Women in Law Firms (Feb. 2014). See Vivia Chen, The Careerist: Female Equity Partnership Rate Is Up! (Just Kidding), *Am. Law.*, Feb. 25, 2014.

③ Jake Simpson, Firms Eyeing Gender Equality Should Adopt a Corporate Culture, *Law* 360, Apr. 22, 2014; Nancy Reichman & Joyce Sterling, Parenthood Status and Compensation in Law Practice, *20 Ind. J. Global Legal Stud.* 1203, 1221 (2013); Catalyst, Women in Law; Maria Pabon Lopez, The Future of Women in the Legal Profession: Recognizing the Challenges Ahead by Reviewing Current Trends, *19 Hastings Women's L. J.* 53, 71 (2008); Joan C. Williams &Veta T. Richardson, New Millennium, Same Glass Ceiling? The Impact of Law Firm Compensation Systems on Women, *The Project for Attorney Retention and Minority Corporate Counsel Association* 14 (2010).

第四章
法律职业的多样性

人。① 性别差异在薪酬方面也同样明显。② 即使在排除了劳动生产率和股权与非股权身份上的差异等因素之后,薪酬差距仍然存在。③

因此,虽然女律师像男同事一样报告了职业上的总体满意度,但是女性在实务活动的关键维度上,如责任级别、对工作的认可和进步机会,经历了更多的不如意。④ 在试图说明这一悖论时,理论家提出了两个解释。第一个涉及价值观。与其他因素(如智力挑战)相比,女性可能对那些对她们不利的工作环境(例如薪酬和晋升)的重视程度较低,这能给女性带

---

① Kathleen J. Wu, "Bossy" Is "Bitch" on Training Wheels, *Tex. Law.*, Apr. 29, 2014 (referring to *Law* 360 survey).

② Sterling, Sandefur, & Plickert, Gender, at 66 (在执业 12 年后,男女之间在薪酬上的差距是 20%); Zach Warren, Average Partner Compensation Growing, Gender Pay Gap Remains Wide, Inside Counsel, Sept. 17, 2014 (引用了梅杰[Major]、林德赛[Lindsey]和阿非利加[Africa]进行的调查,该调查发现,女性合伙人平均薪酬比男性律师的平均薪酬少 248,000 美元,分别为 531,000 美元和 779,000 美元). 女性收取的律师费费率也更低。Jennifer Smith, Legal Fees and Gender Gap, *Wall St. J.*, May 5, 2014, at B4.

③ Marina Angel et al., Statistical Evidence on the Gender Gap in Law Firm Partner Compensation, *Temp. U. Legal Studies*, Research Paper No. 2010-24 (2010); Ronit Dinovitzer, Nancy Reichman, & Joyce Sterling, Differential Valuation of Women's Work: A New Look at the Gender Gap in Lawyer's Incomes, 88 *Soc. Forces* 819, 835-847 (2009).

④ Ronit Dinovitzer et al., *After the JD*: *First Results of a National Study of Legal Careers* 58 (2004); Lopez, The Future of Women, at 69; Nancy J. Reichman & Joyce S. Sterling, Sticky Floors, Broken Steps, and Concrete Ceilings in Legal Careers, 14 *Tex. J. Women & L.* 27, 47 (2004).

来比男性更大的满足感,①第二种理论认为,女性的权利意识之所以较低,在一定程度上是因为她们的对照组是其他女性,或者是因为她们"能坦然接受次好"②。在这两种情况下,女律师对实务活动的关键方面的不满反映在过高的离职率上,这应引起致力于机会平等和多样性的法律职业的关注。

● 种族和少数族裔

种族和少数族裔的进步也很大,但是比白人女性的进展要慢。1960 年,有色人种律师占法律职业的比例不到 1%,③虽然黑人、拉美裔、亚裔美国人和美洲原住民现在占总人口的 1/3 和法学院毕业生的 1/5,但是他们仍然只占律师事务所合伙人的不到 7% 和财富 500 强公司总法律顾问的 9%。④ 在主要的律师事务所,只有 3% 的非合伙律师和不到 2% 的合伙人是非洲裔美国人。⑤ 大约一半的有色人种律师会在 3 年内离

---

① Kay & Gorman, Women in the Legal Profession, 317–318.
② David Chambers, Accommodation and Satisfaction: Women and Men Lawyers and the Balance of Work and Family, *14 Law & Soc. Inq.* 251, 280 (1989).
③ Marc Galanter & Thomas Palay, *Tournament of Lawyers: The Transformation of the Big Law Firm* 39 (1991).
④ National Association for Legal Career Professionals [NALP], Women and Minorities in Law Firms by Race and Ethnicity—An Update. *NALP Bulletin*, Apr. 2013; Minority Corporate Counsel Association, *Diversity and the Bar*, Sept./Oct. 2012, at 30.
⑤ Julie Treadman, Profession Backsliding on Diversity, *Nat'l L. J.*, Jun. 2, 2014, at 1.

职。① 有色人种女性的离职率是最高的,大约75%在其入职后的第 5 个年头之前就离职了,85%会在第 7 个年头前离职。② 对有色人种的律师来说,律师事务所的薪酬较低,其中少数族裔女性处于薪酬等级的最底层。③ 很少有有色人种律师担任领导角色。④

满意度调查反映出混合的、有时自相矛盾的结果。在美国律师协会基金会对年轻律师进行的一项全国性的大型研究中,黑人对他们成为律师的决定和他们的法律工作的实质内容最为满意;白人和亚裔美国人在其工作环境中是最幸福的。⑤ 美国律师协会职业女性委员会发现,在大型律师事务所的律师中,种族群体之间存在着明显的差异。白人男性将其职业满意度评定为 A,白人女性和少数族裔男性将其职业满意度评定为 B,少数族裔女性的职业满意度则在 B-和 C 之间徘徊。⑥

总之,在职业成就的主观和客观量度上,法律界反映出性别、种族和族裔方面的重大差异。但是,就造成这些差异的原

---

① Levit & Linder, *The Happy Lawyer*, at 250 n55.

② Deepali Bagati, Women of Color in U. S. Law Firms 1-2 (2009).

③ American Bar Association Commission on Women in the Profession, Visible Invisibility 28 (2006).

④ Veronica Root, Retaining Color, 47 U. Mich. J. L. Reform 575, 633 (2014).

⑤ Dinovitzer et al., *After the JD II*, at 64.

⑥ Levit & Linder, *The Happy Lawyer*, at 14.

因以及如何处理这些分歧,仍然存在争议。

/ 解释差距 /

- 能力和投入

著名的英国电视连续剧《是,大臣》("*Yes, Minister*")滑稽地模仿了多样性努力,一位古板的白人男性公务员解释了这些举措的愚蠢之处。根据他的逻辑,如果女性有必要的投入和能力,她们就已经在领导职位上有很好的代表了。由于没有那样的很好的女性代表,她们显然缺乏那些能力。同样的观点在美国律师业的领导人中也很常见,这不足为奇。毕竟,负责招聘、决定晋升和薪酬的人,是那些从目前的结构中受益,并且在相信其公平性方面有最大利害关系的人。尽管许多领导人愿意承认社会中普遍存在的经久不衰的偏见,但是他们在自己的机构中不太可能看到这一点。相反,他们将律师的职业道路上的种族、族裔和性别差异归因于能力和投入上的差异。[①]

对于有色人种的律师来说,对代表性不足的最常见解释是业绩不佳,这是以传统的绩效标准衡量的。少数族裔在法学院的人数偏低,并且在法学院的平均成绩低

[①] John M. Conley, Tales of Diversity: Lawyers' Narratives of Racial Equity in Private Firms, *31 Law & Soc. Inq.* 831, 841-842, 851-852 (2006).

第四章
法律职业的多样性

于白人。① 绝大多数律师认为,成绩和法学院排名在招聘方面很重要,因此,种族差异似乎是绩效制度的一个无意但是不可避免的结果。② 对多样性的态度进行的深入研究发现,大型律师事务所的标准叙述大致是这样的:

> 我们知道大多数大型律师事务所都是在一个公然歧视的时代开始的。我们对此感到遗憾,多年来一直试图对此做些什么。我们已经尝试了各种各样的事情,并将继续努力解决这个问题。然而,如果不降低我们的标准就很难解决这个问题,但我们当然不能这样做。所有这一切我们都无能为力。③

在其他工作场所,这种说法大同小异,只是加上进一步的扭曲,即在聘请"合格的"有色人种律师方面,他们不能与大型律师事务所在金钱或者声望上展开竞争。④ 实际上,律师业领

---

① Richard Sander, The Racial Paradox of the Corporate Law Firm, *84 N. C. L. Rev.* 1755, 1775 – 1776 (2006); T. T. Clyesdale, A Forked River Runs Through Law School: Toward Understanding Race, Gender, Age, and Related Gaps in Law School Performance and Bar Passage, *29 Law & Soc. Inq.* 711, 740 (2004).

② 大约80%的男性合伙人和大约70%的女性合伙人持这些观点。Minority Corporate Counsel Association, Sustaining Pathways to Diversity: The Next Steps in Understanding and Increasing Diversity and Inclusion in Large Law Firms 16 (2009).

③ Conley, Tales of Diversity, at 841.

④ Conley, Tales of Diversity, at 844.

导人"宣称被他们创建并维护的制度捕获了"①。

我通过最近对大型律师事务所和财富100强公司法律顾问部门的多样性调查,发现了一个更细致入微的图景。几乎所有的管理合伙人和总法律顾问都提到,多样性是其组织中的一个高度优先事项,许多人对他们取得的进展感到不满。一位管理合伙人表达了一个广为人知的观点:"毫无疑问,[我们]还远远不够成功。"②一些人把有色人种律师的低代表性归为前进中的困难。但是其他人承认了无意识的偏见和"多样性疲劳"。③

相比之下,对"女性问题",通常是从投入和委托人发展方面解释的,而不是从资质方面解释。因为与男性相比,女性要承担高比例的家庭责任,更有可能减少她们的日程安排,或者在工作场所抽出时间,她们被认为不太容易随叫随到,不那么可靠,也不值得进行广泛的指导。在一项调查中,虽然女性和男性报告的工作时间相似,但是超过 1/4 的男性律师认为女性工作时间更少,1/5 的人将这些女性的工作时间评价为"不过如此"。④ 因此,女性在业务发展和支撑这一点的自我推销

---

① Conley, Tales of Diversity, at 850.
② Deborah L. Rhode & Lucy Buford Ricca, Diversity in the Legal Profession: Perspectives from Managing Partners and General Counsel, *Fordham L. Rev.* (forthcoming, 2015).
③ Rhode & Ricca, Diversity in the Legal Profession.
④ Lopez, The Future of Women, at 65.

第四章
法律职业的多样性

方面,也往往被认为不那么擅长。①

这些态度可能有助于解释许多律师对多样性行动计划作出的相对乐观的评价。在一项由 Catalyst 进行的调查中,只有11%的白人律师和15%的白人男性认为多样性的努力未能解决微妙的种族偏见,相比之下,几乎半数的有色人种女性和40%的白人女性这么认为。②

然而,下面的研究表明,许多律师低估了无意识偏见的影响,高估了当前回应的有效性。现行制度在人才筛选上有很大的缺陷;大量的研究表明,雇主在预测绩效时,严重高估了成绩和法学院声望等资质的有效性。③ 借用雪莉·桑德伯格(Sheryl Sandberg)的话,女性仅凭"进取(lean in)"就可以解决自己的问题的假设,也没有根据。正如"法律中的女性中心"执行主任琳达·夏诺(Linda Chanow)所指出的那样,"女性可以随心所欲'进取',以至于快到了争先恐后的地步。但是,律师事务所的文化及其持续的隐性偏见,会破坏和妨害女

---

① Bagati, Women of Color 37 (2009); Tiffani Darden, The Law Firm Caste System: Constructing a Bridge Between Workplace Equity Theory and the Institutional Analyses of Bias in Corporate Law Firms 30 Berkeley J. Emp. & Lab. L. 85, 125 (2009); Lopez, The Future of Women, at 73.

② Bagati, Women of Color, at 13.

③ David B. Wilkins & G. Mitu Gulati, Why Are There So Few Black Lawyers in Corporate Law Firms? An Institutional Analysis, 84 Cal. Rev. 493, 526-527 (1996); James B. Rebitzer & Lowell J. Taylor, Efficiency Wages and Employment Rents: The Employer-Size Wage Effect in the Job Market for Lawyers, 13 J. Lab. Econ. 678, 690 (1995).

性的成功。"①真正致力于创造一个公正和包容的工作场所的律师,需要更好地理解在这条道路上会得到什么。这包括更深入地了解种族、族裔和性别刻板印象是如何对绩效评价、绩效本身以及具体业绩量度所附的相对价值产生影响的。

/ 种族、族裔和性别刻板印象 /

种族、族裔和性别刻板印象,在美国文化中起着充分但是往往未被意识到的作用,法律工作场所也不例外。不同群体的刻板印象各不相同。例如,非洲裔美国人和拉美裔人都奋起反对关于他们资格不足的假设。许多人报告说,他们的能力不断受到质疑,即使他们毕业于精英法学院,他们也被认为是平权行动的受益者,而不是英才教育的选择。② 自信的黑人面临被认为愤怒或者具有敌意的风险。③ 亚裔美国人背负着"少数族裔模范"的神话;他们被认为聪明,勤勤恳恳,但是也

---

① Simpson, Firms Eyeing Gender Equality.
② Root, Retaining Color, at 612; Maria Chávez, *Everyday Injustice* 72 (2011); Jill L. Cruz & Melinda S. Molina, Hispanic National Bar Association National Study on the Status of Latinas in the Legal Profession, Few and Far Between: The Reality of Latina Lawyers, *37 Pepp. L. Rev.* 971, 1010 (2010); Garner K. Weng, Racial Bias in Law Practice, *Cal. Mag.*, Jan. 2003, at 37-38; Lu-in Wang, Race as Proxy: Situational Racism and Self-Fulfilling Stereotypes, *53 DePaul L. Rev.* 1013, 1014 (2004).
③ ABA Commission, Visible Invisibility, at 25; Weng, Racial Bias, at 37-38.

第四章
法律职业的多样性

不够自信,无法获得委托人和法律团队的信任。① 有色人种女性遭遇着特殊的耻辱感,她们经常被误认为是秘书、法庭记录员或者翻译。②

其结果是,有才华的少数族裔缺乏赋予白人男子的称职性推定;崭露头角的白人按部就班就可以快速升迁,而少数族裔则需要展现绩优。③ 咨询公司最近的一项研究表明,无意识的种族偏见持续存在。该研究的负责人在一份法律备忘录中插入了22个错误,小到轻微的拼写和语法错误,大到事实和分析的错误。60个律师事务所的合伙人收到了备忘录的复制件,他们被告知这一备忘录是一页"写作分析研究"。一半的合伙人被告知,作者是一个名叫托马斯·梅耶(Thomas Meyer)的非裔美国人,另一半被告知作者是一个名叫托马斯·

---

① Institute for Inclusion in the Legal Profession, The State of Diversity, at 76; LeeAnn O'Neill, Hitting the Legal Diversity Market Home: Minority Women Strike Out, *The Modern American*, Spring 2007, at 7, 9; Bagati, Women of Color, at 37; ABA Commission, Visible Invisibility, at 25; Sonia M. Ospina & Erica G. Foldy, A Critical Review of Race and Ethnicity in the Leadership Literature: Surfacing Context, Power, and the Collective Dimensions of Leadership, *20 Leadership Q.* 876, 880 (2009).

② ABA Commission, Visible Invisibility, at 18; Cruz & Molina, Few and Far Between, at 1010; O'Neill, Hitting the Legal Diversity Market Home, at 8; Gladys Garcia-López, "Nunca Te Toman En Cuenta [They Never Take You into Account]": The Challenges of Inclusion and Strategies for Success of Chicana Attorneys, *22 Gender & Soc'y* 590, 601–603 (2008).

③ David A. Thomas, The Truth about Mentoring Minorities: Race Matters, *Harv. Bus. Rev.*, Apr. 2001, at 99, 104.

梅耶的白人。评审人员为白人所写的备忘录打分4.1(满分是5),而为非洲裔美国人所写的备忘录打分3.2。在白人就其潜力和分析技能受到表扬的同时,非洲裔美国人被认为充其量是平均水平,还需要"大量的工作"。①

即使有色人种律师具有杰出能力,也无助于消除传统的刻板印象和无意识偏见。心理学家把这称为"冬季开花"效应。② 一个典型的例子是参议员约瑟夫·拜登(Joseph Biden)在2008年总统竞选期间就巴拉克·奥巴马所作的描述,即他是"第一个主流的非洲裔美国人,他口齿伶俐、聪明、干净、看起来很帅"③。尽管这位杰出的律师得到了特殊的优待,但是其他渴望这种地位的人仍然被传统的刻板印象束缚。

性别刻板印象也将女性置于双重标准和双重约束之下。尽管最近取得了进展,但是女性与少数族裔一样,往往不能得到白人男子所享有的称职性推定。④ 在一项全国性调查中,

---

① Arin N. Reeves, Written in Black & White: Exploring Confirmation Bias in Racialized Perceptions of Writing Skills 3 (2014), available at http://www.nextions.com/wp-content/files_mf/1413987796_magicfields__attach_1_1.pdf; Debra Cassens Weiss, Partners in Study Gave Legal Memo a Lower Rating When Told Author Wasn't White, *ABA J.*, Apr. 21, 2014.

② Ella L. J. Edmondson Bell & Stella M. Nkomo, *Our Separate Ways: Black and White Women and the Struggle for Professional Identity* 145 (2001).

③ Lynette Clemetson, The Racial Politics of Speaking Well, *N. Y. Times*, Feb. 4, 2007, Sec. 4, at 1.

④ 关于称职性,see Eli Wald, Glass Ceilings and Dead Ends: Professional Ideologies, Gender Stereotypes and the Future of Women Lawyers at Large Law Firms, 78 Fordham L. Rev. 2245, 2256 (2010); Cecilia L. Ridgeway (转下页)

第四章
法律职业的多样性

1/3 到 3/4 的女律师认为,雇主对她们的要求要比其同事更高。① 对绩效评估的研究证实了这些看法;在表现相似的情况下,对女性的评定比男性更低。② 男性的成就更有可能被归因于能力,而女性的成就则更可能被归因于外在因素,这就是社会科学家所描述的模式:"他很老练,她很幸运。"③

即使那些全时工作的母亲,也被认为不太可能随叫随到和全身心投入,而对于父亲则不会有这样的假设。④ 在一项有

(接上页)& Paula England, Sociological Approaches to Sex Discrimination, in *Sex Discrimination in the Workplace* 189, 195 (Faye J. Crosby, Margaret S. Stockdale, & S. Ann Rupp, eds., 2007). 关于女性需要更加努力, see Lopez, Future of Women, at 73. 即使在男性和女性的绩效在客观上平等的实验情况下,女性也被要求达到更高的标准,她们的称职性也被评分更低。Martha Foschi, Double Standards in the Evaluation of Men and Women, *59 Soc. Psychol. Q.* 237 (1996). 就有色人种女性面临的特殊压力, see Garcia-López, They Never Take You into Account, at 598, 603-604.

① Deborah L. Rhode & Joan Williams, Legal Perspectives on Employment Discrimination, in *Sex Discrimination in the Workplace*, at 235, 245; Minority Corporate Counsel Association, Sustaining Pathways, at 32.

② Monica Beirnat, M. J. Tocci, & Joan C. Williams, The Language of Performance Evaluations: Gender-Based Shifts in Content and Consistency of Judgment, *3 Soc. Psych. & Pers. Sci.* 186 (2011).

③ Janet K. Swim & Lawrence J. Sanna, He's Skilled, She's Lucky: A Meta-Analysis of Observers' Attributions for Women's and Men's Successes and Failures, *22 Pers. & Soc. Psychol. Bull.* 507 (1996); Jeffrey H. Greenhaus & Saoj Parasuraman, Job Performance Attributions and Career Advancement Prospects: An Examination of Gender and Race Effects, *55 Org. Behav. & Hum. Decision Processes* 273, 276, 290 (1993).

④ Amy J. C. Cuddy, Susan T. Riske, & Peter Glick, When (转下页)

代表性的研究中,将近3/4的女性律师报告说,在生育或者领养孩子时,她们的职业投入受到了质疑。只有9%的白人男性同事和15%的少数族裔男性同事面临类似的挑战。① 然而,没有家庭关系的女性有时会面临不同的偏见:她们可能被视为"不太正常",因此"不太像是当领导的材料"。②

在与领导力相关的资格方面,如自信、竞争力和业务发展,女性的评分也低于男性。③ 尽管女性更有可能使用有效的领导风格,但是人们更容易相信男性更有领导能力,也更容易接受男性领导人。④ 对超过100项研究的综述证实,女性在采

(接上页)Professionals Become Mothers, Warmth Doesn't Cut the Ice, *60 J. Soc. Issues* 701, 709 (2004); Kathleen Fuegen, Monica Biernat, Elizabeth Haines, & Kay Deaux, Mothers and Fathers in the Workplace: How Gender and Parental Status Influence Judgments of Job-Related Competence, *60 J. Soc. Issues* 737, 745 (2004).

① ABA Commission, Visible Invisibility, at 83. For other research, see Reichman & Sterling, Sticky Floors, at 63-64.

② Sylvia A. Hewlett et al. , The Sponsor Effect: Breaking Through the Last Glass Ceiling, *Harv. Bus. Rev.* , Jan. 2011, at 24; Michele Mayes & kara Sophia Baysinger, *Courageous Counsel* 129 (2011) (quoting Dana Mayer).

③ Deborah L. Rhode & Barbara Kellerman, Women and Leadership: The State of Play, in *Women and Leadership: The State of Play and Strategies for Change* 7 (Barbara Kellerman & Deborah L. Rhode, eds. , 2007); Catalyst, Women Take Care, Men Take Charge: Stereotyping of Business Leaders (2005); Linda L. Carli & Alice H. Eagly, Overcoming Resistance to Women Leaders: The Importance of Leadership Styles, in *Women and Leadership*, at 127 - 129; Wald, Glass Ceilings, at 2256.

④ Alice Eagly, Female Leadership Advantage and Disadvantage: Resolving the Contradictions, *31 Psych. Women Q.* 1, 5, 9 (2007); Carli & Eagly, Overcoming Resistance, at 128-129; Laurie A. Rudman & Stephen E. Kilianski, Implicit and Explicit Attitudes toward Female Authority, *26 Pers. & Soc. Psych. Bull.* 1315 (2000).

用威权性的、看似男性化的风格时,评分更低,尤其是当评估者是男性时,或者当女性的角色通常由男性担任时。① 一个男人的自信,放在女性领导身上则是粗暴,女性领导人似乎要么是太女性化,要么是不够女人味。她们要么显得过于"软弱",要么则是过于"尖刻",要么无法作出艰难的决定,要么为了博得尊重而过于固执己见和傲慢。②

在男性中可以接受的自抬身价,在女性中被认为是没有吸引力的。③ 在斯坦福商学院的一项生动的研究中,参与者拿到了一个案例,这涉及一个有着出色的人际关系处理技能的重要风险投资者。一半的参与者被告知,此人是霍华德·罗森

---

① D. Anthony Butterfield & James P. Grinnell, Reviewing Gender, Leadership, and Managerial Behavior: Do the Decades of Research Tell Us Anything? in *Handbook of Gender and Work* 223, 235 (Gary N. Powell, ed., 1998); Jeanette N. Cleveland, Margaret Stockdale, & Kevin R. Murphy, *Women and Men in Organizations: Sex and Gender Issues at Work* 106-107 (2000).

② Alice Eagly & Steven Karau, Role Congruity Theory of Prejudice toward Female Leaders, *109 Psych. Rev.* 574 (2002); Alice H. Eagly, Achieving Relational Authenticity in Leadership, *16 Leadership Q.* 470 (2005); Catalyst, The Double Bind Dilemma for Women in Leadership: Damned if You Do, Doomed if You Don't (2007); Linda Babcock & Sara Laschever, *Women Don't Ask: The High Cost of Avoiding Negotiation—and Positive Strategies for Change* 87–89 (2007); Mayes & Baysinger, *Courageous Counsel*, at 131.

③ Carli & Eagly, Overcoming Resistance, at 130; Williams & Richardson, New Millennium, at 48; Laurie A. Rudman, To Be or Not to Be (Self-Promoting): The Consequences of Counterstereotypical Impression Management, in *Power and Influence in Organizations* 290 (Roderick M. Kramer & Margaret A. Neale, eds., 1998).

(Howard Roizen);另一半被告知她是海蒂·罗森(Heidi Roizen)。参与者认为两位企业家同样称职,但是发现霍华德更可爱、真诚和亲切,而海蒂则更咄咄逼人,自抬身价,对权力如饥似渴。① 即使最有成就的律师也会遇到这种偏见。布鲁克斯利·波恩(Brooksley Born)在担任商品期货委员会主席时因努力规制高风险的衍生品而受到广泛赞誉,被解雇的时候则被认为"作风粗暴""尖刻",是一个"无足轻重的怪人"。② 在评论这些描述时,她的一位前助手指出,"她是认真而专业的,她坚持自己的立场,反对那些不赞同她的立场的人。我不赞同把她没有'魅力'说成是尖酸刻薄。"③希拉里·克林顿(Hillary Clinton)受到更刻薄的描述:"渴望权力""阉人""希特勒作风"和"极端女权主义"。④ 在她竞选总统期间,她处理了"克林顿胡桃夹子"*,这让男人想起厉声责骂的母亲或者第

---

① Francis Flynn, Cameron Anderson, & Sebastien Brion, Too Tough Too Soon, Familiarity and the Backlash Effect (2011) (Stanford Business School, unpublished paper).

② Rick Schmidt, Prophet and Loss, *Stan. Mag.*, Mar./Apr. 2009 (quoting Arthur Levitt), available at https://alumni.stanford.edu/get/page/magazine/article/?article_id=30885; Michael Hirsh, *Capitol Offense: How Washington's Wise Men Turned America's Future Over to Wall Street* 12, 1 (2010) (quoting Robert Rubin and unnamed staffer).

③ Schmidt, Prophet and Loss (quoting Michael Greenberger).

④ Katha Pollitt, Hillary Rotten, in *Thirty Ways of Looking at Hillary: Reflections by Women Writers* 16-18 (Susan Morrison, ed., 2008).

* 被设计成克林顿形象的胡桃夹子,其有冒犯性和嘲笑意味。——译者注

第四章
法律职业的多样性

一任妻子的指责,以及举着要求"给我熨衬衫"的牌子的起哄者等问题。①

其他认知偏差加剧了传统刻板印象。人们更倾向于注意和回忆那些证实了他们的刻板假设的信息,而不是与这些假设相抵触的信息;这样一来,不和谐一致的事实就被过滤掉了。② 例如,当律师认为一个工作的母亲不太可能全身心投入于她的职业生涯时,他们更容易记住她的早退而不是晚走。同样,当女性和少数族裔的律师被认为有效性较低时,人们更容易想起他们的失败而不是他们取得的成就。女性和少数族裔所犯的错误也更难以被容忍。③ 这反过来又可能使律师不愿寻求能够展示杰出能力的有风险的"延展性任务"。对律师的投入或者能力的偏见也会影响到工作的分配。其结果是防止女性和少数族裔获得能够证明或者增强其能力的机会,从

---

① Marie Cocco, Misogyny I Won't Miss, *Wash. Post*, May 15, 2008, at A14; Kathleen Deveny, Just Leave Your Mother out of It, *Newsweek*, Mar. 17, 2008, at 32.

② David L. Hamilton & Jim W. Sherman, Stereotypes, in *Handbook of Social Cognition* 1-68 (Robert S. Wyler & Thomas K. Scrull, eds., 1994);关于确认偏差,see Paul Brest & Linda Krieger, *Problem Solving, Decision Making and Professional Judgment* 277-289 (2010).

③ Robin Ely, Herminia Ibarra, & Deborah M. Kolb, Taking Gender into Account: Theory and Design for Women's Leadership Development Programs, *10 Acad. Mgmt. Learning & Educ.* 474, 477 (2010); Martha Foschi, Double Standards in the Evaluation of Men and Women, at 237; ABA Commission, Visible Invisibility, at 27.

而形成了一个自我实现的预言的循环。①

/ 群体内部偏见:指导、后援、人际关系网和工作分配 /

一组相关的障碍包括群体内偏见。广泛的研究表明了个人对自己群体成员的偏好。对于与其上级在包括性别、种族和族裔等在内的重要方面类似的人而言,忠诚、合作、有利的评价、指导以及奖励和机会的分配会更多。② 因此,女性和少数族裔在发展这些"社会资本"方面,面临着困难,她们难以获得建议、支持、后援、合心合意的任务和新的业务机会。③ 有色

---

① Linda Hamilton Krieger, The Content of Our Categories: A Cognitive Bias Approach to Discrimination and Equal Employment Opportunity, 47 Stan. L. Rev. 1161, 1234 (1995).

② Williams & Richardson, New Millennium, at 49-50; Ridgeway & England, Sociological Approaches, at 197; Marilyn B. Brewer & Rupert J. Brown, Intergroup Relations, in The Handbook of Social Psychology 554-594 (Daniel T. Gilbert, Susan T. Fiske, & Gardner Lindzey, eds., 1998); Susan T. Fiske, Stereotyping, Prejudice and Discrimination, in The Handbook of Social Psychology, at 357-414.

③ 这一术语来自于 Pierre Bourdieu, The Forms of Capital, in Handbook of Theory and Research for the Sociology of Education 241, 248 (John G. Richardson, ed., 1986). 关于法律情境下的讨论,see ABA Commission, Visible Invisibility, at ix; Cindy A. Schipani, Terry M. Dworkin, Angel Kwolek-Folland, & Virgina G. Maurer, Pathways for Women to Obtain Positions of Organizational Leadership: The Significance of Mentoring and Networking, 16 Duke J. Gender L. & Pol'y 89 (2009); Fiona Kay & Jean E. Wallace, Mentors as Social Capital: Gender, Mentors, and Career Rewards in Legal Practice, 79 Soc. Inq. 418 (2009).

第四章
法律职业的多样性

人种律师经常报告被隔绝和边缘化,而许多白人女性也同样经历了"老同学"关系网的排斥。① 在美国律师协会的研究中,62%的有色人种女性和60%的白人女性觉得被排除在正式和非正式的关系网机会之外,但是只有4%的白人男性这么觉得;大多数女性和少数族裔都希望得到更好的指导。②

问题在一定程度上反映在了数字上。许多组织的高层缺乏足够的女性和少数族裔。他们的问题一般不是缺乏投入。最近的研究发现没有证据显示蜂王综合征,即脱颖而出的女性使其他女性无法出人头地。③ Catalyst 的一项研究显示,在积极参与指导的女性中,几乎有 3/4 的人在培养女性同事,而与此相比,男性仅有 30%。④ 但是,女性担任领导职务的人数不足,再加上女性承担家庭责任的时间压力,使得潜在导师的人数不足。此外,最近的研究表明,推动女性和少数族裔被雇用和晋升的女性和少数群体在自己的业绩评审中受到了惩

---

① 关于少数族裔,see ABA Commission, Visible Invisibility, at 18; Wilkins & Gulati, Why Are There So Few Black Lawyers in Corporate Law Firms? at 493. 关于女性,see Reichman & Sterling, Sticky Floors, at 65; Timothy O'Brien, Up the Down Staircase, *N. Y. Times*, Mar. 19, 2006, at A4; Williams & Richardson, New Millennium, at 16-17.

② ABA Commission, Visible Invisibility, at 35; Jill Schachner Chanen, Early Exits, *ABA J.*, Aug. 2006, at 36.

③ Sarah Dinolfo, Christine Silva, & Nancy M. Carter, High Potentials in the Pipeline: Leaders Pay It Forward 7 (2012), available at http://www.catalyst.org/knowledge/high-potentials-pipeline-leaders-pay-it-forward.

④ Dinolfo, Silva, & Carter, High Potentials, at 7.

罚,这可能不利于她们获得能够进行有效指导的职位。①

虽然越来越多的组织有正式的指导计划,但是这些组织并不总是提供足够的培训、奖励或者监督,以确保有效性。② 这些正式的程序也不能替代那些自然发展的关系,后者不是简单的顾问,而是后援人,他们作为倡导者,处在能够提供机会的职位上。正如美国律师协会一项研究的参与者所指出的那样,女性导师可能有"良好的意愿",但是她们已经被竞争性的工作和家庭义务步步紧逼,或者"没有太多的权力,所以她们不能真正帮助你。"③对发生性骚扰的担忧,使一些男性无法与初级女性律师建立指导关系。对种族和少数族裔问题的不安,也使一些白人律师无法越过肤色的鸿沟。④ 在跨种族指导关系中,坦率的对话可能特别困难。被指导的少数族裔可能不愿意提出偏见的问题,担心这可能过于敏感。白人导师可能不愿意向少数族裔非合伙律师提供坦率的反馈,因为他们担心这看起来有种族主义色彩或者是在鼓励他们离职。

---

① David Hekman, Does Valuing Diversity Result in Worse Performance Ratings for Minority and Female Leaders? (论文发表于管理学会2014年会议), discussed in Rachel Feintzeig, Women Penalized for Promoting Women, Study Finds, *Wall St. J.*, Jul. 24, 2014, at D3.

② See studies cited in Rhode, From Platitudes, at 1071-1072.

③ ABA Commission, Visible Invisibility, at 14.

④ 关于对性问题的担心所起的作用,see Hewlett et al., Sponsor Effect, at 35. 关于指导中与种族有关的障碍,see Monique R. Payne-Pikus, John Hagan, & Robert L. Nelson, Experiencing Discrimination: Race and Retention in America's Largest Law Firms, *44 Law & Soc'y Rev.* 553, 561 (2010).

结果是,中层的有色人种律师可能发现自己"被软评估打了个措手不及"——"你的技能不是他们所预期的,但是你不知道,因为从来没有人告诉你。"①

关于投入和能力的假设,也让导师不去投资于那些似乎不太可能留下来或者成功的女性和少数族裔。② 这种动力也给这些律师施加了压力,迫使他们融入主流的规范。正如一位有色人种律师所说的那样,"在一家大型律师事务所里,成功的唯一方法就是让他们忘记你是拉美裔。"③如果少数族裔律师"就是不能与人相处",人们会想当然地认为问题在于个人,而不是机构。④

在分配工作和委托人发展机会方面,群体内偏私也很明显。许多组织都使用非正式的系统,将看似有才华的初级律师(极高比例的白人男性)输送到领导层,同时把其他人降级到"干活"的岗位上。⑤ 在美国律师协会的研究中,44%的有色

---

① ABA Commission, Visible Invisibility, at 27. See also Thomas, The Truth about Mentoring Minorities, at 105; Julie Treadman, The Diversity Crisis: Big Firms' Continuing Failure, *Am. Law.*, May 2014.

② ABA Commission, Visible Invisibility, at 15-16; Marc Galanter & William Henderson, The Elastic Tournament, *60 Stan. L. Rev.*, 1 (2008); Payne-Pikus, Hagan, & Nelson, Experiencing Discrimination, at 576.

③ Institute for Inclusion in the Legal Profession, The State of Diversity, 46.

④ Bagati, Women of Color, at 16; ABA Presidential Initiative Commission on Diversity, Diversity in the Legal Profession: The Next Steps 43 (2010).

⑤ ABA Commission, Visible Invisibility, at 21; Wilkins & Gulati, Why Are There So Few Black Lawyers in Corporate Law Firms? at 493, 565-571.

人种女性、39%的白人女性和25%的少数族裔男子报告说,对他们而言合心合意的任务被视而不见;只有2%的白人男性有类似的经历。① 其他研究同样发现,女性和少数族裔常常被排除在委托人业务之外。②

有色人种律师也会遇到"种族匹配";他们接受某些工作是因为他们的身份,而不是他们的兴趣,以便在法庭、委托人会见、招聘和营销工作中塑造正确的"外观"。虽然这一策略有时会带来有益的机会,但是它也可以说是将律师当成了"吉祥物",而他们并没有就此培养自己的职业技能。③ 琳达·马布里(Linda Mabry)是旧金山一家律师事务所的第一个少数族裔合伙人,她叙述了一个例子:她被要求加入对一个公司的汇报,该公司的总法律顾问是非洲裔美国人。"当律师事务所就该事务所的相关专业知识进行介绍时,我对这些知识是一无所知,很明显,我在那里的唯一原因就是要展示律师事务所的多样性,但这实际上是不存在的。在那一刻,我就想从那个设施完备的会议室的玻璃窗口跳下去……"④当有色人种律师被假定拥有他们实际上缺乏的技能和密切关系时,种族匹配特别令人恼火。例如,一个日裔美国人被要求参加一个会议来

---

① ABA Commission, Visible Invisibility, at 21.
② Williams & Richardson, New Millennium, at 42.
③ ABA Commission, Visible Invisibility, at 21; O'Neill, Hitting the Legal Diversity Market, at 10.
④ Linda A. Mabry, The Token, *Cal. Law.*, Jul. 2006, at 76.

第四章
法律职业的多样性

招揽一个韩国委托人;一个拉丁美洲人被分配了西班牙文的文件,即使她解释说她的西班牙语并不流利。① "哦,你会没事的",她被告知。"[有什么不熟悉的就去]查查字典。"②

/ 工作场所结构和性别角色 /

对工作场所需求的不断升级和工作场所结构的僵化,对多样性和包容性构成了进一步的障碍。在过去的1/4世纪里,对工时的要求有了显著的增长,而没有改变的是一天的小时数。让律师有可能在家工作的技术使得越来越不可能在家不工作。随叫随到已经成为新的规范,律师以电子方式被拴在了他们的工作场所。代价由女性过度承担,因为她们很可能承担主要的家庭责任。

结构性反应的不足使问题复杂化。尽管作出了一些努力,但是正式政策和造成有关工作与生活冲突的实际做法之间仍存在着巨大差距。虽然超过90%的美国律师事务所报告说有着允许非全职工作的政策,但是只有约6%的律师实际使

---

① ABA Commission, Visible Invisibility, at 26; David Wilkins, From "Separate Is Inherently Unequal" to "Diversity Is Good for Business": The Rise of Market-Based Diversity Arguments and the Fate of the Black Corporate Bar, *117 Harv. L. Rev.* 1548-1595 (2004).

② ABA Commission, Visible Invisibility, at 26.

用这些政策。① 许多律师有充分的理由认为,减少工作时间或者不能随叫随到,都将危及他们的职业生涯。② 非全职身份和在工作场所之外的工作,通常会带来收入上的长期损失以及成为合伙人的机会减少。③ 对密歇根大学法学院毕业生的一项调查显示,只要有一年不在岗,成为合伙人的机会就会降低 1/3,收入会减少 38%。④ "比子弹还快"的产假太常见了。女性在医院产房测定宫缩时间时在起草文件,这样的令人沮丧的故事也很常见。如果你以 6 分钟为一个收费时段,为什么要浪费一个? 那些在育儿假后选择缩减日程安排的人,往往会发现付出了太大的代价。他们的日程不受尊重,他们的工作时间在攀升,他们的工作质量在下降,他们的工资不成比

---

① National Association for Law Placement, Most Lawyers Working Part Time Are Women—Overall Number of Lawyers Working Part Time Remains Small (Dec. 17, 2009, news release).

② Paula A. Patton, Women Lawyers: Their Status, Influence, and Retention in the Legal Profession, *William & Mary J. Women & L.* 173, 180 (2005). For lower partnership rates, see Beiner, Not All Lawyers Are Equal, at 326; Dau-Schmidt, Galanter, Mukhopadhaya, & Hull, Men and Women of the Bar, at 49; Mona Harrington & Helen Hsi, MIT Workplace Center, Women Lawyers and Obstacles to Leadership, 28-29 (2007), available at http://nysbar.com/blogs/general-practice/2007/05/women_lawyers_and_obstacles_to.html.

③ David Leonhardt, Financial Careers Come at a Cost to Families, *N. Y. Times*, May 27, 2009, at B1; Dau-Schmidt, Galanter, Mukhopadhaya, & Hull, Men and Women of the Bar, at 95-96; Beiner, Not All Lawyers Are Equal, at 326.

④ Noonan & Corcoran, The Mommy Track, at 130, 146.

例,他们被诬蔑为"混子"①。

虽然这不仅是"女性的问题",但是女性付出的代价最大。尽管过去20年来,男子的家务劳动大幅度增加,但是女性仍然承担着主要的任务。② 女性依然有可能像联邦区法官南希·盖特纳(Nancy Gertner)那样,在其即将坐到审判席时接到电话:"妈妈,我的[午餐]没有巧克力布丁。"③在美国律师协会基金会对年轻律师的调查中,女性非全职工作或者离岗的概率比男性高出7倍,这主要是因为要照看孩子。④ 在密歇根大学的研究中,42%的女性休过育儿假,但只有1%的父亲休过育儿假。⑤ 造成这些差异的部分原因是,选择成为全职看护人的少数父亲会受到特殊惩罚。与作出同样选择的女性同事相

---

① See Deborah L. Rhode, Balanced Lives for Lawyers, *70 Fordham L. Rev.* 2207, 2213 (2002);关于污名,see Holly English, *Gender on Trial* 212 (2003)(报告了对混子的看法); Lopez, Future of Women, at 95; Cynthia Thomas Calvert, Linda Bray Chanow, & Linda Marks, The Project for Attorney Retention, Reduced Hours, Full Success: Part-Time Partners in U. S. Law Firms (2009)(报告说,即使是成了合伙人的律师,也有大约40%感到采用兼职日程安排所带来的污名), available at http://amlawdaily.typepad.com/files/part-timepartner.pdf.

② Deborah L. Rhode, *What Women Want: An Agenda for the Women's Movement* 59-60 (2014); Bureau of Labor Statistics, American Time Use Survey 2010 (2011).

③ Nancy Gertner, *In Defense of Women: Memoirs of an Unrepentant Advocate* 246 (2011).

④ Dinovitzer et al., *After the JD II*, at 62.

⑤ Noonan & Corcoran, The Mommy Track, at 137.

比，男性律师会承担更严重的经济损失和晋升不利后果。①

这些问题可能会增加。"千禧年"律师的期望与现行规范是不符的。② 越来越多的男性和女性都表达了更好地平衡工作与生活的愿望，而且坚持这一点的各年龄段的律师都越来越多。《纽约时报》一篇文章的标题是，"他为乐队演出而请假"，报道说奥巴马总统愿意离开关键会议，以便在6点前回家吃饭或者参加他女儿的学校的集会。③

尽管律师业领导人普遍承认工作与生活的平衡问题，但是他们通常会把解决该问题的责任推向其他地方。在私人实务活动中，委托人在一定程度上要承担责任。法律是一个服务性行业，委托人对随叫随到的期待，使律师减少时间安排难以被接受。监督者的反对也同样成问题。在竞争激烈的工作环境中，他们有明显的理由偏爱能够招之即来的律师。④ 在我最近对大型律师事务所和公司法律顾问办公室的调查中，许多管理合伙人和总法律顾问对这个问题评论说：

> 每个人都感到压力……这就是我们所选择的职业。

---

① Dau-Schmidt, Galanter, Mukhopadhaya, & Hull, Men and Women of the Bar, at 112-113; Levit & Linder, *Happy Lawyer*, at 12-13.

② Marci Krufka, The Young & the Restless, *Law Prac.*, Jul./Aug. 2004, at 48; Galanter & Henderson, Elastic Tournament, at 1922-1923.

③ Sheryl Gay Stolberg, He Breaks for Band Recitals, *N. Y. Times*, Feb. 12, 2010.

④ Galanter & Henderson, Elastic Tournament, at 1921.

> 我们每周营业7天,每天营业24小时……我们有一份艰难而又占用时间的工作。
>
> 这是一个非常棘手的问题。我们为解决这个问题确实设置了项目,但是我不确定人们是否有时间参加。①

然而,问题并不像人们经常设想的那样难以克服。现有的证据并不表明委托人对减少日程安排有很大的抵触情绪。他们关心的是及时反应性,而兼职律师通常都能提供。② 在最近一次对兼职合伙人的调查中,大多数受访者报告说,他们甚至没有将他们的地位告知委托人,而且他们的日程安排进行了调整,以适合委托人的需要。③ 会计也是一个服务性行业,但是绝不会对底线问题漠不关心,它们发展了一种商业模式,通过增加留职率来抵消工作与家庭平衡的成本。④ 大量证据表明,法律实务活动也可以做到这一点,并获得更高的士气、较低的招聘和培训费用,以及更少地中断与委托人和同事的关系等好处。⑤ 虽然某些领导职位可能难以与家庭需求相调和,但是许多女性可以在照顾孩子的负担减轻的时候,随时

---

① Rhode &Ricca, Diversity in the Legal Profession.

② Calvert, Chanow, & Marks, Reduced Hours, at 13, 22.

③ Calvert, Chanow, & Marks, Reduced Hours, at 9, 13, 21.

④ Deloitte and Touche has been a leader. See Susan Sturm, Second Generation Employment Discrimination: A Structural Approach, *101 Colum. L. Rev.* 458, 493 (2001).

⑤ Levit & Linder, *Happy Lawyer*, at 170; Wal-Mart Legal News, Nov. 2009, at 1; Calvert, Chanow, & Marks, Reduced Hours, at 10-12.

准备担任这些职务。挑战在于创造工作场所结构,使男女律师都能更容易地满足个人和职业生活的需要,并确保那些暂时离职或者减少工作负荷的人不会长期被这个决定所耽搁。

/ 抵触情绪 /

实行多样性和性别平等行动计划的最后障碍是抵触情绪。人们担心解决这些问题可能会带来新的问题,因此不能解决问题。那些看似支持对女性和少数群体进行"特殊"对待的领导人,不得不担心白人男性的不满情绪。在少数族裔公司法律顾问协会的一项研究中,白人男子常常认为"与绩效和能力相比,多样性应当退居其次"[①]。在他们看来,太多的"逆向歧视"会引起抵触情绪,而"勉强雇用不合格的少数族裔的员工有时会破坏……对多样性和包容性的接受"[②]。正如一位白人男性律师所说的那样:"从那些有本事的人那里拿走机会……给那些种族、性别方面的少数群体,只能迫使我们分裂,而不是团结在一起……在一个表面不看肤色、任贤用能的社会里,我想不出比这更糟糕的事情。"[③]在给《国家法律杂志》编辑的一封信中,一个自我描述为"年轻、白人、直男,并

---

① Minority Corporate Counsel Association, Sustaining Pathways, at 16.
② Minority Corporate Counsel Association, Sustaining Pathways, at 25.
③ Minority Corporate Counsel Association, Sustaining Pathways, at 15.

第四章
法律职业的多样性

且碰巧在政治上要求进步的律师",同样抗议裁员的决定,部分原因在于"这是为了迎合一个重要委托人新提出的多样性要求"。在他看来,"如果以增加多样性的名义行保持同质性之实,仅仅(哪怕是一定程度上)基于不可改变的特点来解雇一个人,都是不公正的。"①许多白人律师似乎同意这一点。在美国律师协会的一项调查中,只有42%的人支持平权行动。②

相比之下,92%的非洲裔美国人对此表示支持。③ 完全做到不看肤色,经过几代人就能做到,但是要等几个世纪,则为时太晚。正如哈佛大学法学教授戴维·威尔金斯(David Wilkins)所言,多样性行动计划仍然是必要的,以"发现和纠正当前实务活动中无数微妙的,但是仍然无处不在的……差异化地对待某些[有色群体]的做法"。④

/ 法律的界限 /

虽然反歧视法律提供了一些免受公然偏见的保护,它不适合于解决当代的种族、族裔和性别障碍。近50年的民权立法经验表明,几乎没有对涉及律师事务所的歧视行为的终局

① Ben Martin, Letter to the Editor, Nat'l L. J., Nov. 6, 2006, at 23.
② Walter La Grande, Getting There, ABA J., Feb. 1999, at 54.
③ La Grande, Getting There, at 54.
④ Wilkins, From "Separate Is Inherently Unequal," at 1572-1573.

判决。① 非正式和解的发生率是无法估量的,但是有效救济措施的障碍是巨大的。在一定程度上,问题在于歧视的法律定义与造成歧视的社会模式之间的不匹配。为了在涉及职业就业的案件中胜诉,诉讼当事人一般必须证明,他们受到的不利对待是基于被禁止歧视的特征,如种族、族裔或者性别。② 然而,正如前面的讨论所指出的那样,女性和少数族裔的许多不利因素,并不涉及这种公然的歧视性对待。

考虑到评价标准的主观性,个人往往不可能知道或者证明他们遭遇了歧视。证据障碍往往是无法克服的,因为律师一般都很聪明,会避免留下关于歧视的书面痕迹,还因为有确凿证据的同事不愿意提供这种证据,以免危及自己的地位。③ 即使那些认为自己经历过歧视的人,也没有什么动机挺身而出,因为投诉的代价高昂,但胜利的可能性很小,并且存在被拉入非正式黑名单的风险。④ 许多女性和少数族裔不希

---

① See Eyana J. Smith, Employment Discrimination in the Firm: Does the Legal System Provide Remedies for Women and Minority Members of the Bar? *6 U. Pa. J. Lab. & Emp. L.* 789 (2004).

② 联邦《民权法》第七编禁止基于种族、肤色、宗教、性别或者来源国而进行雇用歧视。42 US. Code Section 2000 (e)(2). 关于概述,see Katherine T. Bartlett, Deborah L. Rhode, & Joanna Grossman, *Gender and Law: Theory, Doctrine, Commentary* 89 (6th ed., 2013).

③ Rhode & Williams, Legal Perspectives on Employment Discrimination, at 243; *Riordan v. Kaminers*, 831 F. 2d 690, 697 (7th Cir. 1987).

④ 总的来看,关于雇用歧视诉讼确实存在这样的问题。See (转下页)

第四章
法律职业的多样性

望看起来"太咄咄逼人"或者"有对抗性",看起来像一个"泼妇",或者被类型化为"愤怒的黑人"。① 表示关切的律师经常被告知,"就忘掉前嫌吧",或者"风物长宜放眼量"。② 坦诚对话的渠道太少了。大多数律师事务所没有给非合伙律师提供对他们的监督者进行反馈的机会;而提供了此类评价的律师,只有大约5%报告说发生了更好的变化。③ 在许多律师事务所文化中,传达的信息是:"抱怨永远不会让你得到什么……[你会被视为]不是团队的成员"。④

坚持自己的抱怨的律师,将他们的职业生涯置于严峻的考验中,而浮现出来的图景却很少是完全令人愉快的。一个同性恋非合伙律师就晋升的偏见起诉了华尔街律师事务所

(接上页)Laura Beth Nielsen & Robert L. Nelson, Rights Realized? An Empirical Analysis of Employment Discrimination Litigation as a Claiming System, *2005 Wis. L. Rev.* 663; Linda Hamilton Krieger, The Watched Variable Improves: On Eliminating Sex Discrimination in Employment, in *Sex Discrimination in the Workplace*, at 296, 309–310.

① ABA Commission, Visible Invisibility, at 20 (咄咄逼人,泼妇); Williams & Richardson, New Millennium, at 38 (对抗性); Reichman & Sterling, Sticky Floors, at 65 (泼妇); Marcia Coyle, Black Lawyer's Life, Suit Told by a White Author, *Nat'l L. J.*, Jan. 11, 1999, at A14 (quoting Mungen) (愤怒的黑人)。

② 关于建议,see Robert Kolker, The Gay Flannel Suit, *N. Y. Mag.*, Feb. 26, 2007, available at http://nymag.com/news/features/28515/; ABA Commission, Visible Invisibility, at 21. 关于对薪酬投诉后的消极后果,see Williams & Richardson, New Millennium, at 38.

③ National Association for Law Placement Foundation, How Associate Evaluations Measure Up, A National Study of Associate Performance Assessments 74 (2006).

④ ABA Commission, Visible Invisibility, at 27.

Sullivan and Cromwell。他在新闻中被描述为"虚情假意",一个"有迫害情结的偏执的孩子"。① 在同样臭名昭著的性别歧视诉讼中,费城的 Wolf, Block, Schorr 和 Solis-Cohen 律师事务所拒绝晋升南希·艾佐尔德(Nancy Ezold),因为律师事务所领导人认为她缺乏分析能力和其他可能弥补该缺陷的特点。按照一位合伙人的说法,"她就像一名丑陋的女孩。每个人都说她个性不错。事实证明,[艾佐尔德]甚至连很好的个性都没有。"②然而,她所做的就是用充分的证据在审判中占上风。在她被拒绝成为合伙人的时候,该公司的诉讼部门的 55 个合伙人中只有 1 名女性;相比之下,在全国范围内,大约 11% 的大型律师事务所的合伙人是女性。③ 与艾佐尔德一起工作的合伙人对其进行了积极的评价,而被提拔的男性非合伙律师所接受的绩效考核,至少与她所受的考核一样严格。这些人的描述包括"空洞浅薄、不成熟""比牛排还爱作声"和"不是真正的聪明人"。④ 该记录还揭示了性别刻板印象,例如一些合伙人认为艾佐尔德过于"自信",过于专注于"女性问题"。⑤ 尽管有

---

① Kolker, Gay Flannel Suit.

② Deborah L. Rhode, What's Sex Got to Do with It: Diversity in the Legal Profession, in *Legal Ethics: Law Stories* 233, 246 (Deborah L. Rhode & David Luban, eds., 2005) (quoting Charles Kopp).

③ Rhode, What's Sex Got to Do with It, at 235.

④ *Ezold v. Wolf, Block, Schorr & Solis-Cohen*, 751 F. Supp. 1175, 1184-1186 (E. D. Pa. 1990), reversed, 983 F. 2d 509 (3d Cir. 1992), *cert. denied*, 510 U. S. 826 (1993).

⑤ *Ezold v. Wolf, Block, Schorr & Solis-Cohen*, 751 F. Supp. 1175.

这些证据,上诉法院还是作出了有利于律师事务所的判决。在法院看来,对艾佐尔德投反对票的 2/3 的合伙人,并没有"明显或者公然地"表现歧视。① 然而,鉴于给该律师事务所的声誉和招聘活动所带来的损害,这场胜利很难说是完全在理的。在反思没有作出就问题进行和解的决定时,律师事务所一名领导人总结道,"这本是一个不值得去打赢的案件"。②

在减少工作时间后发现自己被剥夺了具有挑战性的任务和职业发展机会的女性,也存在证据方面的困难。在驳回母亲们对彭博新闻提起的集团诉讼时,地区法院发表了广泛流行的观点:法律"并没有规定工作与生活之间的平衡"。在一个"明确地期待全身心奉献的组织中,作出家庭优先于工作的决定,会带来负面后果"③。遭遇此类后果的律师很少看到除退出以外的其他选项。一家律师事务所的一位做了母亲的律师休假 3 年后回来,发现她的处境毫无希望:"我被从所有的工作中排除了,没有经过任何询问和讨论……这就像是我已经脱离了这个星球。"④

---

① 983 F. 2d 509 528 (3d Cir. 1992). See Rhode, What's Sex Got to Do with It, at 243.

② Rhode, What's Sex Got to Do with It, at 245 (quoting Robert Segal).

③ *Equal Opportunity Commission v. Bloomberg*, 778 F. Supp. 2d 458, 485 (S. D. N. Y 2011).

④ Amelia J. Uelman, The Evils of Elasticity: Reflections on the Rhetoric of Professionalism and the Part-Time Paradox in Large Firm Practice, *33 Fordham Urb. L. J.* 81, 83 (2005).

目前的反歧视法不仅没有为个人提供充分的补救办法,而且对机构解决无意识的偏见激励不足。关于多样性的判例法处于不断变化中,表明有种族意识的雇用,特别是政府雇主进行的雇用,需要特别关注。① 哥伦比亚法学教授苏珊·斯特姆(Susan Sturm)的研究还表明,对责任的恐惧,可能会阻止组织收集"揭示问题……或者排外模式的信息,因为这将增加其被起诉的可能性"②。

然而,尽管法律为多样性行动计划没有提供足够的压力,但是其他因素正在大力向这一方向推进。无论是关于多样性的伦理上的理由还是商业上的理由,都应当激励法律界领导人在其机构中以及在他们自己的阶层中建立包容性。

/ 支持多样性的商业理由 /

从20世纪80年代末开始,律师业领导人发起了一系列旨在增加少数族裔在该行业的代表性和影响力的行动计划。他们根据在公司领域产生影响力的观点,强调了多样性的商业理由。就像少数族裔公司法律顾问协会所说的那样,

> 律师事务所致力于变得多样化,是因为它们的未来、市场份额、人才的保留、与公司委托人的现有关系的延续

---

① *Fisher v. University of Texas*, 570 U.S. (2013).
② Sturm, Second Generation, at 468, 470-41, 475-476.

第四章
法律职业的多样性

和业绩,都取决于了解和预测日益多样化的劳动力和市场的需求。①

美国律师协会多样性行动计划委员会2010年的一份报告同样强调,"聘请律师来反映来自世界各地的公民、委托人和客户的多样性,是很有商业意义的。事实上,公司委托人越来越要求律师的多样性,如果没有提供这种多样性,他们就会把业务带到别处去"②。在我最近的调查中,来自管理合伙人和总法律顾问的评论强调,多样性不仅仅是"正确的做法",而且对于组织的经济成功而言,也是至关重要的:

一个多样化的团队是一个更有效的团队:它有更广泛的经验基础,委托人将得到更好的产品。

我们是在做人力资本生意。[多样性]是获得最佳人才和最佳决策的一种方式。③

两性平等的倡导者采取了类似的做法。被广泛认可的2009年《法律中的女性宣言》详细阐述了商业理由。其核心原则指出,

A. 女律师人才库的深度和广度清楚地表明,法律界

---

① Wilkins, From "Separate Is Inherently Unequal," at 1570 n1010 (quoting Scott Mitchell).

② ABA Presidential Initiative Commission on Diversity, Diversity in the Legal Profession, at 9.

③ Rhode & Ricca, Diversity in the Legal Profession.

有必要招募、保留、发展和推进丰富的人才资源。

B. 女性越来越多地在整个社会中发挥影响；法律雇主必须在其领导层中实现性别多样性，这样才能培养一批在其委托人和法律职业成员心目中具有正当性的领导人。

C. 多样性会在无数方面为法律雇主带来附加值——从加强委托人代理的有效性，到在对话和决策中插入具有多样性观点和批判性观点。[1]

为了支持这些主张,拥护者收集了各种证据。例如,一些社会科学研究表明,多样性观点鼓励批判性思维和创造性地解决问题；他们扩大了可以考虑的选项的范围,能抵消团体迷思。[2] 一些研究还发现律师事务所以及财富500强企业的多样性和盈利能力之间存在着关联。[3] 其他的研究利用信号理

---

[1] Center for Women in Law at the University of Texas School of Law, Austin, Manifesto on Women in Law, May 1, 2009.

[2] Cedric Herring, Does Diversity Pay? Race, Gender and the Business Case for Diversity, 74 Am. Soc. Rev. 208, 220 (2009); Elizabeth Mannix & Margaret A. Neale, What Differences Make a Difference? The Promise and Reality of Diverse Teams on Organizations, 6 Psychol. Sci. Pub. Int. 31, 35 (2005); Douglas E. Brayley & Eric S. Nguyen, Good Business: A Market-Based Argument for Law Firm Diversity, 34 J. Legal Prof. 1, 13 (2009).

[3] See Brayley & Nguyen, Good Business, at 13-14; David A. Carter et al., Corporate Diversity and Firm Value, 38 Fin. Rev. 33, 51 (2003). 关于对这一证据及其方法的局限性的审查,see Deborah L. Rhode & Amanda K. Packel, Diversity on Corporate Boards: How Much Difference Does Difference Make? 39 Delaware J. Corp. L. 377, 384-390 (2014).

第四章
法律职业的多样性

论,认为多样性传达了对机会平等的可信承诺,对多样性利益相关者作出了回应。①

然而,重要的是不要夸大多样性的商业理由。并非所有的社会科学研究都能从多样性中发现强大的绩效效益。② 如果管理不善,多样性会加剧冲突和交流问题,或者给人一种不同意见被压制的感觉。③ 也不是所有的研究都发现了多样性和盈利性之间的相关性。④ 就那些发现了这一相关性的研究而言,也不清楚因果关系是什么。财务上的成功有时可能会比不成功更能提高多样性;具有雄厚资金基础的组织可以更好地投资于多样性行动计划和良好的职业培训,指导如何平衡工作与生活,这些既促进了多样性,也提高了盈利能力。⑤

然而,总的来说,存在有力的理由来支持多样性行动计

---

① Lissa Lamkin Broome & Kimberly Krawiec, Signaling through Board Diversity: Is Anyone Listening? 77 U. Cinn. L. Rev. 431, 446-448 (2008).

② 参见该文所讨论的研究: Rhode & Packel, Diversity on Corporate Boards, at 384-390.

③ 参见下文所讨论的研究:Brayley & Nguyen, Good Business; Frank Dobbin & Jiwook Jung, Corporate Board Diversity and Stock Performance: The Competence Gap or Institutional Investor Bias, 89 N. Carolina L. Rev. 809 (2011); David L. Levine & Aparna Joshi, Do Birds of a Feather Shop Together? The Effects on Performance of Employees' Similarity with One Another and with Customers, 25 Org. Behav. 731 (2004); Wilkins, From "Separate but Equal," at 1588-1590.

④ 参见下文所讨论的研究: Rhode & Packel, Diversity on Corporate Boards, at 387; Dobbin & Jung, Corporate Board Gender Diversity.

⑤ Brayley & Nguyen, Good Business, at 34; Rhode & Packel, Diversity on Corporate Boards; Kathleen A. Farrell & Philip L. Hersch, Additions to Corporate Boards: The Effect of Gender, 11 J. Corp. Fin. 85 (2005).

划。正如美国律师协会多样性行动计划委员会所指出的那样,越来越多的公司委托人在分配工作时,把多样性作为优先事项。超过 100 家公司签署了《行动号召:法律职业的多样性》,它们在其中保证"要结束或者限制……与那些表现缺乏多样性的律师事务所的关系"。① 越来越多的委托人设定了具体的要求,包括就律师事务所内部的多样性、事务工作的团队的多样性,以及律师事务所相关的政策和行动计划进行报告。② 沃尔玛提出了最公开、最详细的要求,明确要求律师事务所必须有灵活的时间政策,并在与该公司打交道的合伙人候选人中至少包括一名女性律师和一名有色人种律师。它还终止了与那些未能达到其多样性标准的律师事务所的关系。③ 盖璞(Gap)公司还对灵活的时间政策进行了调查,并对未能实现其目标的律师事务所提出了改进的期望。④ 微软公

---

① Minority Corporate Counsel Association, A Call to Action: Diversity in the Legal Profession Commitment Statement.

② Neta Ziv & Christopher Whelan, Privatizing the Profession: Clients' Control of Lawyers' Ethics, *80 Fordham L. Rev.* 2577 (2012).

③ Ziv & Whelan, Privatizing the Profession, at 2597-2600; Claire Tower Putnam, Comment: When Can a Law Firm Discriminate among Its Own Employees to Meet a Client's Request? Reflections on the ACC's Call to Action, *9 U. Pa. J. Lab. & Emp. L.* 657, 660 (2007); Karen Donovan, Pushed by Clients, Law Firms Step Up Diversity Efforts, *N. Y. Times*, Jul. 21, 2006, at C6.

④ California Minority Counsel Program, Diversity Business Matters: Corporate Programs Supporting Business for Diverse Outside Counsel 18 (2011).

第四章
法律职业的多样性

司也为律师事务所实现其多样性目标提供了激励措施。①

同样,重要的是不要夸大这些举措的影响力。几乎没有任何研究可用于评估这些政策的影响,以确定它们在多大程度上可以共享,或者确定那些承诺在适当情况下减少或者结束代理的公司是否实际上这么做了。在我最近对大型律师事务所的研究中,只有一家律师事务所报告说因为这个问题而失去了业务,许多律师事务所因委托人要求提供关于多样性的详细信息却未能跟进或者奖励这方面表现良好的律师事务所而感到失望。② 不过,委托人关注的方向是明确的,在今天的竞争环境中,杰出的公司的经济和外在形象的影响力不应不被重视。

此外,多样性行动计划还有其他好处。如前所述,一些政策,如涉及工作与家庭平衡的政策,是具有商业意义的。培养不同的观点并有效地管理它们之间的冲突也是这样。许多改善女性律师和有色人种律师条件的做法都是为更广泛的组织利益服务。更好的指导计划、更公平的薪酬和工作分配以及对监督律师更多的问责,都有可能有长期的回报,尽管难以精确量化。通常,对于多样性的商业理由持怀疑态度的人对其进行怀疑时,就好像采用当前模式的商业理由是不言而喻的。

---

① Melanie Lasoff Levs, Carrot Money to Diversity, *Diversity and the Bar*, Sept./Oct. 2008, at 59.
② Rhode & Ricca, Diversity in the Legal Profession.

很少有律师事务所的管理专家会同意这一点。①

关于多样性的好处缺乏数据,这一事实是避免夸大其重要性的理由,但是不是排除其相关性的理由。在这个人才有一半是女性、1/5 是有色人种律师的世界里,如果律师事务所不能有效地招募和留住这些群体,那么就有理由认为律师事务所会面临一些竞争劣势。这种不利情况难以量化的部分原因是,关于多样性的比较数据传统上很难得到。现在,随着更加完整和可近用的数据库的出现,求职者和关心种族、族裔和性别平等的委托人可以作出更明智的决定。他们的决定很可能是重要的,尤其是在当今竞争日益激烈的法律市场上,多样性至少具有潜在的决胜属性。

然后,问题就变成了组织如何帮助将多样性制度化和建立包容性文化。同样重要的是,女性和少数族裔如何才能增加自己的职业选项?

/ 个人战略 /

为了提高成功的机会,女性和少数族裔应当明确自己的目标,寻求富有挑战性的任务,征求经常性的反馈,发展指导关系,建立职业联系,并培养关于有效性的声誉。为了成功完

---

① 关于对批评意见的取样,see Williams & Richardson, New Millennium, at 51-55.

第四章
法律职业的多样性

成这些任务,还需要注意对职业生涯产生不利影响的无意识的偏见和排除异己的人际关系网络。

例如,有抱负的女律师需要在"过于自信"和"不够自信"之间寻求平衡。调查研究强调了形成一种适合本组织并使"男性感到舒适"的领导风格的重要性。① 这一研究结果对一些律师来说,是非常令人恼火的。在美国律师协会一次关于女性领导地位的峰会上,许多与会者抨击要求女性适应男性需要的说法。为什么焦点总是集中在女性身上?但是正如其他人所指出的那样,这也是一个女人栖息的世界,不仅仅是男性会觉得过于独断或者自我吹嘘的风格令人气恼。为了使效率最大化,女律师需要有一种果断有力而不显得傲慢自大的方式。专家建议,在不退缩的情况下,"温柔地坚持"②。策略包括经常微笑、表达赞赏和关注、援引共同利益、强调他人的目标和自己的目的,以及采取解决问题而不是批评性立场。③ 成功的律师,例如桑德拉·戴·奥康纳(Sandra Day O'Connor),就以这种能力著称。一位政治评论员评估她在亚利桑那州立法机构取得成功时指出,"桑迪(Sandy)是一个机敏的女孩",有着"如钢铁般的头脑和陷阱般细密的心思……她[也]

---

① Catalyst, Women in Corporate Leadership, 15, 21; Eleanor Clift & Tom Brazaitis, *Madame President* 321, 324 (2003).
② Linda Babcock & Sara Laschever, *Ask for It* 252 (2008).
③ Babcock & Laschever, *Ask for It*, at 252-262.

有着可爱的微笑,应当经常使用它。"① 她就是这么做的。

正式的领导力培训和指导,可以帮助培养人际交往的风格,以及诸如风险承担、冲突解决和战略远景等能力。为女性或者少数群体设计的领导项目,为应对其特殊挑战提供了特别有利的环境。② 成功的律师的剖析,也可以提供个人行动计划的指导性例子,从而开启职业机会。这些律师没有去等电话响起。米歇尔·梅耶斯(Michele Mayes)是美国最著名的非洲裔美国人总法律顾问之一,她回忆说,在得到一位女导师的鼓励后,她找到公司的首席法律官,"告诉他我想要他的工作"。③ 在震惊结束后,他列出了她需要具有的技能和经验清单。他还招募她跟随他到了下一个总法律顾问岗位。她从来没有取代他,但是在他的帮助下,她做好了在其他财富500强公司担任相应职务的准备。路易斯·帕伦特(Louise Parent)是美国运通的总法律顾问,她描述了面对具有挑战性的工作如何学会"举手",并愿意屈尊以获得她需要的经验。④ 特里·麦克卢尔(Terry McClure)是联合包裹服务公司的总法律顾问,她被告知如果她想在公司升迁,就需要直接接触商业运营。在

---

① Joan Biskupic, *Sandra Day O'Connor* 56 (2009) (quoting Benie Wynn).

② Ely, Ibarra, & Kolb, Taking Gender into Account; Erin White, Female Training Classes Flourish, *Wall St. J.*, Sept. 25, 2006, at B3. 法律多样性领导委员会也为担任领导的少数族裔提供了一个奖学金项目。

③ Mayes & Baysinger, *Courageous Counsel* 82 (2011).

④ Mayes & Baysinger, *Courageous Counsel*, at 69.

第四章
法律职业的多样性

接受了地区经理的职位后,她突然发现自己作为一名"律师,一个黑人女性,没有任何操作经验,与所有卡车司机一起走进了……[仓库]"①。她在这一职位上的成功,使她成为了总法律顾问的候选人。

设置优先事项和管理时间也是关键的领导技能。建立边界、将家庭任务交给他人并放弃完美,对那些有大量家庭负担的人来说,是至关重要的,"比完美更重要的是去做。"②律师不应当牺牲的是与有影响力的导师建立关系的时间。③ 为了建立这些战略关系,律师需要认识到,他们寻求帮助的人在同样的时间压力下。最好的导师通常会指导最好的受指导者,即那些理性、专注于自身需求且确保这种关系互惠互利的人。

暂时离职的律师应当找到保持职业活跃性的方法。志愿者活动、付费的临时项目、继续法律教育、再入职计划,等等,都有助于回归时的过渡。

最后,最重要的是,律师需要选择合适的合伙人。正如 Norton Rose Fulbright 律师事务所的管理合伙人琳达·艾迪生(Linda Addison)所说的那样,"如果你的事业对你的合伙人而

---

① Mayes & Baysinger, *Courageous Counsel*, at 75.
② Linda Addison Delivers Advice to All with a "Lawyer's Dozen," *Forbes*, Apr. 25, 2014, available at http://www.forbes.com/sites/gaygaddis/2014/04/25/linda-addison-delivers-advice-to-all-with-alawyers-dozen (quoting Xerox CEO Ursula Burns).
③ Susan A. Berson, The Rules (for Women), *ABA J.*, Jan. 2012, at 28; Chanow & Rikleen, Power in Law, at 15.

言,并不像对你而言那么重要,你就没有机会。"①

/ 组织战略 /

确保平等获得职业机会的最重要因素,是对这一目标的忠信,这一点反映在组织政策、优先事项和奖励结构上。② 该忠信需要从顶层开始。一个组织的领导不仅需要承认多样性的重要性,而且还要建立促进它的组织结构,并让个人对结果负责。最成功的办法一般是让具有多样性的成员组成工作组或者委员会,这些成员要得到同事信任,并且与结果有利害关系。③ 该群体的任务应当是找出问题、制定对策并监控其有效性。

就像美国律师协会多样性行动计划委员会所承认的那

---

① Linda Addison Delivers Advice.
② Frank Dobbin, Alexandra Kalev, & Erin Kelly, Diversity Management in Corporate America, *Context*, Fall 2007, at 21; Catalyst, Advancing Women in Business, at 6, 12-13; Catalyst, Women of Color in Corporate Management, at 69.
③ Frank Dobbin & Alexandra Kalev, The Architecture of Inclusion: Evidence from Corporate Diversity Programs, *30 Harv. J. L. & Gender* 279, 283 (2007); Jeanine Prime, Marissa Agin, & Heather Foust-Cummings, Strategy Matters: Evaluating Company Approaches for Creating Inclusive Workplaces 6 (2010), available at http://www.catalyst.org/knowledge/strategy-matters-evaluating - companyapproaches - creating - inclusive - workplaces; Beiner, Not All Lawyers, at 333.

第四章
法律职业的多样性

样,自我评估应当是所有多样性行动计划的关键部分。① 领导人需要了解政策在实践中是如何影响包容性的。这就需要收集定量和定性的数据,例如晋升、留任、工作分配、满意度、指导活动和家庭冲突方面的数据。正如早先的讨论所表明的那样,许多律师事务所在灵活和缩减日程安排方面都有官方政策,但是在实践中却行不通。定期调查、关注相关群体、与前雇员或者即将离职的雇员面谈,以及对监督者的自下而上的评价,都可以为女性和少数族裔所经历的问题带来启示。监控不仅在查明问题和作出反应方面很重要,而且对使人们认识到他们的行动正在被评估也至关重要。要求个人证明自己的决定的正当性,可以帮助减少无意识的偏见。②

无论雇主选择什么样的监督结构,一个核心优先事项应当是建立有效的评价、奖励、分配领导和职业发展机会的制度。女性和少数族裔需要在管理和薪酬委员会等关键职位上拥有举足轻重的代表。③ 监督者需要对在与多样性相关的问题上的表现负责,并且该表现应当是自我评估和自下而上的

---

① ABA Presidential Initiative Commission on Diversity, Diversity in the Legal Profession, at 23.

② Emilio J. Castilla, Gender, Race, and Meritocracy in Organizational Careers, *113 Am. J. Soc.* 1479, 1485 (2008); Stephen Benard, In Paik, & Shelley J. Correll, Cognitive Bias and the Motherhood Penalty, *59 Hastings L. Rev.* 1359, 1381 (2008).

③ Simpson, Firms Eyeing Gender Equality.

评估结构的一部分。① 如果没有重大奖励或者制裁措施,包括多样性在内的绩效评估则不太可能会影响人们的行为。② 像 King and Spaulding 律师事务所的备忘录(该备忘录为律师"更多地参与"多样性活动提出了路径建议)这样的行动计划,也不会很好地服务于组织。该备忘录中的建议包括邀请"具有多样性"的律师参加午餐或者周末社交活动,或者"花 20 分钟问女律师或者具有多样性的律师'你想从这里去哪里?'"此外,律师亦被提醒把花在与这些同事交流上的时间计入收费时间。该备忘录在互联网上流传,标题是"这是你见过的最令人讨厌的误导性的多样性备忘吗?"③

然而,我们对能发生作用的策略知之甚少。什么有助于律师事务所对付那些在多样性方面表现不佳的强大的合伙人?像指导奖和大笔奖金这样的激励,是否能有效地改变组织文化?更多的试验和信息分享,有助于各个组织将口头承诺转化为机构优先事项。

---

① Bagati, Women of Color, 49; Rhode & Kellerman, Women and Leadership, at 27; Ridgeway & England, Sociological Approaches, at 202; Ely, Ibarra, & Kolb, Taking Gender into Account, at 481; Joanna Barsh & Lareina Lee, Unlocking the Full Potential of Women at Work 11 (2011), available at http://www.mckinsey.com/client_service/organization/latest_thinking/unlocking_the_full_potential.

② Dobbin & Kalev, The Architecture of Inclusion, at 293-294; Dobbin, Kalev, & Kelly, Diversity Management, at 23-24.

③ See http://jezebel.com/is-this-the-most-offensively-misguided-office-memo-youv-1568180278.

第四章
法律职业的多样性

我们特别需要了解更多关于培训的知识。一些被调查的律师对多样性教育的用处"不冷不热",而一些研究其有效性的专家则更是缺乏热情。① 在对横跨多个行业的多样性行动计划进行大规模评审时,培训项目并没有显著增加目标群体的代表性或者进步。② 问题的一部分是,这些项目通常只关注个人行为,而不是机构问题;它们也没有提供用于贯彻所建议的做法的激励措施,有时还会激起非自愿参与者的抵触情绪。③ 然而,我最近对管理合伙人和总法律顾问的调查结果表明,情况更为乐观,他们就无意识偏见培训报告的反应主要是正面的。律师"不知道他们不知道什么",而设计良好的教育项目可以帮助"打开对话,让人们意识到问题"④。

另一个共同的战略是为女性和少数族裔建立人际关系网

---

① Darden, The Law Firm Caste System, at 85-100. 关于对有效性的有限研究和混合或者消极的研究结果, see Deborah L. Rhode, Social Research and Social Change: Meeting the Challenge of Gender Inequality and Sexual Abuse, *30 Harv. J. L. & Gender* 11, 13-14 (2007); Elizabeth Levy Paluck, Diversity Training and Intergroup Contact: A Call to Action Research, *62 J. Soc. Issues* 577, 583, 591 (2006).

② Dobbin & Kalev, The Architecture of Inclusion, at 293-295; Dobbin, Kalev, & Kelly, Diversity Management, at 23-25.

③ Darden, The Law Firm Caste System, at 117; Diane Vaughan, Rational Choice, Situated Action, and the Social Control of Organizations, *32 Law & Soc'y Rev.* 23, 34 (1998).

④ Rhode & Ricca, Diversity in the Legal Profession.

络和亲和团体。① 这些做法在有效性上各有不同。有效的做法能够提供有用的建议、角色榜样、联络方式和非正式的指导关系。② 通过将律师聚集在共同利益的周围,这些人际关系网络还可以就与多样性有关的问题结成联盟,并提出有益的改革建议。③ 然而,在这个问题上的唯一的大规模研究表明,人际关系网络对职业发展没有显著的积极影响,他们增强了参与者的共同体意识,但是没有做足够的事情来让个人"与他们应当知道的事情或者人员相接触"④。

最有效的干预措施之一是指导,这可以直接解决女性和少数群体在获得职业发展所必需的支持方面存在的困难。许多组织都有正式的指导计划,以匹配雇员或者允许个人选择他们自己的配对者。精心设计的评估和奖励指导活动的举措,可以提高参与者的技能、满意度和留任率。⑤ 然而,大多数

---

① NALP National Survey on Retention and Promotion of Women in Law Firms, Nov. 2007, at 15.

② Schipani et al., Pathways, at 131; Alexandra Kalev, Frank Dobbin, & Erin Kelly, Best Practices or Best Guesses: Assessing the Efficacy of Corporate Affirmative Action and Diversity Policies, 71 Am. Soc. Rev. 589, 594 (2006); Rhode & Kellerman, Women and Leadership, at 30.

③ Bob Yates, Law Firms Address Retention of Women and Minorities, Chi. Law., Mar. 2007.

④ Dobbin, Kalev, & Kelly, Diversity Management, at 25.

⑤ Kalev, Dobbin, & Kelly, Best Practices, at 594; Rhode & Kellerman, Women and Leadership at 30; Schipani et al., Pathways 89, 100-101 (2009); Abbott, The Lawyer's Guide to Mentoring, at 25, 32-33.

项目并不要求评估或者就该关系具体规定会面的频度和目标。[1] 相反,他们允许"有什么事随时打电话给我"的方法,这使得太多的初级律师不愿负担指导义务。[2] 无效匹配系统使问题更加复杂;律师最终分配到的导师往往与他们没有共同点。[3] 正式程序也难以激发最关键的后援活动。女性和少数群体需要支持者,而不是简单的顾问,这种支持不能强行为之。这些组织的教训是,它们不能简单地依赖于正式的结构。它们需要培养和奖励对女性和少数族裔的支持,并监控指导项目的有效性。识别和培养高水平的工作者,应当是一个优先事项。[4]

各组织还可以通过奖学金和其他教育行动计划来支持扩大合格少数族裔群体的努力。美国律师协会《渠道多样性名录》(*Pipeline Diversity Directory*)描述了全国大约400个这样的项目。[5] 一个突出的例子是,Skadden Arps 律师事务所为一个

---

[1] Minnesota State Bar Association, Diversity and Gender Equity in the Legal Profession, Best Practices Guide, available at http://msba.mnbar.org/.

[2] Minnesota State Bar Association, Diversity and Gender Equity.

[3] Minority Corporate Counsel Association, Mentoring Across Differences, available at http://www.mcca.com/_data/n_001/rsrources/live/GoldBookExecutiveSummary.pdf.; Leigh Jones, Mentoring Plans Failing Associates, *Nat'l L. J.*, Sept. 15, 2006, available at http://www.law.com/jsp/nlj/PubArticleNLJ.jsp?id=900005462642.

[4] Catalyst, The Pipeline's Broken Promise 5 (2010).

[5] American Bar Association, Search the Pipeline Diversity Directory, available at http://www.americanbar.org/groups/diversity/diversity_pipeline/resources/pipeline_diversity_directory.html. 关于对该等项目的讨论,see Jason P. Nance & Paul E. Madsen, An Empirical Analysis of Diversity in the Legal Profession (2014).

为期10年的项目作出了提供1000万美元的承诺,这个项目为少数群体学生提供法学院入学资助。① 在对该例子进行评论时,美国律师协会一位官员指出:"这是我们需要的扭转乾坤的真金白银……现在我们需要的就是其他500家律师事务所采取行动。"②

要使所有这些改革成为可能,就不能把它们视为"女性"或者"少数族裔"问题,而是要视为女性和少数群体有特定利害关系的组织性优先事项。正如顾问们强调的那样,"包容只能通过包容来建立……变革需要发生在与组织内人员的合作上,而不是发生在他们身上。"③剩下的挑战是创造这种团结感,并将口头承诺转化为组织的优先事项。

---

① Sara Eckel, Seed Money, *Am. Law.*, Sept. 2008, at 20.
② Eckel, Seed Money, at 20 (quoting Ruth Ashby).
③ Frederick A. Miller & Judith H. Katz, The Inclusion Breakthrough: Unleashing the Real Power of Diversity 37-38 (2002).

05
Chapter

第五章
法律职业的规制

- 规制结构
- 跨司法辖区执业
- 多行业执业
- 非律师人员投资
- 继续法律教育
- 惩戒
- 可选的规制模式：国外经验
- 对规制结构的反思

美国律师协会大张旗鼓地建立了伦理20/20委员会,以适应技术和全球化的变革,就律师协会伦理规则的修改提出建议。在提出建议时,委员会遵循了三条原则:"保护公众;维护法律职业的核心价值观;保持一个强大的、独立自主的和自我规制的法律职业。"①这个项目受到其具有根本性的保守的使命("保持"和"维护")的制约,并且受到了不适合创新或者改革的批准程序的限制。② 该委员会完全由律师组成。提议的修改需要经过美国律师协会代表大会的批准,由各州的律师协会审查后,由州最高法院批准。所有这些群体都是由律师或者前律师控制的,他们因为训练和性格倾向而常常抵制变革。③ 当律师自身的地位和经济利益处于危险之中时,这种抵制尤其激烈。④ 因

---

① ABA Commission on Ethics 20/20, Introduction and Overview (2012), available at http//www.americanbar.org/content/dam/aba.

② James E. Moliterno, Crisis Regulation, *2012 Mich. St. L. Rev.* 307, 340-341 (2012).

③ David Maister, The Trouble with Lawyers, *Am. Law.*, Apr. 2008, at 33; Moliterno, Crisis Regulation, at 344. 在一次调查中,不到1/5的律师事务所领导人将其角色描述为领导创新和变革。Leadership Partners or Managing Partners, *10 Law Off. Mgmt. & Ad.*, 1, 20 (Oct. 2010).

④ Benjamin Barton, In Defense of the Status Quo: A Critique of the ABA's Role in the Regulation of the American Legal Profession, *45 Suffolk U. L. Rev.* 1009, 1021-1022 (2012); Deborah L. Rhode, *In the Interests of Justice: Reforming the American Legal Profession* 16 (2000).

此,委员会的工作都没有致力于进行重大改革。① 它所考虑的最为重要的建议是允许非律师人员投资律师事务所,但也被放弃了。全国代表大会1/3的成员甚至企图阻止就这个问题进行辩论。他们支持了一项决议,该决议在没有支持性事实或者论据的情况下指出,任何非律师人员参与,都与法律职业的"核心价值观"不相一致。②

这一过程代表了任何根本性改革所面临的障碍。从规制的角度来看,美国律师业在某种意义上是自己的成功的牺牲品。没有一个国家的法律职业能比它更具有影响力,能够更为有效地保护其获得规制独立性的权利。然而,这种成功,以及保证它的结构性力量,则使得法律职业失去了最能为社会利益服务的责任和创新。规制程序的职业目标与公共目标之间的不匹配恶化了这一问题。从公众的角度来看,这个过程应当保护人们免遭不称职和不合伦理的服务,促进获得具有费效比的帮助,并确保律师独立于政府伸得过长的手。从法

---

① Jack A. Guttenberg, Practicing Law in the Twenty-First Century in a Twentieth (Nineteenth) Century Straightjacket: Something Has to Give, *2012 Mich. St. L. Rev*. 415, 491 (2012); James E. Moliterno, The Future of Legal Education Reform, *40 Pepp. L. Rev.* 423, 436 (2013); Moliterno, Crisis Regulation, at 341.

② James Podgers, Clear Track Ethics 20/20 Commission Can Now Address Issues of Fee Splitting with Nonlawyers, *ABA J.*, Oct. 2012, at 20; Stephen Gillers, How to Make Rules for Lawyers: The Professional Responsibility of the Legal Profession, *40 Pepp. L. Rev.* 365, 399–402 (2013).

第五章
法律职业的规制

律职业的角度来看,这个过程还应当提高律师业的经济和社会地位,维护其规制的自治性。美国律师业的治理制度是由法律职业主导的,不出所料,它更多是为了维护自身利益,而不是为了维护公共利益。

本章探讨律师规制程序存在的问题。这涉及跨司法辖区和多行业执业、非律师人员在律师事务所投资、继续法律教育和律师惩戒。这些都受到了律师行业规制结构的局限性的影响,都要求进行根本性改革。

/ 规制结构 /

律师规制存在两个结构性问题:法律职业对自身治理的无节制控制,以及以州为基础的监督体系。二者都源自司法部门规制法律实务活动的固有的、排他的权力,这些州法院是在20世纪初开始宣称拥有这些权力的。① 这一权力根植于司法、行政和立法部门三权分立的宪法要求,在很大程度上排斥立法干预。② 法院难以受到公众的影响,并且它们愿意在治理

---

① Laurel Rigertas, Stratification of the Legal Profession: A Debate in Need of a Public Forum, *2012 Prof. Law.* 79, 111 (2012). See generally Charles W. Wolfram, Lawyer Turf and Lawyer Regulation: The Role of the Inherent Powers Doctrine, *12 U. Ark. Little Rock L. J.* 1 (1989).

② Rigertas, Stratification, at 112; Charles Wolfram, Barriers to Effective Public Participation in the Regulation of the Legal Profession, *62 Minn. L. Rev.* 619, 636-641 (1978).

问题上让律师协会"就主要问题"和"大多数非主要问题"发号施令,这种隔绝状态由此被强化。①

尽管该固有权力原则在保证法律职业独立于政府的干预方面发挥了宝贵的作用,但其代价也是巨大的。其结果实质上使法律职业无法受到公众问责。就像康奈尔大学法学院教授查尔斯·沃尔夫勒姆(Charles Wolfram)所说过的那样,该原则"是一种强有力的屏障,使得法律职业不受任何批评……法律职业已经这样认定和'保护'了委托人和公众的利益,但是不允许他们以任何方式参与这些过程。"②这种缺乏参与的做法,导致了一个过于自利的规制框架。③ 法官与他们所声称进行规制的人员有着同样的背景和世界观。法律职业的独特规范、行为和思维方式,构建了一个制度性身份,影响了决策过程。④ 正如田纳西州法学教授本杰明·巴顿(Benjamin Barton)所指出的,大多数州法官都是选举产生的,并依赖于律师的认可、

---

① 关于难以受到公众影响,see Benjamin H. Barton, An Institutional Analysis of Lawyer Regulation: Who Should Control Lawyer Regulation— Courts, Legislatures, or the Market? 37 *Ga. L. Rev.* 1167, 1200 (2003). 关于律师协会的角色,see Wolfram, Lawyer Turf and Lawyer Regulation, at 16.

② Wolfram, Lawyer Turf and Lawyer Regulation, at 17.

③ Gillian K. Hadfield, Higher Demand, Lower Supply? A Comparative Assessment of the Legal Resource Landscape for Ordinary Americans, 37 *Fordham Urb. L. J.* 129, 154 (2011).

④ Barton, An Institutional Analysis, at 1176; Benjamin H. Barton, Do Judges Systematically Favor the Interests of the Legal Profession?, 59 *Ala. L. Rev.* 453, 456, 459 (2008); Benjamin H. Barton, *The Lawyer-Judge Bias in the American Legal System* (2010).

第五章
法律职业的规制

排名和竞选捐款。① 即使在基于考绩遴选法官的州,州和地方律师协会也会施加重大影响。② 司法机构在薪金和预算方面,也有赖于律师协会的支持,并很容易受到律师在会议、年会和社交聚会上进行的非正式游说的影响。③ 相反,消费者的利益很少有这种施加影响的机会。

另外一个问题是,公众缺乏信息和激励措施,无法在涉及律师协会治理的问题上被动员起来。很少有选民知道法院在规制法律职业方面所扮演的角色,亦没有任何强势团体试图将这些问题与司法选举联系在一起。④ "帮助废除法律暴政"(Help Abolish Legal Tyranny, HALT)这个唯一致力于改革法律职业的全国性组织,宣称只有大约 2 万名成员。⑤ 其资源和影响不能与代表近乎 100 万律师的地方和全国性律师协会相比。⑥ 也没有消费者保护机构愿意干预和创造公平竞争

---

① Barton, An Institutional Analysis, at 1187, 1195; Barton, Do Judges Systematically Favor the Interests of the Legal Profession?, at 458.

② Kelly Armitage, Denial Ain't Just a River in Egypt: A Thorough Review of Judicial Elections, Merit Selection, and the Role of State Judges in Society, 29 *Cap. U. L Rev.* 625, 656 (2002); Barton, An Institutional Analysis, at 1199.

③ Barton, *The Lawyer-Judge Bias*, at 133; Barton, Do Judges Systematically Favor the Interests of the Legal Profession?, at 458; Barton, An Institutional Analysis, at 1200.

④ Barton, An Institutional Analysis, at 1203.

⑤ HALT, http://www.halt.org/about_halt/.

⑥ 美国律师协会本身有几乎 40 万名会员。See http://www.americanbar.org/membership.html.

的环境。①

同样存在问题的是美国律师协会在起草《职业行为示范规则》方面的主导作用,州法院在采纳该规则时几乎没有加以修改。② 美国律师协会不仅是一个高度自利的组织,它的决策过程也很不可取。正如参加美国律师协会规则制定的一位资深人员所指出的那样,"把伦理规则展现给 400 个律师,并试图通过两三分钟的发言说服他们这么做很明智,我想不出一个比这更繁琐和更难的规定伦理规则的方法了"。③

规制过程中的第二个结构性问题,涉及其以州为基础的框架,它未能适应法律实务活动日益增加的全国性和跨国性。许多律师的工作,反映了其委托人业务的跨司法辖区性质。其结果是,以州为基础的规制制度越来越脱离生活实际。

/ 跨司法辖区执业 /

一般而言,律师协会的职业行为规则禁止未取得某一州

---

① Ted Schneyer, Thoughts on the Compatibility of Recent UK and Australian Reforms with U. S. Traditions in Regulating Law Practice, *2009 J. Prof. Law.*, 13, 25.

② Gillers, How to Make Rules for Lawyers: The Professional Responsibility of the Legal Profession, at 365, 372.

③ Elizabeth J. Cohen, Modest Changes That Ethics 20/20 Urged Can be Seen as Positive, or Lost Opportunity, *29 ABA/BNA Law. Man. Prof. Conduct* 690, 691 (2013) (quoting George Jones).

第五章
法律职业的规制

的执照的律师在该州提供任何法律服务。① 传统上,希望在其被准入执业的司法辖区之外代理委托人的律师,必须挂靠于当地律师,如果涉及诉讼,就需要请求法院对他们进行临时准入,即仅限此次(pro hac vice)的准入。法院在宪法上没有义务提供仅限此次的准入,并且可能设定诸如挂靠于当地律师之类的要求。② 一些司法辖区允许内部律师代表其雇主在该州以外的办事处提供法律服务,前提是他们登记并向当地律师规制机构提出了申请。③

在这个国家的大部分历史中,各州对律师颁发执照是有意义的,因为法律问题通常只局限于某个州,律师对当地法律的了解尤为重要。④ 但是,传统的方法不适用于当代的实务活动。许多法律事务和律师的交流是通过电话、电子邮件、传真和互联网进行的,而这并不在律师被许可执业的司法辖区之内。在虚拟律师事务所的时代,也不是所有的律师都被束缚

---

① ABA Model Rules of Professional Conduct, Rule 5.5.
② *Leis v. Flynt*, 441 U. S. 956 (1979).
③ ABA Report of the Commission on Multijurisdictional Practice (Aug. 2002), available at http://www. abanet. org/cpr/mjp/final_mjp_rpt_5- 13. pdf.
④ Bruce A. Green, Assisting Clients with Multi-State and Interstate Legal Problems: The Need to Bring the Professional Regulation of Lawyers into the 21st Century (2000), available at http://www. americanbar. org/groups/professional_responsibility/committees_commissions/commission_on_multijurisdictional_practice/mjp_bruce_green_report. html.

在一个实际的处所。① 此外,正如纽约大学法学教授史蒂夫·吉勒斯指出的那样,"与律师取得执照的司法辖区的物理边界相比,职业知识往往更能保证律师的称职性……俄亥俄州的《统一商法典》专家比印第安纳州的产品责任专家更了解印第安纳州的《统一商法典》。"②

在总结这些趋势时,美国律师协会跨司法辖区执业委员会说,

> 在委员会作证的人一致承认,律师通常从事跨州法律实务活动。此外,普遍的共识是,这种实务活动正在增加,这种趋势不仅不可避免,而且是必要的。技术的爆炸和法律实务活动的日益复杂化,使得律师有必要越过州界,为委托人提供称职的代理……
>
> 现行的律师规制制度是而且应当是许多律师重点关注的事项。即使在司法辖区的限制明确适用的情况下,例如在州法院的诉讼程序中,也会因不同州的仅限此次准入规定之间缺乏一致性、法院在个案中适用这些规定的不可预测性、某些情况下这些规定的过度严格性而造成问题。然

---

① Stephen Gillers, A Profession, if You Can Keep It: How Information Technology and Fading Borders Are Reshaping the Law Marketplace and What We Should Do About It, *63 Hastings L. J.* 953, 976-978 (2012); Stephanie L. Kimbro, Regulatory Barriers to the Growth of Multijurisdictional Virtual Law Firms and Potential First Steps to Their Removal, *13 N. C. J. L. & Tech.* 165 (2012).

② Gillers, A Profession, at 998, 996.

第五章
法律职业的规制

而,更令人关切的是,在诉讼范围之外,司法辖区限制的范围也是非常不确定的,而且可能是限制更多……现行的律师规制制度给委托人带来了成本。例如,出于对司法辖区限制的担心,律师可能会谢绝提供他们能够娴熟和合乎伦理地提供的服务……①

为了回应日益增长的关切,美国律师协会批准了跨司法辖区执业委员会的建议,修正了《职业行为示范规则》。就州外律师临时提供法律服务的非法执业禁止,修订后的示范规则第5.5条规定了某些"安全港"。其中一个例外是"该服务是与在本司法辖区获准执业并且积极地参与的律师合作办理的"②。但是增加一名律师大大增加了委托人的费用,除遵守旨在使本州律师受益的保护主义规制之外,可能不会带来任何价值。

另一项重要的例外是,该服务源于律师获准执业的司法辖区的律师业务,或者与此合理相关。同样,如果服务与律师的实务活动有合理关系,而不是与"未决或者潜在的仲裁、调停或者其他争端解决程序"有合理关系,则可获得安全避难所。最后,律师可向律师的雇主或者其附属组织提供帮助。

许多论者认为,即使有这些例外情况,示范规则第5.5条的方法也过于复杂和有局限性。就像法学教授伊莱·瓦尔德

---

① ABA Report of the Commission on Multijurisdictional Practice, 10-12 (2002).
② ABA Model Rules of Professional Conduct, Rule 5.5 (c)(1).

(Eli Wald)所指出的那样,它只允许"与律师取得执照的州有强烈的事实或者法律联系的临时……[或者]附带性全国性实务活动"①。规则之所以仍然存在,是因为当地律师协会是制定规制政策时的一股强大的力量,放宽对州外律师的限制,会让他们遭受很大的损失。②尽管大型律师事务所的律师将从自由化中受益,但是他们也没有什么动力去推动它,因为他们面临强制执行的风险很小。"偷偷摸摸地"越过司法辖区边界的行为被广泛容忍。③律师协会惩戒机构很少有足够的信息或者资源来强制禁止州外实务活动。当外州的律师认为需要挂靠于当地律师时,他们会把这些费用转嫁给委托人。

然而,从社会的角度来看,这一体制带来了巨大的成本。在这个规则被藐视的情况下,它滋生了对法律的不敬。在律师遵守了该规则的情况下,就要挂靠当地律师,它会扼杀竞争,并给委托人增加额外的费用。④

---

① Eli Wald, Federalizing Legal Ethics, Nationalizing Law Practice, and the Future of the American Legal Profession in a Global Age, *48 San Diego L. Rev.* 489, 506 (2011).

② Wald, Federalizing Legal Ethics, at 528; Stephen Gillers, Protecting Their Own, *Am. Law.*, Nov. 1998, at 118.

③ Charles Wolfram, Sneaking Around in the Legal Profession: Interjurisdictional Unauthorized Practice by Transactional Lawyers, *36 S. Tex. L. Rev.* 665, 685 (1995); Christine R. Davis, Approaching Reform: The Future of Multijurisdictional Practice in Today's Legal Profession, *29 Fla. St. L. Rev.* 1339, 1344-1345 (2002); Wald, Federalizing Legal Ethics, at 501; James Moliterno, *The American Legal Profession in Crisis* 198 (2013).

④ Guttenberg, Practicing Law, at 415, 424.

第五章
法律职业的规制

试图通过在多个司法辖区内获得准入而避免非法执业的律师,会遇到巨大的障碍。有些州要求通过自己的律师考试,不论律师经验多么丰富。有些州要求居住于本地,包括在当地有办事处,而另一些则只对那些向他们州的律师提供同样特权的州的律师免除考试要求。从消费者保护的角度来看,这种互惠规则是难以得到证成的。如果有经验的外州律师有能力在本司法辖区执业,那么他们所在的地方的律师协会如何对待竞争者又有什么关系呢?

最明显的矫正措施,是一个全国性的律师考试和准入制度,但这因为与州法院固有的规制权力不一致而被排除了。律师担心,管理该制度所需的中央集权科层机构将容易受到政治的影响,并对法律职业的独立性造成不必要的风险。[1] 这种方法的一个更有希望的变体,是避免全国性颁照机构,这是在仿效澳大利亚的做法。在那里,律师在一个州或者领地获准执业,但是依据的是统一标准,他们的准入因此在全国被承认。[2] 在这个国家,州最高法院可以保留准入律师的权力,但是要基于有统一录取分数线的全国性考试。

另一种选择是开放边界制度,在这一制度中,执业执照与

---

[1] Wolfram, Sneaking Around, at 706; Anthony E. Davis, Multijurisdictional Practice by Transactional Lawyers—Why the Sky Really Is Falling, *Prof. Law.*, Winter 2000, at 1359.

[2] Murray Hawkins, Australian Legal Education and Bar Admissions, *B. Exam.*, Feb. 2008, at 18.

驾驶执照相似。由律师的居住地所在的州测试其称职性,其他司法辖区则将遵从它的评断,只要律师的存在是临时性的。① 各州仍然可以就在当地发生的不端行为对律师实施惩戒,包括未能熟悉当地的规则。如果一些额外的保护被证明是必要的,州可以要求非当地居民的律师通过对这些规则的掌握程度的测试考试。为了防止"逐底竞赛",即申请者涌向准入标准最宽松的司法辖区,然后在其他地方执业,律师可能需要在来源地司法辖区有最低限度的执业经历。②

一项相关的建议是,仿效欧洲共同体 15 个成员国的做法。《罗马条约》允许在一个成员国取得执照的律师在另一国提供法律服务,但是特别保留给该国律师协会成员的活动除外,例如在法庭上的代理活动。根据欧洲理事会的指令,在一个成员国执业的律师在该国和欧洲联盟执业 3 年以上后,可以在另一国准入为律师。仅在一个国家准入的律师,也可以在另一国提供临时法律服务,但是需要遵守某些要求。③ 律师必须将其行为限制为偶尔的活动,同意遵守当地的

---

① 类似的开放边界的建议,see Wald, Federalizing Legal Ethics, at 538-539; Davis, Multijurisdictional Practice, at 27; Gillers, Protecting Their Own, at 118.

② Wald, Federalizing Legal Ethics, at 537; Davis, Multijurisdictional Practice, at 1359.

③ See James M. Moliterno & George C. Harris, *Global Issues in Legal Ethics* 7-22 (2007); Roger J. Goebal, The Liberalization of Interstate Legal Practice in the European Union: Lessons for the United States? 34 *Int'l L.* 307 (2000).

第五章
法律职业的规制

伦理规则和执行程序,并购买有律师不当执业保险。①

在美国,科罗拉多州率先制定了一项开放边界政策。它允许在另一司法辖区持照的律师在该州从事诉讼活动,只要他们不在此定居或者开设办事处。② 这些律师必须遵守当地的伦理规则,并服从州的惩戒程序。③ 在美国律师协会伦理20/20委员会作证时,该州律师规制办公室的副总法律顾问坚持认为,该规则"行之有效"。④ 美国律师协会前会长卡洛琳·拉姆(Carolyn Lamm)回应说,鼓吹这种做法会损害委员会的可信度,并且"这不会在美国律师协会代表大会上讨论"⑤。这一异议,凸显了在规制政策上赋予律师协会如此多的权力的问题,律师协会与影响职业竞争的问题是有利害关系的。目前的框架迫切需要改革,但是很难看到在一个如此受制于保护主义冲动的制度中,改革的动力将从何而来。

---

① See Geoffrey C. Hazard, Jr., The New Shape of Lawyering, *Nat'l L. J.*, Jul. 23, 2001, at A21.

② Colorado Rules of Professional Conduct Rule 5.5 (2010). See Robert R. Keating et al., Colorado Adopts Rules Governing Out-of-State Attorneys, *Colo. Law.*, Feb. 2003, at 27.

③ Colorado Rules Civil Procedure, 220.

④ Joan C. Rogers, Ethics 20/20 Commission Gets Earful About Its Draft Proposals on Foreign Lawyers, MJP, *27 ABA/BNA Law. Man. Prof. Conduct* 669, 671 (2011) (quoting James Coyle).

⑤ Rodgers, Ethics 20/20 Commission, at 671 (paraphrasing Carolyn Lamm).

/多行业执业/

另一个对社会来说可取但是在政治上有问题的问题,是律师协会对多行业执业的禁止,因为这涉及与非律师人员分享费用。① 该禁令越来越引起争议,因为委托人对多行业服务的兴趣越来越明显。其他西方工业国家一般允许非律师人员提供庭外法律服务,并允许他们雇用或者与律师结成合伙关系。② 因此,大型会计师事务所主宰了全球法律市场。它们在138个国家派驻人员,并正在增加对美国市场的侵入。联邦法律规定,税务咨询和在税务法院的代理不构成法律实务活动。这种传统的非法执业的例外,使得律师能够为会计师事务所的委托人提供服务,只要该等工作可以被界定为税务而不是法律帮助。在过去的十年中,会计师事务所就这一界定有了越来越大的自由度,并增加了其内部的法律工作人员,在税

---

① ABA Model Rules of Professional Conduct, Rule 5.4. 这一关于多行业执业的讨论,是基于:Deborah L. Rhode, David Luban, & Scott L. Cummings, *Legal Ethics* 776-779 (6th ed., 2013).

② 欧洲律师协会职业行为守则并没有提到多行业执业,而仅仅是规定禁止与非律师人员分享律师费,除非是在法律和职业伦理规则允许这么做的司法辖区。关于欧洲做法的概述,see Rees M. Hawkins, Not "If," but "When" and "How": A Look at Existing De Facto Multidisciplinary Practices and What They Can Teach Us about the Ongoing Debate, 83 N. C. L. Rev. 481, 494-496 (2005).

务、金融、房地产规划、知识产权、替代性争端解决和诉讼支持等方面提供了与律师事务所相同的服务。美国律师事务所在与这些会计师事务所竞争时,面临着越来越大的困难,因为这些组织通常提供更广泛的服务、有更大的经济体量以及更有效的营销和经营能力。就像法学教授杰弗里·哈泽德(Geoffrey Hazard)所说的那样,会计师正在"吃我们的午餐"。①

多行业执业的支持者强调"一站式购物"给委托人带来的好处,以及律师能够吸引更多的资金和专门知识,这使他们与其他资本雄厚的服务提供者相比,更有竞争优势。这些好处,不仅会扩展到大型律师事务所和商业委托人,还会延伸到有着跨行业需求的自然人委托人的小型律师事务所和独立执业者。因此,例如,一个专门从事老年法的律师事务所,可能会发现与医务和社会工作者一起共事的优势。②

- 对多行业实务活动的反对

相反,反对者担心,律师要对来自不同传统的非律师人员监督者负责,而这些监督者的保密、利益冲突和公益服务的标准不

---

① Geoffrey Hazard, Accountants vs Lawyers: Let's Consider Facts, *Nat'l L. J.*, Nov. 9, 1998, at A24.

② See sources cited in Hawkins, Not "If" but "When." The Brave New World of Multidisciplinary Practice, Future of the Profession: A ymposium on Multidisciplinary Practice, *84 Minn. L. Rev.* 1083 (2000). See also Mary C. Daly, Choosing Wise Men Wisely: The Risks and Rewards of Purchasing Legal Services from Lawyers in a Multidisciplinary Partnership, *13 Geo. J. Legal Ethics* 217 (2000).

那么严格。在批评者看来,随着行业界限的模糊和薄弱,法律将成为另一项业务,在非律师人员干预律师的职业判断的情况下,委托人将付出代价。① 在一些论者看来,安然事件中的不端行为,反映了会计师审计和咨询职能之间的利益冲突,并证明了为什么律师不应当参与提供这种服务的合伙。②

在1999年,美国律师协会多行业执业委员会发表了一份报告,承认这些伦理上的顾虑,但是提出了未能加以足够禁止的策略。委员会建议在多行业事务所中让非律师人员像律师那样适用同样的利益冲突和保密的伦理标准。此外,委员会建议作出特别审计规定,防止非律师人员干预律师的职业判断。在这一框架下,可以将律师—委托人特免权扩展到非律师人员,或者可以向委托人发出有关该特免权不可适用的警告。③

美国律师协会代表大会两次否决了委员会的建议。代表大会成员最初投票反对放宽对多行业合伙的禁令,"除非进一步的研究表明,这种变革将促进公众利益,而不牺牲或者损害律师的独立性和法律职业忠诚于委托人的传统"。然而,正

---

① 关于这些观点的抽样,see New York State Bar Association, Special Committee on the Law Governing Firm Structure and Operation, Preserving the Core Values of the American Legal Profession: The Place of Multidisciplinary Practice in the Law Governing Lawyers 324 (2000).

② Steven C. Krane, Let Lawyers Practice Law, *Nat'l L. J.*, Jan. 28, 2002, at A16; Geanne Rosenberg, Scandal Seen as Blow to Outlook for MDP, *Nat'l. L. J.*, Jan. 21, 2002, at A1.

③ American Bar Association Commission on Multidisciplinary Practice, Report to the ABA House of Delegates, reprinted in *10 Prof. Law.* (1999).

第五章
法律职业的规制

如委员会所回应的那样,在消除"非法污点"之前,无法评估在此类做法方面的公共利益。尽管如此,委员会还是从商业委托人和消费者团体那里得到了更多的证言,他们都敦促协会允许多行业合伙。没有一个法律服务用户表示反对。① 在律师事务所和多行业合伙中工作的律师在委员会作证时都指出,这两种组织的伦理文化除有关利益冲突的规则外没有明显差异。许多提供证言的多行业合伙人也提供了与律师事务所的公益服务记录相媲美的公共服务记录。尽管有这种积极的反馈,代表大会还是解散了该委员会,并拒绝与非律师人员分享任何费用,因为这与"法律职业的核心价值观"不符。② 整个辩论花了不到一小时的时间,凸显了美国律师协会作为决策机构的问题。就像一位代表介绍审议情况时所说的那样,

> 在美国律师协会会议的讨论中,焦点几乎完全集中在多行业合伙将如何影响律师、他们的实务活动、他们的适正性以及他们对提供法律服务的控制上。几乎没有考虑到对提供法律服务进行限制将如何影响委托人及其需求……③

---

① Paul D. Paton, Multidisciplinary Practice Redux: Globalization, Core Values, and Reviving the MDPDebate in America, *78 Fordham L. Rev.* 2193, 2209 (2010). See also MDP Rides Again, *ABA J.*, Feb. 2000, at 96.

② American Bar Association Center for Professional Responsibility Recommendation 10F, available at http://www.abanet.org/cpr/md;/mdprecom10f.html.

③ Robert R. Keating, Colorado and Denver in the House: MDP Declared Heresy by the ABA House of Delegates, *Colo. Law.*, Sept. 2000, at 48.

● 对反对的答复

关于多行业执业的争论引发了人们所认为的"地盘大战"或者"圣战"。多行业合伙的反对者把这场斗争形容为大难临头。这一职业的独立性和核心价值,现在受到了追求利润最大化的异端的侵犯,这些人在保密、利益冲突和公益服务等方面所要遵守的标准不太严格。多行业合伙的支持者以不那么崇高的角度看待这场斗争。从他们的角度来看,关键是地位和金钱。职业主义是保护主义的门面;不能或者不愿参与竞争的律师,试图把错位的精明利益作为公共价值。

解决这些争端的部分困难在于,与其他组织相比,多行业组织缺乏关于其伦理问题的范围以及拟进行的回应的有效性的系统信息。然而,值得注意的是,美国律师已经面临着限制职业独立性的压力,而且这与在多行业环境下出现的压力没有本质的区别。内部律师、政府律师和为会计师事务所或者预付的法律服务计划工作的律师都需要使非律师管理层满意。① 即使可以证明在多行业合伙中,发生利益冲突和保密问题的可能性要比律师事务所大,但是全面禁止不一定是最佳对策。为什么不让委托人选择权衡多行业合伙的风险和利益,并为解决滥权行为而量身定做伦理限制呢?②

---

① Commission on Multidisciplinary Practice, Report to the House of Delegates.
② 关于对这些观点的讨论,see David Luban, Asking the Right Questions, 72 Temp. L. Rev. 839 (1999); Rhode, In the Interests of Justice, at 138.

不论如何解决这些问题,某些形式的多行业合作可能会增加。法律和非法律咨询的整合有强大的市场需求和正当的社会需要。如果州律师协会禁止多行业合作,多行业实务活动就可能采取其他形式。例如,纽约州允许律师事务所(并且一些美国的律师事务所正在发展)与职业服务事务所的"战略联盟"。在这些安排下,这些事务所同意分享委托人,有时还会分享资本和市场营销能力。① 在其他司法辖区,律师和非律师人员通过不涉及费用分享的协作提供综合服务。② 这些安排是否能像完全整合的多行业合伙那样有效地满足委托人的需要,还有待观察。如果它们不能做到这一点,则应当重新审视律师协会的做法。

/ 非律师人员投资 /

美国律师协会的规则被证明存在的另一个问题,涉及非律师人员投资律师事务所问题。③ 此类投资在澳大利亚、英

---

① New York State Bar Association Committee on Professional Ethics, Op. 765, Jul. 22, 2003(批准了非排他性的互惠转介安排); see also Hawkins, Not "if" but "When," at 498.

② See Hawkins, Not "if" but "When," at 511, 512(描述了"波士顿法律协作"公司,它雇用了7名律师、1名心理医生、1名财务规划师和1名工作顾问,来处理雇用、家庭和商业事务)。

③ 这一关于非律师人员投资的讨论,是基于:Deborah L. Rhode, Reforming American Legal Practice and Legal Education: Rethinking Licensing Structures and the Role of Nonlawyers in Delivering and Financing Legal Services, 16 Legal Ethics 243 (2013).

格兰、威尔士、苏格兰、德国、荷兰、新西兰和加拿大部分地区已经被允许。① 然而,2012 年,美国律师协会伦理 20/20 委员会就美国的非律师人员投资提出了一个温和的建议。该建议要求律师事务所只从事法律实务活动,非律师人员的投资上限是 25%,非律师人员要积极参与律师事务所的运营,他们要达到一个适合成为所有权人(fit-to-own)的标准,这类似于律师准入所要求的品性和适当性标准。② 美国律师协会的决策再次被证明已经沦为职业利益而非公共利益的人质。

- 反对非律师人员投资

对这类投资的反对是基于三个理由。第一,股东对利润的关注会对职业独立性构成威胁。③ 美国律师协会《职业行为示范规则》第 5.4 条禁止与非律师人员分享费用,这种禁止被认为是"保护律师的职业独立判断"所必需。④ 根据伦理 20/20 委员会的报告,反对者认为,不受律师协会职业伦理守则约

---

① ABA Commission on Ethics 20/20, For Comment, Issues Paper Concerning Alternative Business Structures, Apr. 5, 2011, at 7-17.

② ABA Commission on Ethics 20/20, at 7-19.

③ Katherine H. Reardon, It's Not Your Business! A Critique of the UK Legal Services Act of 2007 and Why Nonlawyers Should Not Own or Manage Law Firms in the United States, 40 Syracuse J. Intl L. & Com. 155 (2012); New York State Bar Association, Report of the Task Force on Nonlawyer Ownership 73-74 (Nov. 17, 2012).

④ ABA Model Rules of Professional Conduct, Rule 5.4, Comment.

第五章
法律职业的规制

束的非律师人员,可能会促使律师"追逐金钱,而不是遵守职业行为规则"①。对职业象征性和地位的关注也是重要的考虑因素。按照一些论者的说法,非律师人员投资将意味着"淡化律师的真髓"。② 劳伦斯·福克斯(Lawrence Fox)预计,如果沃尔玛可以拥有律师事务所,"这将是法律职业的终结……我们将仅仅成为另一组服务提供者。"③

其他反对意见涉及保密和利益冲突。美国的公司通常需要向股票投资者报告收入、主要委托人和工作细节。④ 然而,共享此类信息可能构成对律师保密义务的违反和对律师—委托人特免权的放弃。另一个令人担忧的问题是战略股本收购可能引起的利益冲突。大型投资者可以购买多个律师事务所的股份,以便在竞争对手试图雇用其中一家律师事务所时,主张利益冲突。⑤

---

① John Eligon, Selling Pieces of Law Firms, *N. Y. Times*, Oct. 29, 2011, at B1 (quoting Andrew Perlman, reporter for Ethics 20/20 Commission).

② Jennifer Smith, Law Firms Split Over Nonlawyer Investors, *Wall St. J.*, Apr. 2, 2012, B1 (quoting David J. Carr).

③ Trio of Federal Suits Challenge Ethics Rule That Stops Private Equity Investment in Firms, 27 *ABA/BNA Law. Man. Prof. Conduct* 382 (2011) (quoting Lawrence Fox).

④ Joanne Stagg-Taylor, Lawyers' Business: Conflicts of Duties Arising from Lawyers' Business Models, *14 Legal Ethics* 173, 183 (2011).

⑤ Stagg-Taylor, Lawyers' Business, at 185; Reardon, It's Not Your Business, at 179.

- 非律师人员投资的基本原理

这些观点中所缺失的,是在允许非律师人员所有权的司法辖区内存在此类问题的证据。美国律师协会伦理20/20委员会审查了哥伦比亚特区的经验,该地区允许非律师人员在律师事务所的所有权,已经超过20年,并没有发现任何有关惩戒问题的记录。① 该委员会也没有发现澳大利亚或者英国存在任何伦理难题,后者最近允许非律师人员投资于"可选性商业结构"。这两个国家都要求任命一名法律执业者董事或者执业负责人,以确保遵守伦理义务。② 这两个国家还要求可选性商业组织与法律职业人员一样,遵守相同的伦理规则,并且非律师所有权人有义务不让律师违反任何职业职责。③ Slater and Gordon 这个澳大利亚律师事务所,是世界上第一个成为上市公司的律师事务所,它在招股说明书中明确表示,对法院和委托人的义务优先于股东的利益。④ 根据其执行主任的数据,上市不仅保持了职业独立性,而且与传统合伙相比,增加的收入使律师更为远离商业压力。⑤ 回应性法律制度的消费

---

① ABA Commission on Ethics 20/20, Discussion Paper on Alternative Practice Structures, Dec. 2, 2011, at 4.

② ABA Commission on Ethics 20/20, Issues Paper Concerning Alternative Business Structures, Apr. 5, 2011, at 15.

③ ABA Ethics Commission on Ethics 20/20, Issues Paper, at 9, 115.

④ Andrew Grech & Kirsten Morrison, Slater & Gordon: The Listing Experience, *22 Geo. J. Legal Ethics* 535, 555 (2009).

⑤ Eligon, Selling Pieces of Law Firms (quoting Ken Fowlie).

第五章
法律职业的规制

者组织(Consumers for a Responsive Legal System)的法律和政策总监托马斯·戈登(Thomas Gordon)指出,"并不仅仅是有着外部投资者的律师事务所才有着对经济压力的担忧。独立执业者正面临着支付账单的压力,大型律师事务所的律师们正面临着凑够时数的压力。"①正如其他论者也指出的那样,在美国,已经有很多非律师人员参与了经营。在这种情况下,已经出现了保护职业独立性和保密的战略。例如政府机构、保险辩护、团体法律服务计划、公共利益组织和公司内部法律部门。②然而,对一些反对者来说,这些例子是无关紧要的。在一次激烈的交流中,一位直言不讳的批评者被问及他的看法是否可以通过表明律师事务所的非律师所有权人并未干涉律师的职业判断的实证研究来改变时,他的回答是"不会"。③

反对者不仅没有考虑相关的没有坏处的证据,他们也没有承认注入资金和人才可能带来的好处。与依赖于合伙人的出资或者外部借贷的传统方法相比,股权融资具有许多优势。正如乔治敦大学法学教授弥尔顿·里根(Milton Regan)所指出的那样,"合伙企业的资本基础仅限于其合伙人的财富,其资

---

① Letter from Thomas M. Gordon to the ABA Commission on Ethics 20/20 Working Group on Alternative Business Structures, May 31, 2011.

② Guttenberg, Something's Got to Give, at 473-474.

③ Joan C. Rogers, Speakers Debate Nonlawyers' Role in Firms at First Ethics 20/20 Commission Hearing, ABA/BNA Manual on Professional Conduct, 26 Law. Man. Prof. Conduct, Feb. 17, 2010, at 110.

产是流动性的。"①在横向流动日益增加的时代,不能确定自己或者同事未来计划的合伙人,很难愿意投资于律师事务所的长期需求。这些合伙人可能会同样谨慎地承担贷款义务,因为如果其他人离职,他们将会对律师事务所的债务承担责任。过度依赖贷款是律师事务所解散的诱因之一。② 与此同时,由于全球化、全国化和技术进步,对其他资金来源的需求也在增长。在多个地点为委托人提供服务的需求推动了依赖于额外资源的扩张。同样,发展信息技术以协助诊断法律问题、提供基本帮助和生成文件,都是资本高度密集型的。③ 创新的法律服务提供者通常依赖于非律师人员的融资。④ 禁止外行人投资,使得法律组织不能从天使投资人、风险资本、私募股权和公共资本市场等其他经济领域获得推动创新的资金。⑤

　　律师事务所也会因来自市场营销、金融系统、工程、项目

---

① Milton C. Regan, Jr. , Lawyers, Symbols and Money: Outside Investment in Law Firms, *27 Penn. St. Int'l L. Rev.* 407, 422 (2008).

② See Tyler Cobb, Have Your Cake and Eat It Too: Appropriately Harnessing the Advantages of Nonlawyer Ownership, *54 Ariz. L. Rev.* 765, 777 (2012); Deborah L. Rhode, *Lawyers as Leaders* 167–172 (2013).

③ Mathew Rotenberg, Stifled Justice: The Unauthorized Practice of Law and Internet Legal Resources, *97 Minn. L. Rev.* 709, 729, 738–741 (2012).

④ Rachel M. Zahorsky & William D. Henderson, Who's Eating Law Firms' Lunch? *ABA J.*, Oct. 2013, at 37; Gilliam K. Hadfield, Innovating to Improve Access: Changing the Way Courts Regulate Legal Markets, *Daedalus*, Summer 2014, at 83.

⑤ Hadfield, Innovating to Improve Access.

管理和类似行业的其他职业人员的参与而受益。① 研究发现,这通常是通过与相关领域的互动来进行的。② 正如理查德·萨斯坎德所指出的那样,就像图书管理员没有创造出谷歌(Google)一样,律师也不能创造出在法律服务方面的突破。③ 吸引和留住外部投资者的愿望,也"常常给律师事务所带来经济……方面的历练,其成员没有经历过这方面的严重压力。"④非律师人员投资还可以帮助企业将多种类型的服务(包括法律)捆绑在一起,从而提高便利性和效率。例如,这些业务可能能够因分摊开销或者联合宣传活动而节省成本。⑤

在日常营销方面,对外部资本和专门知识的需求尤其强烈。沃尔玛提供法律服务的可能性(不论怎么令律师感到不快)有可能会吸引许多消费者。⑥ 该连锁店已经提供了各种职

---

① William D. Henderson & Rachel M. Zahorsky, Paradigm Shift, 2011 *ABA J.* 40, 45–47.

② Steven Johnson, *Where Good Ideas Come From*: *The Natural History of Innovation* 41, 58, 166, 246 (2010).

③ Richard Susskind, *The End of Lawyers? Rethinking the Nature of Legal Services* 254 (2008).

④ Thomas D. Morgan, *The Vanishing American Lawyer* 170 (2010).

⑤ Nick Robinson, When Lawyers Don't Get All the Profits: Non-Lawyer Ownership of Legal Services, Access and Professionalism (2014), available at http://papers.ssrn.com/sol3/papers.cfm?abstract_id=2487878.

⑥ Malcolm Mercer, Professionalism and the "Fear of Walmart": Would You Like Some Bananas With That Tort? *Slaw*, Apr. 25, 2014, available at http://www.slaw.ca/2014/04/25/professionalism-and-thefear-of-walmart-would-you-like-some-banannas-with-that-tort/.

业服务,包括医疗、牙科和眼科护理。法律服务将是它下一步合乎逻辑的举措。英国已经开始了类似的演变。WHSmith 这家总部位于伦敦的连锁店,提供有关离婚、遗嘱、房地产交易、基本合同等的法律咨询,这是通过与 QualitySolicitors 合伙运行的法律亭运营的。① Co-operative Legal Services 是超市的一部分,它提供法律帮助,通常与其他相关服务一起打包。② 就像法学教授蕾妮·纳克(Renee Knake)所说的那样,外部投资可能"使法律服务的路径民主化",从而增加得不到服务的消费者近用司法的途径。③ 这是最近一起对禁止外部投资提出质疑的诉讼背后的主张。在该案中,Jacoby & Meyers 辩称,它需要外部资本,以实现提供可承受的例行帮助所需要的规模经济。④

总之,对非律师人员投资的禁止需要反思。正如吉勒斯所指出的那样,援引"核心价值"并不能"替代理性对话,尽管

---

① Renee Newman Knake, Democratizing the Delivery of Legal Services, 73 *Ohio St. L. J.* 1, 7 (2012).

② John Flood, Will There Be Fallout from Clementi? The Repercussions for the Legal Profession After the Legal Services Act 2007, *2012 Mich. St. L. Rev.* 537, 557 (2012).

③ Knake, Democratizing the Delivery of Legal Services. 关于不乐观的评价, see Robinson, When Lawyers Don't Get All the Profits.

④ Jacoby & Meyers, LLP v. Presiding Justices of First, Second, Third & Fourth Departments, Appellate Div. of Supreme Court of New York, 847 F. Supp. 2d 590, 593 (S.D.N.Y. 2012), vacated and remanded, 488 Fed. App'x 526 (2d Cir. 2012).

不幸的是,它似乎有时会被当成理性对话"①。尽管需要进一步研究以评估非律师人员投资的全面影响,但是迄今为止的证据表明,禁止这种选择的理由是不足的。② 考虑到此类投资的潜在好处,以及尽量减少其风险的规制性保障措施的可操作性,一个更超然的讨论将会允许这种做法。

/ 继续法律教育③/

　　问:如果律师在墨西哥的地中海俱乐部、欧洲邮轮、巨人棒球比赛、心血管健康课程、大吃大喝和藏式减压方法上花了一周时间,如何获得税收减免并让雇主报销?

　　答:把这称为"继续法律教育"。

原则上,我们很难反对继续法律教育。除 5 个州之外的其他所有的州都有这样的继续教育要求,谁能反对让律师稍稍努力就能在他们的领域中保持与时俱进呢?④ 然而,在实践

---

① Gillers, How to Make Rules for Lawyers, at 365, 401.
② 关于进一步研究的需要和对迄今为止的证据的概述, see Robinson, When Lawyers Don't Get All the Profits.
③ 这一关于继续法律教育的讨论,是基于:Deborah L. Rhode & Lucy Ricca, Revisiting MCLE: Is Compulsory Passive Learning Building Better Lawyers? 22 Prof. Law. 1 (2014).
④ American Bar Association, MCLE Information by State, available at http://www.americanbar.org/cle/mandatory_cle/mcle_states.html.

中,这个制度还有很多有待改进的地方。为了获得律师的支持,继续法律教育的要求是最低的,并且是使用者高度友好型的。各个州通常只要求每年 10 至 12 小时的被动出勤,"看一下午的伦理电影"、结束于棒球比赛和免费热狗的体育法研讨会、在豪华的地中海度假俱乐部度假的那一周与高等法院法官讨论法律发展,都可以获得课程学分。①

● 强制性继续法律教育的基本理论

支持强制性继续法律教育的观点,经常开始于并且有时结束于这样的前提:"对于所有律师来说,教育都是有价值的,也没有人严肃认真地争辩说不是这样。"②虽然承认缺少证明强制性继续法律教育的价值的研究,密歇根州律师协会主席还是坚持认为,"不需要进行这样的研究。我们知道,教育是好的,会使人们做得更好。律师怎么能拒绝这一基本原

---

① 关于例子, see Carrie Dolan, California Lawyers, Required to Study, Study at Club Med, *Wall St. J.*, May 21, 1992, at A1; George M. Kraw, Classroom Capers, *S. F. Daily J.*, Jan. 7, 1997, at 4; Alan Ogden, Mandatory Continuing Legal Education: A Study of Its Effects, *13 Colo. Law.* 1789 (1984); Lisa A. Grigg, The Mandatory Continuing Legal Education (MCLE) Debate: Is It Improving Lawyer Competence or Just Busy Work? *12 B. Y. U. J. Pub. L.* 417, 429 (1988).

② State Bar of California, MCLE Evaluation Commission Report 15 (2001); Rocio Aliaga, Framing the Debate on Mandatory Continuing Legal Education (MCLE): The District of Columbia Bar's Consideration of MCLE, *8 Geo. J. Legal Ethics* 1145, 1153 (1995).

第五章
法律职业的规制

则呢？"①

这些评论不得要害。反对者反对的不是教育本身,反对的是当前的强制性继续法律教育的形式。如果它的价值如支持者所宣称的那样不言而喻,就不需要强迫。这恰恰是因为许多律师还没有看到州律师协会推行最低要求的继续法律教育的好处。自愿性项目中的出席率差别很大,但是很显然,许多律师在没有受到制裁威胁的情况下,是不会参加的。②

强制性继续法律教育的第二个前提是,即使被迫参加,也会提高能力。特别是对于从小型或者单独执业机构开始的新律师而言,"研讨会可以填补法律实务方面的导师空白。"③对于更多的资深律师来说,继续法律教育是了解最新发展、磨炼专业、探索新的执业领域的一种方法。据说,即使是"反对强制性继续法律教育"的律师,也会去"冒着学到点什么的风

---

① Stuart M. Israel, On Mandatory CLE, Tongue Piercing and Other Related Subjects, *Lab. & Emp. L. Notes*, Spring 1999, at 4 (quoting Thomas Lenga).

② Paul W. Wolkin, On Improving the Quality of Lawyering, *50 St. John's L. Rev.* 523, 544 n82 (1976) (到课率从 5% 到 66% 不等); Cheri A. Harris, MCLE: The Perils, Pitfalls, and Promise of Regulation, *40 Valp. L. Rev.* 359, 370 (2006) (在贯彻要求之前,俄亥俄州和科罗拉多州不到一半的律师经常参加继续法律教育); J. Thomas Lenga, Minimum Continuing Legal Education—Not Your Father's Oldsmobile, *Lab. & Emp. L. Notes*, Spring 1999, at 2 (引用的研究说,密歇根州 35% 到 50% 的律师并不参加继续法律教育课程); Molly McDonough, Mandatory CLE Again Rears Its Pointy Little Head, *Chi. Daily L. Bull.*, May 15, 1988, at 1 (伊利诺伊州不到 30% 的律师到课)。

③ Janis E. Clark, Transition Education: One Step in a Lifetime of Learning for Lawyers, *40 Valp. U. L. Rev.* 427, 435 (2006).

险……强制性继续法律教育当然不会伤害称职性,甚至可能帮助改善它"①。但是问题是,它所做的是否足以证明成本的合理性。这一点上,支持者通常是保持沉默的,尽管偶尔的说法是,转嫁给委托人的成本是"微不足道的"②。

强制性继续法律教育的另一个理由是,它可以提高公众的信任。③ 正如一位论者所承认的那样,"否认公共关系是强制性继续法律教育计划的一部分,就是无视明摆着的事实。"④这个论点的另一个说法是,由于其他州有继续教育要求,没有强制性继续教育要求的州的律师则冒着"[失去]公众信心的风险"。⑤ 类似的说法还有,由于其他职业要遵守继续教育要求,如果律师协会未能照样学样,将危及其自身的公共地位。⑥ 加利福尼亚州律师协会的一份报告详述了其他持照

---

① Grigg, Mandatory Continuing Legal Education, at 427.

② Ogden, Mandatory Continuing Legal Education, at 1789[据估计,如果继续法律教育的平均成本是每学时 20 美元(如果律师的时间也被计算在内,这是一个令人怀疑的假设),那么转嫁给委托人的现金成本将是每小时 60 美分]. But see Paul-Noel Chretien, The Bar's Back-to-School Scam, *Wall St. J.*, Jan. 17, 1996, at A15 (估计公众每年要花费"惊人的 3.5 亿美元").

③ Aliaga, Framing the Debate, at 1160–1161; David Thomas, Why Mandatory CLE Is a Mistake, *6 Utah B. J.*, Jan. 1993, at 14 (describing report by Utah bar).

④ Ogden, Mandatory Continuing Legal Education, at 10.

⑤ Chretien, The Bar's Back-to-School Scam, at A15 (quoting D. C. bar report).

⑥ See Lenga, Minimum Continuing Legal Education, at 2 (提到了医学和会计行业).

行业的义务,其中不仅包括医生和会计师,还有针灸师、理发师、美容师和房地产估价师。该报告得出结论说:"加利福尼亚州律师可以免除继续学习的义务,而加利福尼亚州的其他职业人员以及美国的大多数律师,都必须履行这一职责,这将是傲慢无礼的,和令人震惊的。"①

- 强制性继续法律教育的问题

强制性继续法律教育的核心问题是,没有研究"表明与没有参与的律师相比,参与的律师能提供更好的服务"②。此外,还有理由怀疑,被动地参加课程是否是解决不称职的根源的有效策略。显而易见,"到课并不能证明在学习。"③任何熟悉强制性继续法律教育的人都能记起参加者在读报纸、电子邮件和其他与课程无关的材料的一幕。④ 对于许多成人学习者来说,柏拉图的至理名言仍然是贴切的:"强灌的知识记不牢。"⑤

---

① State Bar of California, MCLE Evaluation Commission Report 10, 154, discussed in Jack W. Lawson, Mandatory Continuing Legal Education and the Indiana Practicing Attorney, *40 Val. U. L. Rev.* 401, 405 (2006).

② Herschel H. Friday, Continuing Legal Education: Historical Background, Recent Developments, and the Future, *50 St. John's L. Rev.* 502, 508 (1975).

③ Wolkin, On Improving the Quality of Lawyering, at 523, 529 (1976).

④ Donald S. Murphy & Thomas Schwen, The Future: Transitioning from Training Lawyers to Improving Their Performance, *40 Val. L. Rev.* 521, 524 (2006); James C. Mitchell, MCLE—The Joke's on Us, *36 Ariz. Att'y*, Aug./Sept. 1999, at 27; Douglas Shaw Palmer, Why the CLE Board Should Allow Credit for Self-Study, *Wash. St. B. News*, Jun. 1985, at 17.

⑤ Plato, The Republic, Book VII, 423 (Classics Club ed., 1942).

此外,大多数继续法律教育课程的安排与成人学习原则不一致。"如果没有提前准备,没有课堂参与、复习和应用,在课堂上听到的是不太可能记住的。"①关于印第安纳州参加者的一项调查报告说,

> 很少有证据表明,法院的最低继续法律教育标准已经以一种有意义的方式,促进了称职性或者职业发展。我们发现,那些参加这些课程的律师获得了新的知识,但是记不住它,很少在他们的工作中应用新获得的知识。近半数的受访者报告说,他们很少将他们在课程中所学到的东西用于实践,20%的人报告说他们不知道自己是否曾经学以致用。尽管被调查人员报告说,培训课程提供了有用的信息和技术,但是大多数没有报告说其技能和知识方面发生了持久变化。大多数律师没有足够的实际应用和跟进,来形成持久的变革。②

在对宾夕法尼亚州律师的调查中,只有大约 1/4 的参与者认为他们在强制性继续法律教育中学到的东西有助于改善他们的实务活动。③ 继续法律教育项目几乎从来没有提供专家认为有利于成人学习的环境,包括准备、参与、评估、问责和

---

① Wolkin, On Improving the Quality of Lawyering, at 529.
② Wolkin, On Improving the Quality of Lawyering, at 525.
③ William S. Stevens, Ethics and CLE, *Phil. Law.*, Winter 1993, at 27.

第五章
法律职业的规制

在实践背景下应用新知识的机会。① 就像对医学继续教育的研究所表明的那样,讲课是一个特别不足的工具。② 有效的培训是一个过程,而在强制性继续法律教育中常见的一次性讲座和小组讨论是不足的。

这些项目也没有解决大多数委托人投诉的根本原因,这些投诉涉及的不是缺乏技术知识,而是疏忽、准备不足、过度收费、未能沟通等问题。③ 在刑事案件中,律师的无效帮助是最令人关切的问题,该问题的主要根源是过多的案件负荷,而继续法律教育并没有做任何事情来解决该问题。④

同样值得怀疑的是,强制性继续教育是否一项有效的公共关系策略。没有证据表明公众"关注我们在强制性继续法

---

① Wolkin, On Improving the Quality of Lawyering, at 530; David A. Garvin, *Learning in Action: A Guide to Putting the Learning Organization to Work* (2000); M. David Merrill, First Principles of Instruction, *50 Educ. Tech. Res. & Dev.* 43, 44-45 (2002); S. D. Brookfield, *Understanding and Facilitating Adult Learning: A Comprehensive Analysis of Principles and Effective Practices* (1986).

② Dave Davis, Impact of Formal Continuing Medical Education, *282 JAMA*, Sept. 1, 1999, at 867, 870. See also D. E. Kanouse & I. Jacoby, When Does Information Change Practitioners' Behavior? *4 Int. J. Technol. Assess Health Care* 27 (1988).

③ Ogden, Mandatory Continuing Legal Education.

④ Rhode, Luban, & Cummings, *Legal Ethics*, at 301-302. Jenna Greene, A Muted Trumpet, *Nat'l L. J.*, Mar. 18, 2013, at A4; Eve Brensike Primus, Not Much to Celebrate, *Nat'l L. J.*, Mar. 18, 2013, at 26. ABA Standing Committee on Legal Aid and Indigent Defendants, *Gideon's Broken Promise: America's Continuing Quest for Equal Justice* 7-14 (2004).

律教育上的努力。经过 20 多年的强制性继续法律教育,人们仍然喜欢去憎恨所有的律师,他们自己的律师除外。"①这个问题在公众的雷达上没有丝毫的亮点……如果取消了这种强制性,则根本不需要向公民提供情感疏导"。② 如果公众确实注意到,一些可以免税和由雇主报销的不必要的事情可以算作继续法律教育的学分,那他们的信心也不会有多大的提高。正如其他论者所指出的那样,公共关系似乎是一个"特别脆弱的钩子,难以与强制性继续法律教育挂在一起。律师可以很容易和有效地向公众宣告……在最近一年,自愿参与了 x 千个小时的继续法律教育"③。

关于继续法律教育的质量问题,一个听众受约束不能走开的强制性制度,可能不会像自愿项目那样为费效比创造更多的激励。④ 在一个纯粹的市场体系下,"具有实质内容和合理费用的项目将会有回报,并将发展壮大。在强制性制度下,这些自然选择力受到严格限制。"⑤因此,质量不足是一个

---

① Israel, On Mandatory CLE, at 3.

② James C. Michell, Colossal Cave-In: Why Reform of MCLE Was DOA, *37 Ariz. Att'y* 36 (2001).

③ Thomas, Why Mandatory CLE Is a Mistake, at 14.

④ Thomas, Why Mandatory CLE Is a Mistake, at 15; Jack Joseph, Mandatory Continuing Legal Education—An Opponent's View, *Ill. B. J.*, Jan. 1997, at 256, 258 (指出未能提供有效项目的自愿性制度,带来的将是空荡荡的教室).

⑤ Joseph, Mandatory Continuing Legal Education, at 258.

普遍性问题。① 许多州的律师协会没有用于监控质量的资源。② 它们也不能监督自学(允许律师证明他们观看了视频、听了录音或者完成了在线项目)的执行情况。由于不要求考试,律师协会官员无法核实是否有任何重大的"学习"发生,或者参与者是否清醒,更不用说是否参与学习过程了。

- 改革战略

我们需要反思强制性继续法律教育。尽管要求参加该教育的理由很薄弱,但是废除它在政治上是困难的。在大多数州,开弓没有回头箭。强制性继续法律教育为律师协会提供了太多的利益,不仅表现在课程的费用,而且表现在律师协会会议的到会率上,因为参加会议可以取得继续法律教育的学分。终止这种要求也有可能被视为公共关系问题。事实证明,一开始很难抵制强制性要求,但现在提出它们不再是必需的可能更困难。

然而,似乎有可能使继续教育项目更有意义。一种可能

---

① See New York City Bar Association Task Force on New Lawyers in a Changing Profession, Developing Legal Careers and Delivering Justice in the 21st Century 63 (2013)(指出项目质量参差不齐,没有互动,没有跟进); Mitchell, Colossal Cave-In, at 36; James C. Mitchel, MCLE—The Joke's on Us, *Ariz. Att'y*, Aug./Sept. 1999; State Bar of California, MCLE Evaluation Commission Report, at 12(指出在电话民意测验中,40%的受访者在适当的体验上,将其领域内项目的可得性评定为一般或者差,在律师协会期刊进行的调查中,半数的受访者将强制性继续法律教育课程评价为不满意).

② State Bar of California, MCLE Evaluation Commission Report, at 14.

是各州可以要求更少的时数,但是要实行更多的质量控制。律师协会官员可能要求通过考试或者至少取消与实践中的表现关系不大的无效工作。应当为符合成人学习所建议的最佳实践标准的课程和提供互动、应用、反馈和跟进的机会的课程,提供更多的激励和律师协会支持。一个例子是纽约市律师协会的试点新律师学院,它提供指导和为期一年的课程,包括针对实务技能、具体的执业管理和职业发展的课程。①

另外,各州可以把强制性方法和自愿性办法结合起来。对于新的律师和受到惩戒、司法或者不当执业处罚的执业者来说,这是强制性的。完成自愿性的课程并通过基本考试的律师可以就其课程获得证明,该证明可以成为更广泛的认证结构的一部分。例如,获得这种证明的律师可以利用这一资质来吸引委托人,并减少其不当执业保险的保费。各州可以通过增加要求参加继续法律教育的专业化项目,并宣传其对消费者的价值,来鼓励这种趋势。②

另一种可能是向为包括培训和监督在内的指定的公益计划提供免费法律服务的律师提供学分。例如,纽约每年允许就公益工作提供3个强制性继续法律教育的学分时数。③ 扩

---

① New York City Bar Association Task Force, Developing Legal Careers, at 64-65.

② Jeremy Perlin, Special Recognition, *ABA J.*, May 1998, at 76.

③ See N. Y. App. Div. Rules of Court Section 1500.222 (2000). See John Caher, State Board Adopts CLE Rules Allowing for Pro Bono Credit, *N. Y. L. J.*, Mar. 6, 2000, at 1.

第五章
法律职业的规制

展的培训和学分制度可能为那些把当前课程视为愚蠢的无用功的律师提供一种建设性的方案。

作为一个抽象的概念,继续教育是很难被反对的。对于法律职业而言,面对变化的法律、不断发展的执业技术和重大的伦理挑战,它的潜在价值是不言而喻的。但是按照目前的管理,该制度远远没有发挥其潜能。法律教育应当是一个持续的投入,而不是许多律师现在所经历的象征性姿态。

/ 惩戒 /

美国的惩戒程序从来不乏批评者。[1] 在过去 40 年中,无论是律师协会的各种委员会,还是独立的学者,都发现了在应对不端行为方面存在的严重的问题。就像加州大学洛杉矶分校法学教授理查德·阿贝尔(Richard Abel)就他们的共识所总结的那样:"被指名、谴责、索赔和处罚的不合伦理的行为太少了。"[2]大多数美国人同意,只有大约 1/3 的公众认为律师协会

---

[1] 这一关于律师惩戒的讨论,是基于:Deborah L. Rhode & Alice Woolley, Comparative Perspectives on Lawyer Regulation: An Agenda for Reform in the United States and Canada, *80 Fordham L. Rev.* 2761, 2764–2769 (2012).

[2] Richard L. Abel, *Lawyers in the Dock: Learning from Lawyer Disciplinary Proceedings* 150 (2008). 美国律师协会关于各州律师协会的惩戒程序的新模式的建议, see ABA Commission on Evaluation of Disciplinary Enforcement, Report to the House of Delegates ix–xvii, 40–45 (1991).

在惩戒律师方面做得很好。① "过于缓慢,过于隐秘,过于宽和,过于自我规制",已经成了广泛的不满。②

● 职业惩戒的缺陷结构

根本问题是结构性的。就像哥伦比亚大学法学教授约翰·科菲(John Coffee)所说的那样,自我规制允许"行会所有、所治、所享的持续的治理"③。对于律师协会的惩戒而言,这意味着对消费者保护的关注过少,对律师的声望关注过多。许多惩戒机构因为资源限制和错误地认为存在其他民事责任救济,甚至没有处理各种各样的不端行为,处理的是"纯粹的"过失和过度收费行为。但是实际上,所有机构都处罚在职业关系之外实施的不端行为,这往往是一种误入歧途的做法,只是为了维护律师的公共形象。

同样,问题的根源在于固有权力学说。州最高法院宣称有规制法律职业的固有权力,但是没有充分的时间、兴趣或者能力来有效地运用该权力。④ 这些法院中的大多数面临难以

---

① See Rhode, *In the Interests of Justice*, at 158; see also Perceptions of the U. S. Justice System 63 (ABA ed. ,1999).

② ABA Commission on Evaluation of Disciplinary Enforcement, Report to the House of Delegates, at xxiv.

③ John C. Coffee, Jr. , The Attorney as Gatekeeper: An Agenda for the SEC, *103 Colum. L. Rev.* 1293, 1316 (2003). 类似观点, see Anthony E. Davis, Professional Liability Insurers as Regulators of Law Practice, *65 Fordham L. Rev.* 209, 231 (1996).

④ 这一观点是基于早先的著作,包括:Deborah L. Rhode, (转下页)

第五章
法律职业的规制

承受的案件负荷,它们的法官既没有资源也没有专门知识来保证进行足够的监督。① 他们也没有什么倾向或者动机来就对于律师具有重要意义但是对于一般公众而言并不处于优先地位的事项,来挑战律师协会。

一个相关问题是,最容易受到律师不端行为侵害的自然人委托人和第三方,缺乏政治影响力和动机来要求进行改革。② 大多数人是"一次性参与者",他们使用律师仅仅是偶尔为之。试图创建更具有公共问责性的惩戒结构的零星举措,因为没有得到消费者的支持,因为法律职业的反对而失败了。③ 因此,法院将日常监督权力交给了律师协会或者名义上独立但是与律师业的利益密切联系的各种组织。律师可以就惩戒处罚上诉于州最高法院,但是对于那些没有对消费者利益作出回应的判决或者程序,消费者并没有有效的救助手段。

律师协会的监督程序几乎完全是被动反应性的,通常仅仅对严重职业不端行为或者关于刑事定罪的投诉作出回应。④ 尽

(接上页) Professional Regulation and Public Service: An Unfinished Agenda, in *The Paradox of Professionalism: Lawyers and the Possibility of Justice* 153, 161–168 (Scott L. Cummings ed., 2011); Rhode, *In the Interests of Justice*, at 158–165.

① Barton, An Institutional Analysis, at 1207.

② Richard Abel, *Lawyers on Trial: Understanding Ethical Misconduct* 476 (2011); Rhode, *In the Interests of Justice*, at 7–8, 208.

③ 关于在加利福尼亚州和佛罗里达州的举措的讨论, see Abel, *Lawyers on Trial*, at 15–59, and Barton, *The Lawyer-Judge Bias*, at 139.

④ Judith L. Maute, Bar Associations, Self-Regulation, and Consumer Protection: Whither Thou Goest? *2008 J. Prof. Law*. 61–65.

管几乎所有司法辖区都有要求律师报告不端行为的证据的伦理规则,但这些要求被广泛忽视,很少被执行。向惩戒机构提出的投诉中,只有大约10%来自法律职业。① 尽管律师不愿意告发同僚是出了名的,但最全面的调查发现,20多年来,针对未能举报违反伦理的行为,仅仅有4个惩戒行动。②

　　结果就是要依赖于委托人投诉,这导致了救济措施涵盖不足。当委托人因不端行为(例如滥用诉讼程序或者欺诈共谋的行为)而受益,或者当委托人缺乏信息或者动机来投诉时,该制度就不能作出反应。商业委托人通常发现,与惩戒制度提供的救济相比,取消业务或者不支付律师费,是更为有效的救济措施。即使是那些缺乏这种选择的弱势消费者,也常常怀疑将投诉提交律师协会是否会得到令人满意的回应。他们的怀疑通常是正确的。绝大多数投诉都未经调查就被驳回了,因为这些投诉未能阐明属于该机构管辖的合理主张;对于其他主张,不足的资源常常限制了回应的有效性。③ 向惩戒机构提出的案件中,只有大约3%导致了公开处

---

① Abel, *Lawyers in the Dock*, at 502.
② Lance J. Rogers, Misconduct: Conference Panelists Call for Clarification of Obligation to Report Peer Misconduct, *23 Law. Man. Prof. Conduct* 297 (2007).
③ Michael S. Frisch, No Stone Left Unturned: The Failure of Attorney Self-Regulation in the District of Columbia, *18 Geo. J. Legal Ethics* 325 (2005); Maute, Bar Associations, at 62 n39, 64-65; Richard L. Abel, Comparative Studies of Lawyer Deviance and Discipline, *15 Legal Ethics* 187, 190 (2012).

第五章
法律职业的规制

罚。① 即使在律师协会发现有重大不端行为的情况下,处罚也常常是敷衍了事的,并不能保证为委托人提供足够的赔偿。② 对违背宣誓的行为和销毁文件,只处以 6 个月的停止执业,长期疏怠委托人和滥用代管账户,仅仅处以 3 个月的停止执业。③ 对于涉及疏忽、过失和律师费争端的轻微不满案件,惩戒机构拒绝处理,不当执业诉讼通常过于昂贵,并且被投诉的律师往往没有民事责任保险。④ 尽管越来越多的州就轻微投诉和律师费争端设立了替代性争端解决制度,但这些项目很少有强制性,对其效果的唯一的研究发现,委托人存在

---

① Mark J. Fucile, Law Firm Risk Management by the Numbers, *20 Prof. Law.* 28 (2010).

② Abel, *Lawyers in the Dock*, at 500; Judith A. McMorrow et al., Judicial Attitudes Toward Confronting Attorney Misconduct: A View from the Reported Decisions, *32 Hofstra L. Rev.* 1425, 1454 (2004). 惩戒组织也缺少处以罚款或者命令赔偿的权力。在没有命令赔偿或者律师缺少充分资产的情况下,故意不端行为的受害者可以从委托人保障基金寻求赔偿,但是它们不足以支付大多数索赔。See Maute, Bar Associations, at 65 and n43, n44; ABA Center for Professional Responsibility, Standing Committee on Client Protection, Survey of Lawyers' Funds for Client Protection 2005-2007, 27 (2008) (说明基金赔付了大约 10% 的索赔).

③ In re Caro, 945 N.Y.S. 2d 285, 287 (1st Dep't 2012); In re Johannes, 883 N.Y.S. 2d 471, 473 (App. Div. 1st Dep't 2009). 关于其他过度宽纵的案例, see Stephen Gillers, Lowering the Bar: How Lawyer Discipline in New York Fails to Protect the Public, 17 *N.Y.U. J. Legis. & Pub. Pol'y* 485, 510-534 (2014).

④ 估计 20% 至 50% 的律师没有责任保险。See Rhode, Luban, & Cummings, *Legal Ethics*, at 974.

重大不满。① 许多州还缺少与造成伦理违规行为的原因相呼应的救济方法。律师常常受到申饬,而不是得到能帮助他们在未来避免发生问题的培训和监督。②

缺乏透明性使得问题进一步复杂化。律师的大多数伦理违规行为或者律师协会不充分的回应,对于公众而言是不可见的。除4个州外,律师协会惩戒机构并不会披露投诉的存在,除非它们已经发现了违纪行为或者有合理证据认为违纪行为已经发生。有着多达20起正在被调查的投诉的律师,在消费者要求获得关于他们的信息时,收到了律师表现良好的证明。有时候在十多年的时间里要积累44个投诉才能导致取消律师的资格。③ 即使在实施了处罚的情况下,公众也缺少得知它们的便利途径。并不是所有的州都公开惩戒处罚信

---

① See Maute, Bar Associations, at 62 n38. 仅有9个州有强制性律师费仲裁程序。See Lawyers.com, Fee Arbitration for Attorney Costs, available at http://alternative-dispute-resolution.lawyers.com/arbitration/Fee-Arbitration-for-Attorney-Costs.html. 关于惩戒制度缺少对工作表现问题的关注和委托人的不满意率的讨论,see Rhode, *In the Interests of Justice*, at 159, 181; Deborah Rosenthal, Every Lawyer's Nightmare, *Cal. Law.*, Feb. 2002, at 23, 24. 在俄勒冈州的律师惩戒制度中,大多数委托人对其投诉的解决方案感到不满。See Oregon State Bar, Annual Report of the Oregon State Bar Client Assistance Office (2006).

② Vivian Berger, Mediation: An Alternative Means of Processing Attorney Disciplinary Complaints, *16 Prof. Law.* 21, 24 (2005).

③ Leslie C. Levin, The Case for Less Secrecy in Lawyer Discipline, *20 Geo. J. Legal Ethics* 1, 2 n9, n10 (2007); see also Rhode, *In the Interests of Justice*, at 160-161.

第五章
法律职业的规制

息,许多州并不在线公开惩戒处罚信息或者以其他消费者能够查阅的形式公开。① 因为绝大多数投诉从没有导致公开处罚,绝大多数不当执业诉讼从没有要求被公开,消费者也常常缺少对律师执业历史的了解。

法律职业和公众都缺少使他们能够评估惩戒程序适当性的信息。很少有州针对投诉的性质、律师的特点和实施的处罚公布综合数据。② 针对投诉的处理缺乏透明性,对于那些委托人很少提起投诉的公司律师缺少积极主动的监督,使得律师们怀疑惩戒制度对小型律师事务所、独立执业者、种族和族裔少数群体存有偏见。③ 迄今为止的研究,并没有对这些关切进行足够的评估。④ 20 个有分流计划的州,也没有就这些计划在防止不端行为和解决委托人关切方面的有效性发布统计数据。⑤

法律职业未能形成足够的规制程序的结果之一,是其他

---

① Levin, The Case for Less Secrecy, at 20-21; Gillers, Lowering the Bar, at 489, 500, 501; Vesna Jaksic, Attorney Discipline Web Data Uneven, *Nat'l L. J.*, Sept. 10, 2007, at 1, 7.

② Lynn Mather, How and Why Do Lawyers Misbehave? in *The Paradox of Professionalism*, at 130.

③ Mather, How and Why Do Lawyers Misbehave? at 111, 119. 例如,几乎半数的俄勒冈州律师认为,惩戒制度是有偏见的,它的结果在很大程度上基于被惩戒的律师所在的律师事务所的规模。伊利诺伊州的大多数非洲裔律师认为,种族是影响惩戒决定的一个因素。但是仅有少数白人律师这样认为。See Levin, The Case for Less Secrecy, at 6-7.

④ Levin, The Case for Less Secrecy, at 7.

⑤ Levin, The Case for Less Secrecy, at 4-6.

决策者挺身而出,来补充或者取代律师协会的监督。例如,律师参与21世纪早期的一些重大金融丑闻没有导致惩戒行动,而是导致了新的重大立法。① 尽管美国律师协会强烈反对,国会还是要求上市公司的律师就可能的欺诈向公司领导层作出内部报告。② 其他联邦和州机构在律师协会的规则之外,也设定了伦理标准的要求,公诉人也在惩戒机构未能采取行动的情况下提起了刑事程序。③ 就像约翰·勒布斯道夫(John Leubsdorf)对这一趋势所总结的那样:"越来越多的规制者试图规制律师业……[并且]变得越来越不愿意遵从律师协会或者法院。"④委托人和商业组织也进入了竞技场。大公司的聘请协议包括了伦理要求,保险公司坚持以与伦理有关的其

---

① 卷入安然事件的律师都没有受到律师协会的处罚。Barton, *The Lawyer-Judge Bias*, at 253-254.

② See Deborah L. Rhode & Paul D. Paton, Lawyers, Enron and Ethics, in *Enron*: *Corporate Fiascos and Their Implications* 625, 628 (Nancy Rappaport &Bala G. Dharan, eds., 2004); Fred C. Zacharias, The Myth of Self-Regulation, *93 Minn. L. Rev.* 1147, 1170 n109 (2009).

③ Paul F. Rothstein, "Anything You Say May Be Used Against You": A Proposed Seminar on the Lawyer's Duty to Warn of Confidentiality's Limits in Today's Post-Enron World, *76 Fordham L. Rev.* 1745, 1749 n16 (2007) (指出因牵涉委托人的犯罪而对律师的刑事检控有上升趋势); Laurel S. Terry, The Future Regulation of the Legal Profession: The Impact of Treating the Legal Profession as "Service Providers," *2008 J. Prof. Law.* 189 (描述了规制律师的组织); Zacharias, The Myth of Self-Regulation, at 1169-1170 (讨论了有关组织的规则和刑事检控).

④ John Leubsdorf, Legal Ethics Falls Apart, *57 Buff. L. Rev.* 959, 961 (2009).

他保障措施作为提供不当执业保险的条件,律师名录和网站有时也含有关于惩戒历史或委托人评价的信息。①

然而,这些行动计划是有不足的。州法院宣称有固有的规制权,这限制了行政和立法干预的范围。② 保险公司的手段也受到了律师协会的影响,州律师协会中只有1个州要求律师有不当执业保险。③ 此外,在某些事务上,例如律师协会对非职业不端行为的监督上,并没有外部的力量来介入,尽管当前的执行做法存在固有的问题。

- 惩戒审查的混乱范围:非职业不端行为

不论就律师—委托人关系内发生的不端行为的回应有多少不足之处,律师协会常常对发生在这种关系之外的刑事犯罪保持着高度警惕。这不应当令人感到惊讶。这样的案件相对容易处理,因为公诉人已经完成了艰难的调查工作,并且无论对于公众而言还是对于法律职业而言,犯罪者都常常是很不值得同情的。实际上,几乎所有的州都有美国律师协会《职业行为示范规则》的某个版本,该规则授权对不利影响律师的称职性、可信性或者作为律师的适当性的犯罪行为,"不诚实、

---

① 关于协议,see Christopher J. Whelan & Neta Ziv, Privatizing Professionalism: Client Control of Lawyers' Ethics, *80 Fordham L. Rev.* 2577, 2582-2583 (2012). 就保险公司,see Davis, Professional Liability Insurers, at 209.

② Wolfram, Lawyer Turf and Lawyer Regulation, at 1, 6-13.

③ 仅有1个州(俄勒冈州)要求有保险,仅有5个州要求律师在没有保险的情况下向委托人进行披露。See Maute, Bar Associations, at 71.

欺诈、欺骗或者不实陈述"的行为以及"有损于司法"的犯罪行为实施惩戒。① 美国律师协会的标准规定了 11 个加重处罚情节和 16 个减轻处罚情节,这允许不同司法辖区甚至同一司法辖区内对类似的犯罪作出截然不同的反应。②

部分困难在于,没有证据将特定行为与律师协会进行惩戒的理由联系在一起。关于对非职业性犯罪进行职业监督,法院阐明了两个主要理由。一是保护公众和司法免受未来违反伦理标准行为的损害。二是维护公众对律师和法律制度的信心。原则上,这二者似乎都毫无争议;实践中,这二者都被证明是高度存在问题的。

公众保护基本原理认为,那些在非职业背景中违反规则的人也可能在职业背景中这么做。然而,各种心理学研究表明,伦理决策是高度情境性的,取决于环境压力和约束。③ 除

---

① Model Rules of Professional Conduct, Rule 8.4 (2011).

② ABA Standards for Imposing Lawyer Sanctions 26-28 (2005), available at http://www.americanbar.org/content/dam/aba/migrated/cpr/regulation/standards_sanctions.authcheckdam.pdf. 关于不一致性, see Gillers, Lowering the Bar, at 510-520.

③ See generally John M. Doris, *Lack of Character* (2002); Philip Zimbardo, *The Lucifer Effect: Understanding How Good People Turn Evil* (2007); Gilbert Harman, Moral Philosophy Meets Social Psychology: Virtue Ethics and the Fundamental Attribution Error, *99 Proc. Aristotelian Soc.* 315 (1999); Walter Mischel & Yuichi Shoda, A Cognitive-Affective System Theory of Personality: Reconceptualizing Situations, Dispositions, Dynamics, and Invariance in Personality Structure, *102 Psychol. Rev.* 246 (1995); Deborah L. Rhode, Moral Character as a Professional Credential, *94 Yale L. J.* 491, 557-559 (1985).

第五章
法律职业的规制

极端的情况外,基于过去的行为来预测不诚实、越轨行为或者其他不端行为的不准确性是出了名的,即使是由心理学专家进行的。① 没有受过培训的惩戒官员和法官不可能做得更好,特别是在导致非职业性不端行为的因素与律师—委托人关系中遇到的因素存在很大差别的情况下。但是许多决策者无视了区分个人不端行为与职业不端行为的情况。

劳拉·柏斯·兰姆(Laura Beth Lamb)就是一个典型例子。兰姆陷入了充满家庭暴力的婚姻中,她在代替其丈夫参加律师资格考试后,丢掉了其已经持有10年的律师执照。② 在考试的时候,她有七个月的身孕,并患有慢性糖尿病并发症。她的丈夫以前曾两次参加考试而没有通过,多次出现暴怒和抑郁的症状,在发作期间他投掷重物,并威胁如果她不替他参加考试的话就要杀掉兰姆和她腹中的胎儿。她同意了,把自己扮作她的丈夫,在大约7,000名申请人中得分第七名。在有人就此匿名向州律师协会举报后,她就假冒和欺骗的重罪进行了有罪答辩。她被罚款2,500美元,缓期执行,并被处以200个小时的社区服务。在她被美国证券交易委员会解雇后,她找了一份法律秘书的工作。她还与她丈夫离了婚,并接受了心理治疗。尽管她的医生得出的结论是兰姆"不可能'再去做哪怕与此有一点点相像的事情'",加利福尼亚州最高法院还

---

① Rhode, Moral Character, at 558–559 (citing sources).
② *In re Lamb*, 776 P. 2d 765 (Cal. 1989).

是认为她的欺骗行为是"极其严重的",应当取消其律师资格。① 在法院看来"日常实务活动的法律、伦理和道德压力有多种形式。除原始的贪婪和自我夸大外,它们还可能包括这种真诚但是误入歧途的愿望,即取悦一个强势的或者霸道的委托人……"②然而,法院将固执己见的委托人带来的压力等同于有虐待行为、精神不稳定的配偶带来的压力,表明法院对殴打孕妇带来的风险是深度麻木不仁的。③

在马萨诸塞州最近的一个案件中,另一个家庭暴力的被害人的执照因为被害人有不允许在任何职业背景中发生的行为而被吊销。④ 福恩·巴里洛(Fawn Balliro)是一名地区检察官助理,她在田纳西州遭到了一名与其有感情纠葛的人的殴打。邻居报了警,这导致了轻罪殴打指控。被告对巴里洛施加压力要求撤诉,因为他因毒品犯罪而正在缓刑期间,如果他被定罪,就会被收监,这样就没有人来抚养他的两个未成年女儿。巴里洛未能阻止检控,当作为证人被传唤作证时,她作伪证说她的伤害是摔倒造成的。案件被驳回,田纳西州的公诉人将

---

① *In re Lamb*, at 767–768.

② *In re Lamb*, at 769.

③ Pan-Am Health Org., Domestic Violence During Pregnancy 1–2 (2000), available at http://www.planetwire.org/files.fcgi/2368_ violencepregnancy.PDF; Loraine Bacchus et al., Domestic Violence: Prevalence in Pregnant Women and Associations with Physical and Psychological Health, *113 Eur. J. Obstet. Gynecol. &Reprod. Biol.* 6 (2004).

④ *In re Balliro*, 899 N.E.2d 794, 805 (Mass. 2009).

其涉嫌伪证的行为通知了雇用她的马萨诸塞州地区检察官办公室。该办公室让巴里洛休假，直到她同意接受心理辅导，并向惩戒机构报告她的行为。她这么做了，律师协会建议公开申诉，这在一定程度上是因为心理学家的证言表明她完全不可能再实施这样的行为。① 然而，马萨诸塞州最高法院认为，宣誓后的虚假证言不能被宽恕，"无论情节如何"，并处罚其暂停执业6个月。② 在这样的裁决中，法院注意到了不公平的情况，即给予她的处罚，重于对曾殴打其分居妻子的律师进行的停止执业2个月的处罚。③ 然而，在法官看来，宣誓后撒谎是一个比殴打更为严重的犯罪，尽管存在减轻情节。

在大多数涉及非职业行为的公开判决中，法院甚至不想费心去考虑在职业关系中重现的可能性。有关行为威胁到了法律职业的声望就足以处罚。一个具有代表性的例子是，阿尔伯特·布德罗（Albert Boudreau）这名路易斯安那州律师被判定进口了几本儿童色情杂志和一份儿童色情录像。④ 布德罗是在荷兰购买的这些东西，在那里这些杂志都是合法的，模特都到了可以拍摄裸体的法定年龄。然而，根据美国的界定，她们都是未成年人。⑤ 路易斯安那州最高法院同意惩戒委员会

---

① *In re Balliro*, at 796–798.
② *In re Balliro*, at 804.
③ *In re Balliro*, at 804–805 [citing *In re Grella*, 777 N. E. 2d 167 (Mass. 2002)].
④ *In re Boudreau*, 815 So. 2d 76, 76 (La. 2002).
⑤ *In re Boudreau*, at 78.

的意见,即有关行为构成了"法律职业的污点",并明确反映了律师"从事法律实务活动的伦理适当性问题"。① 尽管以前没有惩戒记录,而且其个人行为与职业行为之间没有任何关系,法院还是判令取消其律师资格。②

如果这些处罚的目标是确保公众的信心,那更好的策略肯定是使监督程序更充分地回应职业不端行为,对非职业犯罪的回应少一些特异性。当实施了这种犯罪的律师受到的对待完全不同,关注点是职业声望而不是公众保护时,人们对律师惩戒制度的尊重很少能够提高。现在对毒品犯罪、逃税和家庭暴力的处罚,从申饬到取消律师资格不等,作出惩戒决定的人常常就同样的案件的处理有不同意见。③ 就像前最高法

---

① *In re Boudreau*, at 78–79.
② *In re Boudreau*, at 79–80.
③ 关于毒品, see *Florida Bar v. Liberman*, 43 So. 3d 36, 37 (Fla. 2010)(因为为朋友提供了少量甲基苯丙胺和摇头丸而被取消律师资格);*In re Lewis*, 651 S. E. 2d 729, 730 (Ga. 2007)(因持有可卡因而被处以 2 年停止执业);*In re Vegter*, 835 N. E. 2d 494 (Ind. 2005)(因为持有大麻而受到公开申饬);State *ex rel. Okla. Bar Ass'n v. Smith*, 246 P. 3d 1090, 1095 (Okla. 2011)(公开申饬,以及暂停执业 1 年);Brian K. Pinaire et al. , Barred from the Bar: The Process, Politics, and Policy Implications of Discipline for Attorney Felony Offenders, *13 Va. J. Soc. Pol'y & L.* 290, 319 (2006). 关于逃税, see Pinaire et al. , Barred from the Bar, at 319;Tax Evasion Aggravated by High Lifestyle Nets Year-Long Suspension for Two Lawyers, *26 Law. Man. Prof. Conduct* 14 (2010). 就家庭暴力, see Ignascio G. Camarena II, Comment, Domestically Violent Attorneys: Resuscitating and Transforming a Dusty, Old Punitive Approach to Attorney Discipline into a Viable Prescription for Rehabilitation, *31 Golden Gate L. Rev.* 155, 173 (2001). 关于同一事实存在不同意见的例子, see(转下页)

院大法官罗伯特·H. 杰克逊(Robert H. Jackson)在相关背景下所指出的那样,像"道德败坏"这样的标准,允许根据"特定法官对特定犯罪的反应"作出决定,是在怂恿心血来潮和陈词滥调。② 一个关注自己规制的正当性的职业,肯定应当努力去做得更好。

- 改革战略

更为有效的惩戒程序,应当就职业表现加强监督,增加救济方法,并减少对非职业犯罪的关切。惩戒机构的管辖权应当扩大,包括疏忽、过失和律师费在内。律师协会应当增加资源来确保进行足够的调查和救济回应。与其几乎完全依赖于委托人投诉(并以重罪定罪判决为补充),规制人员不如根据法院的处罚和不当执业判决发动调查。应当就轻微不端行为采用强制性争端解决程序。应当要求律师购买不当执业保险,救济措施应当包括委托人赔偿。为存在精神健康、药物滥用、办公室管理和短期经济困难等问题的律师提供支持服务和分流计划,应当帮助这些执业者制定适当的救济计划,并监

(接上页)*In re Lever*, 869 N. Y. S. 2d 523, 524, 528 (App. Div. 2008),在该案中一名非合伙律师使用其办公的计算机装作 13 岁的女孩进行性引诱。公断人建议暂停执业 6 个月,法院判处暂停执业 3 年,两名法官投票要取消他的律师资格。

② *Jordan v. DeGeorge*, 341 U. S. 223, 239 (1951) (Jackson, J. dissenting).

督他们的遵守情况。① 还应当采取进一步措施来追踪这些计划的有效性,并处理累犯问题。

这个程序还需要变得更加透明。应当要求律师就其惩戒和不当执业记录向委托人或者集中式数据库提供信息。② 被调查的美国人中,4/5 表达了对这种资源的渴望,医生行业的模式是可复制。③ 如果相关监督机构发现有进行调查的合理根据,也应当将惩戒投诉公开。尽管律师通常反对这一建议,理由是披露毫无根据的投诉将会不公正地损害他们的声望,但没有证据表明在少数有着公开程序的州存在这种损害。既然民事投诉和警察逮捕都要进行公共记录,为什么对律师提出的投诉应当受到特别保护?④ 因为调查发现消费者对于不公开程序存在深深的怀疑,即使是美国律师协会自己的惩戒委员会,也建议披露合理的投诉。⑤

---

① Abel, *Lawyers in the Dock*, at 512–514; Rhode, *In the Interests of Justice*, 163–164; Diane M. Ellis, A Decade of Diversion: Empirical Evidence That Alternative Discipline Is Working for Arizona Lawyers, *52 Emory L. J.* 1221 (2003).

② Abel, *Lawyers in the Dock*, at 514; Rhode, *In the Interests of Justice*, at 162–163; Leslie L. C. Levin, Misbehaving Lawyers: Cross-Country Comparisons, *15 Legal Ethics* 357 (2012).

③ Steven K. Berenson, Is It Time for Lawyer Profiles? *70 Fordham L. Rev.* 645, 651–657, 680 (2001). 关于这些改革和其他改革,see Rhode, *In the Interests of Justice*, at 162–165.

④ Levin, The Case for Less Secrecy, at 21–22.

⑤ ABA Commission on Evaluation of Disciplinary Enforcement, Lawyer Regulation for a New Century 33 (1992); Levin, The Case for Less Secrecy, at 22.

第五章
法律职业的规制

在对非职业不端行为的审查中,公共保护关切应当变得更加突出。考虑到难以从不相关的过去的不端行为来预测未来的犯罪,在经验上最站得住脚的方法,就是将律师协会的监督限定在涉及欺诈、不诚实和其他与职业有关的行为上。[①] 如果这种限制在政治上是讲不通的,另一个可能将是适用在其他颁发执照背景下适用的标准。至少,法律职业应当努力更为一致地对待相似行为,将保护公众作为主要关切,而不是公共形象。

/ 可选的规制模式:国外经验 /

考虑到美国法律职业规制结构的缺陷,对具有类似法律制度的其他国家的方案进行研究是有益的。英国和澳大利亚提供了具有启发性的模式。

- 英国

2003年,英国大法官向会计师、英国银行的前副行长戴维·克莱门蒂(David Clementi)发出了下列命令:

- 审酌什么样的规制框架能够在高效和独立的法律领域最大化地促进竞争、创新以及维护公共与消费者

[①] 关于例子,see *Attorney Disciplinary Board v. Keele*, 795 N. W. 2d 507, 513-514 (Iowa 2009) (拒绝惩戒一名非法持有火器的律师,因为该犯罪与其作为一名律师的能力之间没有关系)。

利益。

• 推荐一个独立代表公共和消费者利益,全面、负责、一致、灵活、透明,不会有显然超乎情理的限制或者负担的框架。①

这项职责要求是对律师行业在处理惩戒投诉及与竞争相隔绝方面普遍存在的问题所作出的回应。② 就在任命克莱门蒂之前,公平贸易办公室发表了一份白皮书,对律师业的做法感到非常不满。③ 克莱门蒂的报告同样挑剔,其建议为通过2007年《法律服务法》进行的根本性改革铺平了道路。

对于比较目的而言,最有启发意义的是克莱门蒂为审查确定的以消费者为导向的目标,以及那些为随后的《法律服务法》奠定基础的目标。克莱门蒂的报告确定了法律服务规制的6个目标:

维护法治;

近用司法;

保护和促进消费者利益;

促进竞争;

鼓励一个自信、强大、有效的法律职业;

---

① David Clementi, Review of the Regulatory Framework for Legal Services in England and Wales: Final Report 1 (2004).
② Flood, Will There Be Fallout from Clementi? at 537, 540–542.
③ Office of Fair Trading, Competition in Professions: Progress Statement (2002).

促进公众对公民法律权利的理解。①

根据这些目标,《法律服务法》允许包含非律师人员投资的可选性商业结构。这给消费者带来的好处包括额外的选项、更低的价格和更好的质量、更多的非律师人员的专门知识和资源,以及一站式购物和规模经济的近用和便利。② 因为可选性商业结构往往在提供非法律服务方面已经建立了很强的声誉,因此在提供法律帮助时,它们将有强烈的动机来维护这种声誉。③

对于那些在美国担心近用司法、服务的费效比和惩戒程序的回应性的人来说,《法律服务法》改革和进行这些改革的程序,有许多值得赞赏的方面。该法建立了一个独立的法律服务理事会来负责监督英格兰和威尔士的法律服务,该理事会大多数成员是非法律人员,其主席也是非法律人员。该理事会为每一类持照的法律服务提供者核准了一个第一线的规制者。核准的规制者对于指控严重职业不端行为的投诉,保

---

① Clementi, Review of the Regulatory Framework, at 15-17. The Legal Services Act lists "protecting and promoting the public interest" as its first objective. Legal Services Act, 2007, c. 29 Section 1 (U.K.). 关于讨论, see Laurel S. Terry, Steve Mark, & Tahlia Gordon, Adopting Regulatory Objectives for Legal Profession, 80 *Fordham L. Rev.* 2685, 2699 (2012).

② Department for Constitutional Affairs, The Future of Legal Services: Putting Consumers First 40 (2005).

③ Department for Constitutional Affairs, The Future of Legal Services, at 40.

留了惩戒责任,但是必须创设一个基本独立的机构来进行监督。① 此外,最大的规制者的治理机构[事务律师规制局(Solicitors Regulation Authority)]的大多数成员是外行成员。② 如果核准的规制者在行使其权力方面过于缓慢或者无效,理事会可以对规制者处以罚款、作出救济命令,或者撤销其监督权力。③

涉及工作表现问题的不太严重的投诉,由法律监察专员来处理。法律监察专员是法律投诉办公室根据法律服务理事会的授权创设的,负责审议自然人和小企业对其收到的法律服务质量的投诉。法律监察专员在确定律师与委托人之间的结果是否"公平和合理"时,要考虑法院会如何看待律师与委托人之间的关系、相关的行为规则。法律监察专员可以要求律师就经济损失或者"不便或麻烦"进行赔偿,还可以采取措施纠正"任何具体的错误、疏漏或者其他不足"④。法律监察专员也可能要求律师退还或者免除费用。⑤

● 澳大利亚

在澳大利亚,被广泛宣传的丑闻也促使州政府创建更可

---

① Legal Services Act of 2007, Part 4. 事务律师的核准规制者是英格兰和威尔士事务律师协会,惩戒管辖权归属事务律师规制局。

② See Law Society General Regulations, s. 14(6), available at http://www.lawsociety.org.uk/documents/downloads/generalregulations.pdf.

③ Schneyer, Thoughts on the Compatibility, at 13, 27.

④ Legal Ombudsman Scheme Rules, Rule 5.38.

⑤ Legal Ombudsman Scheme Rules, Rule 5.40.

第五章
法律职业的规制

问责和以消费者为取向的规制程序。2004年,一个总检察长常设委员会制定了《法律职业示范规定》,该文件最终被除一个州之外的所有州和领地修订为《法律职业法》。① 尽管这些法律在某些方面有所不同,但它们都致力于提高监督程序的透明度和反应性。例如,在新南威尔士,独立法律服务专员(Legal Services Commissioner)接受所有投诉,并将它们移送给以消费者为导向的调解机构或者移送给律师协会自己的规制机构。对结果不满意的投诉者可以要求法律服务专员进行审查,法律服务专员有权代之以新的决定。该专员还监督处理投诉的程序,可以接管特定的调查或者建议作出一般的更改。② 昆士兰州有一个独立的法律服务委员会,由非律师人员担任领导。③ 它的惩戒制度包括一个委托人关系中心(解决轻微争端)和一个法律实务活动裁判庭(由1名最高法院法官、1名非律师人员和1名执业者组成)。称职和勤勉问题也会受到惩戒,所有的惩戒行动都公布在法律服务专员网站上。

除一个州之外的所有澳大利亚的州和领地也允许"公司

---

① Bobette Wolski, Reform of the Civil Justice System 25 Years Past: Inadequate Responses from Law Schools and Professional Associations and How Best to Change the Behavior of Lawyers, 40 Common L. World Rev. 40, 67 (2011).

② Christine Parker & Adrian Evans, Inside Lawyer's Ethics 54-55 (2007).

③ Legal Profession Act of 2007; Parker & Evans, Inside Lawyer's Ethics, at 56; Leslie C. Levin, Building a Better Lawyer Discipline System: The Queensland Experience, 9 Legal Ethics 187, 193-194 (2006).

化法律执业机构(Incorporated Legal Practices)"(ILPs),这种结构允许非律师人员拥有所有权。这些执业机构的规制框架正在扩大到其他律师事务所。它要求律师事务所必须至少有一名执业者负责贯彻适当的管理制度,以确保遵守职业行为规则。在新南威尔士(它有着最发达的监督结构之一),公司化法律执业机构的积极主动的管理制度必须就常常引发投诉的事项,例如称职性、交流、监督、信托资金、利益冲突,处理好十个目标。[1] 所有公司化法律执业机构必须进行自我审计,以评估它们对这些目标的遵守情况。[2] 公司化法律执业机构如果评定自己并没有做到全面遵守,必须与法律服务专员办公室合作来改进它们的业务管理系统。[3] 如果公司化法律执业机构的自我审计或者委托人投诉引发了关切,法律服务专员可以发起独立审计。[4] 对新南威尔士的法律执行机构框架进行的一项综合研究发现,要求公司化法律执业机构通过自我评估程序经常进行内部改革,因而委托人投诉量仅仅是其他律师事务所的1/3。[5] 几乎2/3的被调查律师认为,这一过程

---

[1] Christine Parker, Tahlia Gordon, & Steven Mark, Regulating Law Firm Ethics Management: An Empirical Assessment of an Innovation in Regulation of the Legal Profession in New South Wales, 37 J. Law & Soc'y 466, 472 (2010).

[2] Parker, Gordon, & Mark, Regulating Law Firm Ethics Management, at 473.

[3] Parker, Gordon, & Mark, Regulating Law Firm Ethics Management, at 473.

[4] Parker, Gordon, & Mark, Regulating Law Firm Ethics Management, at 473.

[5] Parker, Gordon, & Mark, Regulating Law Firm Ethics Management, at 488, 493.

是"使[他们的]事务所能够更好地为委托人服务";只有15%的人不同意这一说法。①

昆士兰州的规制创新是另一种模式。该州现在正在制定外部审计程序,以确保在没有过度干扰或者繁冗要求的情况下,能够进行充分监督。这些程序包括就伦理文化、收费做法和投诉管理制度等事项对公司化法律执业机构的执业者和员工进行网上调查。② 结果将使得公司化法律执业机构根据同行的表现来标定自己的表现,并帮助法律服务专员评估不同的规制程序的有效性。这一框架的成功,将会导致传统的律师事务所以及那些有着可选性执业结构的律师事务所采用这种做法。③

这种以积极主动管理为基础的规制结构,可以很容易地适用于美国。正如亚利桑那州法学教授泰德·谢尼尔(Ted Scheneyer)所指出的那样,美国律师协会《职业行为示范规则》第5.3条要求律师事务所的合伙人"尽合理努力,保证律师事务所采取有效措施合理地保证所有律师遵守《职业行为示范

---

① Susan Forney & Tahlia Gordon, Adopting Law Firm Management Systems to Survive and Thrive: A Study of the Australian Approach to Management-Based Regulation, *10 U. St. Thomas L. J.* 152, 175 (2012).

② John Briton & Scott McLean, Incorporated Legal Practices: Dragging the Regulation of the Legal Profession into the Modern Era, *11 Legal Ethics* 241, 250-251 (2010).

③ Briton & Mclean, Incorporated Legal Practices, at 253.

规则》"①。该规则的强制执行非常少见。② 州最高法院可以要求这种积极主动的管理制度作为遵守《职业行为示范规则》的一种方式，或者采用澳大利亚框架的其他方面。这种改革将明显改善美国的被动的、投诉驱动的程序,该程序已经被证明不足以胜任监督任务。

/ 对规制结构的反思 /

没有其他任何国家的法律界能够对自己的规制过程施加如此巨大的影响。这种规制权力的一个后果,就是使律师协会不受公共问责的影响,并与如何最好地应对市场力量的公正看法隔离开来。跨司法辖区和多行业执业、非律师人员投资、继续法律教育以及律师惩戒等方面的缺陷是很明显的。显而易见的解决方案是朝着英国和澳大利亚的方向迈进,走向一种共同规制模式,在该模式中,律师协会与由非律师人员控制的独立监督机构分享权力。

---

① Model Rules of Professional Conduct, Rule 5.3 (a) (2002). See Ted Schneyer, The Case for Proactive Management-Based Regulation to Improve Professional Self-Regulation for U.S. Lawyers, *42 Hofstra L. Rev.* 233 (2013); Ted Schneyer, On Further Reflection: How "Professional Self Regulation" Should Promote Compliance with Broad Ethical Duties of Law Firm Management, *53 Ariz. L. Rev.* 577, 619-628 (2011).

② Schneyer, Proactive Management-Based Regulation, at 254.

无论这样的制度理论上多么有吸引力,在实践中可能很难实现。这将需要一个具有前瞻性的州法院,它愿意承受律师协会的反对。如果这被证明要求太多,那么至少有可能说服法院在考虑修改《职业行为示范规则》或者律师协会的惩戒程序时,对律师协会少一点顺从。

在美国律师协会的赞助下,哈佛大学法学教授罗斯科·邦德(Roscoe Pound)在一篇关于法律职业的历史的有广泛影响的论文中,向他的赞助者保证,它不是"与零售杂货商协会类似的协会"[1]。如果他是对的,那是出于错误的理由。律师正如杂货商一样,受他们自己的职业利益驱动。美国律师协会与众不同的一点是,它有能力将自我规制伪装成一种社会价值。法院和消费者应当看穿这种伪装,并要求采取符合公共利益而非职业利益的规制方法。

---

[1] Roscoe Pound, *The Lawyer from Antiquity to Modern Times* 7 (1953).

06
Chapter

第六章
法律教育

- 财务
- 结构
- 课程
- 价值观
- 法律评论
- 战略

"美国法律教育处在危机中",《纽约时报》的一篇专栏文章如此宣称。① 其他论者也纷纷同意。② 对于许多批评者来说,"法学院不是有待修缮,而是已经毁掉了。几十年来,它的问题无人理睬。"③法律教育最忠诚的辩护者也承认,它在一个艰难的环境中运作,其特点是成本上升、入学率下降、就业减少以及学生心怀不满。④

本章将探讨法学院面临的挑战。问题的部分原因在于对问题是什么缺乏共识。教员和规制机构正在形成的对法学院困境的症状而不是原因的反应是不足的,尽管这种反应是善

---

① Legal Education Reform, *N. Y. Times*, Nov. 26, 2011, at A16. 本章以前的版本是: Legal Education: Rethinking the Problem, Reimagining the Reform, *40 Pepp. L. Rev.* 437 (2013).

② 关于综述, see Brian Tamahana, *Failing Law Schools* (2012). 就例子, see sources cited in Eli Wald & Russell G. Pearce, Making Good Lawyers, *9 St. Thomas L. Rev.* 403, 403-404 n1, n4, n5 (2011).

③ Wes Reber Porter, Law Schools' Untapped Resources: Using Advocacy Professors to Achieve Real Change in Legal Education, IAALS Online, Jul. 16, 2013, available at http://online.iaals.du.edu/2013/07/16/advocacy-professors-can-help-law-schools-achieve-real-change/.

④ 关于入学, see Karen Sloan, Enrollment Slump Continues, *Nat'l L. J.*, Jul. 21, 2014, at A1. 上一次入学率如此之低是在 1975 年,当时比现在少将近 40 个法学院。Mark Hansen, Law School Enrollment Down 11 Percent This Year Over Last Year, 24 Percent Over 3 Years, Data Shows, *ABA J.*, Dec. 17, 2013.

意的。对法律教育成本的关注,使人们的注意力偏离了对其结构和优先事项的更广泛关切。正如法学教授威廉姆·亨德森(William Henderson)所指出的那样,我们的职业没有"认真对待这些问题"①。

/ 财务/

● 认可

美国法律教育与托马斯·杰斐逊(Thomas Jefferson)的这一观点有相当大的距离:"法学院学生所必需的一切,就是进入图书馆和按照什么顺序读书的指示。"②美国律师协会法律教育和准入委员会规定了大量成本高昂的认证要求,包括3年的研究生学习、教师的工作保障、丰富的图书馆和有形场地,并限制可以在线或者由兼职教授讲授的课程数量。③ 申请认证也是一个昂贵的过程。一个具有讽刺意味、没有逃过低

---

① William Henderson, Waking Up Law Professors, *Nat'l L. J. L. Sch. Rev.*, Nov. 3, 2011, available at http://legaltimes.typepad.com/lawschoolreview/2011/11/waking-up-law-professors.html; Mavlik Shah, The Legal Education Bubble: How Law Schools Should Respond to Changes in the Legal Market, 23 *Geo. J. Legal Ethics* 843, 846-847 (2010).

② Thomas Jefferson, *Selecting Writings* 966 (Merrill P. Peterson, ed., 1984).

③ ABA Standards and Rules of Procedure for Approval of Law Schools, http://www.americanbar.org/groups/legal_education/resources/standards.html.

预算申请人的注意的事情是,7名管理人员不得不从田纳西州飞往波多黎各,在认证委员会开会的丽思·卡尔顿(Ritz Carlton)酒店去作简短介绍。①

其结果是法学院之间的"单调乏味的雷同"②。僵化的认证标准阻碍了可以大大降低成本的创新和不同的法律教育模式。

• 排名

在许多法律教育者看来,排名对成本的影响比认证更为重要。③《美国新闻和世界报道》这个"错误的测量指标之母"严重扭曲了法学院的优先事项。④ 在这场竞争中,学校最容易提高排名的方法之一,就是在《美国新闻和世界报道》的计算方法所看重的领域花更多的钱。一个例子是每个学生的支出在该排名生效后的几十年中急剧攀升。⑤ 另一个因素是学生的中位

---

① David Segal, The Price to Play Its Way, *N. Y. Times*, Dec. 18, 2011, at B4.

② 戴维·R·班尼泽(David R. Barnhizer)提出了这一观点,但是并没有将其与认可联系在一起。See David R. Barnhizer, The Purposes and Methods of American Legal Education, *36 J. Legal Prof.* 1, 40 (2011).

③ U. S. Government Accountability Office, Higher Education: Issues Related to Law School Cost and Access (2009). See also Martha Daugherty et al., American Bar Association Report of the Special Committee on the U. S. News and World Report Rankings 3-4(2010), available at http://ms-jd.org/files/f.usnewsfinal-report.pdf.

④ Steven J. Harper, *The Lawyer Bubble*: *A Profession in Crisis* 16 (2013).

⑤ Shah, The Legal Education Bubble, at 847; Debra Cassens Weiss, Study Partly Blames Higher Law School Tuition on 40 Percent Leap in Faculty Size, *ABA J.*, Mar. 2010. See also Gene R. Nichol, Rankings, Economic Challenge, and the Future of Legal Education, *61 J. Legal Educ.* 345, 349 (2012) (讨论了法学院为提高排名而增加支出的方式).

GPA 和法学院入学考试(LSAT)分数,学校有动机将更多的奖学金用于吸引高分申请者。因为这些人也可能在学业上表现最好,并且获得报酬最高的工作,这一做法相当于反罗宾汉效应,最贫困的学生的学费作为奖学金补贴给了富人。① 法学院还试图通过增加旨在提高其声望的支出提高其排名,其中包括对教师五花八门的学术出版物提供补贴。② 此外,占每个学校排名比重40%的声望调查,是教育质量的一个特别不足的表象。③ 被调查者很少有足够的知识来作出准确的比较判断。大多数参与者依靠的是口碑和先前的排名,这使得该过程能够自我延续。过去的认可创造了光环效应,即使评估人员对学校目前的表现一无所知,也会打出很高的分数。这就解释了为什么普林斯顿和麻省理工学院的法学院在调查中表现很好,尽管它们并不存在。④ 此外,排名制

---

① Richard A. Matasar, The Viability of the Law Degree: Cost, Value, and Intrinsic Worth, *96 Iowa L. Rev.* 1579, 1581 (2011); David Yellen, The Impact of Rankings and Rules on Legal Education Reform, *45 Conn. L. Rev.* 1389, 1397 (2013); American Bar Association Task Force on the Future of Legal Education, Report and Recommendations 2 (2014).

② Yellen, The Impact of Rankings and Rules, 1895.

③ 关于排名方法, see Robert Morse & Sam Flanagan, Law School Rankings Methodology, Mar. 14, 2011, available at http://www.usnews.com/education/best-graduate-schools/top-law-schools/articles/2014/03/10/methodology-2015-best-law-schools-rankings.

④ Stephen P. Klein & Laura Hamilton, Association of American Law Schools, The Validity of the U.S. News and World Report Rankings of ABA Law Schools (1998); Roger L. Geiger, *Knowledge and Money* 149 (2004); Terry Carter, Rankled by the Rankings, *ABA J.*, Mar. 1998, at 46, 48-49. Deborah L. Rhode, *In Pursuit of Knowledge* 7 (2006).

第六章
法律教育

度排除了许多严重影响学生教育经历的因素,如近用临床课程、公益机会以及具有多样性的教员和学生团体。①

排名对法学院的决策产生了其他不利影响。在某些情况下,学校在计算每名学生的支出时,编造事实或者使用了"安然型会计准则"。② 在其他情况下,学校的短期岗位会雇用自己的毕业生,以提高他们的就业率。

这并不是说排名完全没有价值。对一些相关的特征可以进行客观评估,学校应当对它们的表现负责。在缺乏比较数据的情况下,法学院的申请者将会遇到教育上的"沃博艮湖"(Lake Woebegon)③,每个学校都声称高于平均水平。但是,《美国新闻和世界报道》的排名制度是存在严重的缺陷和不当影响的。它为不完备的量度任意分配权重,使用向不知情者进行的声望调查作为质量的表象,并且强迫学校在造成成本飞涨的学术军备竞赛中竞争。然而,超过 4/5 的法学院学生说,在申请时,法学院的排名对于决定去哪里是重要的或者非常重要的。④ 它与捐

---

① Klein & Hamilton, The Validity of the U. S. News Rankings.
② Tamanaha, *Failing Law Schools*, at 78, 84 (quoting William Henderson).
③ 这里讲的是沃博艮湖效应,即人类高估自身能力的一种自然倾向。这是由心理学家戴维·迈尔斯(David Myers)以小说中虚构的同名小镇命名的。"所有的女人都很强壮,所有的男人都很英俊,所有的孩子都超过平均水平",这句话被用来描述一种真实而普遍的人类倾向,即高估自己的成就和能力。——译者注
④ Harper, *The Lawyer Bubble*, at 15; Karen Sloan, Prospective Law Students Still Have Stars in Their Eyes, *Nat'l L. J.*, Jun. 19, 2012.

赠者、雇主和教员同样具有影响力。① 华盛顿大学法学教授布莱恩·塔玛纳哈(Brian Tamanaha)直言不讳地说:"排名扼住了法学院的咽喉。"②

- 成本上升和就业岗位减少

排名和认证要求一起,助长了学费的快速增长。取消学生贷款上限的做法也在向类似的方向行进。③ 在过去的30年中,法律教育价格的增长比家庭平均收入的增长快了大约3倍。④ 从1989年到2009年,大学教育费用增长了71%,而法学院学费则上涨了317%。⑤ 现在法学院毕业生的平均债务达到10万美元。⑥ 只有57%找到了专职法律工作,而那些找到工作并

---

① Olufunmilauyo Arewa, Andrew P. Morriss, & William Henderson, Enduring Hierarchies in American Legal Education, Legal Studies Research Paper Series No. 2013-141, University of California at Irvine 76 (2013).

② Tamanaha, *Failing Law Schools*, at 78.

③ Benjamin H. Barton, Glass Half Full: *America's Lawyer Crisis and Its Upside* (forthcoming, 2015).

④ William Henderson, Law School 4.0: Are Law Schools Relevant to the Future of Law? *Legal Prof. Blog*, Jul. 2, 2009, available at http://lawprofessors.typepad.com/legal_profession/2009/07/law-school-40are-law-schools-relevant-to-the-future-of-law.html.

⑤ David Segal, Law School Economics: Ka-Ching, *N.Y. Times*, Jul. 17, 2011, at B6.

⑥ Brian Z. Tamahana, How to Make Law School Affordable, *N.Y. Times Op. Ed.*, Jun. 1, 2012, at A23; U.S. News and World Report, http://www.usnews.com./education/best-graduate-schools/the-short-list-grad-school/articles/2012/03/22/10-law-schools-that-lead-to-the-most-debt.

报告收入的人往往赚得太少,无法涵盖债务。① 根据西北大学法学院前院长戴维·凡·赞德(David Van Zandt)的计算,超过40%的美国法学院毕业生的起薪不足以偿还平均债务。② 毫无疑问,债务负担的分布是不均的,这加剧了种族和阶级劣势。③

学生贷款在破产时一般不能免除,并经常造成巨大的困难。一个代表性的例子是芝加哥的洛约拉(Loyola)大学法学院的一名毕业生,她放弃了成为检察官的计划,因为她有20万美元的债务,在为一家中型公司工作时,她仍然无法还清。

---

① Karen Sloan, Bright Spots amid Glum Jobs Outlook, *Nat'l L. J.*, Apr. 21, 2014; NALP, Law School Grads Face Worst Job Market Yet—Less Than Half Find Jobs in Private Practice, NALP press release, Jun. 7, 2012, available at http://www.nalp.org/2011selectedfindingsrelease, http://www.nalp.org/classof2011; William D. Henderson & Rachel M. Zahorsky, The Law School Bubble: How Long Will It Last If Law Grads Can't Pay Bills? *ABA J.*, Jan. 2012, at 32, 36; Martha Neil, In "Perfect Storm" of Hard-to-Find Jobs and Stagnant Pay, Law Grads Can't Escape Hefty Student Loans, *ABA J.*, Feb. 6, 2012, available at http://www.abajournal.com/news/article/more_recent_law_grads_likely_are_filing_for_bankruptcy. 这些报告收入的人可能是在薪酬曲线的高端,因此实际的中位数可能更低。

② Political Calculations, Does It Pay to Go to Law School, Jul. 20, 2010, available at http://politicalcalculations.blogspot.com/2010/07/does-it-pay-to-go-to-law-school; Barton, *Glass Half Full*.

③ Bourne, The Coming Crash(指出非洲裔美国人和来自低收入背景的人有着更高的债务负担); American Bar Foundation and National Association for Law Placement, *After the JD III: Third Results from a National Study of Legal Careers* 80-81(黑人和西班牙裔律师的债务负担过高)。

就像她告诉《纽约时报》的那样，

> 现在，贷款控制着我生活的方方面面。就我的实际生活而言，它控制着我将要养活的孩子的数量，就我住的地方而言，它控制着我能住的房子的类型。我真的相信我还没有还清贷款就会成为祖母。我还没有就此取得有效的进展。①

尽管联邦政府和大多数法学院向那些从事公共利益工作的毕业生提供贷款偿还援助，但是法学院的项目往往资金不足，联邦项目在为公共利益工作10年后才能够全额免除。② 这些项目也没有解决根本的问题，即缺少工作岗位（无论是公共利益工作还是其他工作），这使得法学院成为一个值得怀疑的投资。近年来，只有约半数的应届毕业生获得了法律学位优先录用的专职长期就业机会。③ 托马斯·杰斐逊（Thomas Jefferson）法学院的一名毕业生描述了找到足够的就业机会以偿还15万美元贷款的困难：

---

① Segal, The Price to Play, at B5 (quoting Keri-Ann Baker).

② College Cost Reduction and Access Act of 2007, 21 Stat. 784, Public Law 110-184 (2007); Philip G. Schrag & Charles W. Pruett, Coordinating Loan Repayment Assistance Programs with New Federal Legislation, *60 J. Legal Educ.* 584 (2010). See ABA Commission on Loan Repayment and Forgiveness, Lifting the Burden: Law School Debt as a Barrier to Public Service (2003).

③ Joe Palazzolo, Law Grads Face Brutal Job Market, *Wall St. J.*, Jun. 26, 2012, at A1, A2; William Henderson, A Blueprint for Change, *40 Pepp. L. Rev.* 461, 476 (2013).

第六章
法律教育

八年来,我从未有过一份稳定的工作,只是断断续续的文件审查工作……这些年来,我已经发出了几千份简历。在"好"的年份里,我一周工作 80 小时,我的工资的一半用于偿还学生贷款。在过去的"糟糕"的几年里,我还不能还清我的贷款,而且工作太不稳定了,我被赶出了公寓,不得不使用食物券。此外,尽管八年过去了,我的贷款余额仅仅减少了 10%。我永远不会跳出这个债务陷阱,永远不会拥有我自己的房子,也不会有能力养活孩子。我考虑过自杀……①

随着越来越多的债务拖欠,现行制度在政治和经济上变得不那么可持续发展。② 那些背负着难以承受的债务负担的人的背叛感,在那些以"温柔地雇我来当托儿""失业的法律博士"和"揭露法学院骗局"为标题的博客中可见一斑。③

然而,对律师供应过剩和失业的担忧并不新鲜,也并非总是永久性的。1927 年,斯坦福大学法学院院长宣称,

我们今天的律师比现在所有合法需求所需要的律师

---

① Steven J. Harper, Suffering in Silence, *Am. Law.*, Sept. 2011, at 83.
② 半数以上学生贷款被拖欠或者延期,see Bill Hardekopf, More Than Half of Student Loans Are Now in Deferral or Delinquent, *Forbes*, Feb. 1, 2013, available at http://www.forbes.com/sites/moneybuilder/2013/02/01/alarming-number-ofstudent-loans-are-delinquent/. 关于当前制度的不可持续发展性,see Henderson, A Blueprint for Change, at 462.
③ 进一步的例子,see Lauren Carasik, Renaissance of Retrenchment: Legal Education at a Crossroads, *44 Ind. L. Rev.* 735, 745-746 (2011).

都要多。事实是,我们只是被那些有抱负的年轻律师所淹没,他们中的大多数将在准入后的几年内沦落到房地产、保险和相关行业,而这并不是一个旨在帮助我们提高职业声誉的过程。①

一些论者认为,随着婴儿潮一代人变老、人口的增加和法律的日益复杂化,退休率将增至3倍,目前的情况将会改善。②

然而,大多数论者认为,由于法律服务市场的结构变化,毕业生目前面临的困难要比往年更加严重和持久。③ 更多的雇主依靠律师助理、技术、外包和合同律师来做以前要由应届毕业生所从事的工作,而资金拮据的公共部门即使面临重大需求,也无法扩大雇用。④

---

① Marion Kirkwood, quoted in John W. Reed, On Being Watched: Modeling the Profession During Uncertain Times, B. Exam., Jun. 2011, at 6, 8.

② René Reich-Graefe, Keep Calm and Carry On, 27 Geo. J. Legal Ethics 55, 63-66 (2014).

③ Bill Henderson, A Counterpoint to "the most robust legal market that ever existed in this country," Legal Whiteboard, Mar. 17, 2014, available at http://lawprofessors.typepad.com/legalwhiteboard/2014/03/a-counterpoint-to-the-most-robust-legal-market-the-ever-existedin-this-country.html.; Bernard A. Burk, What's New about the New Normal: The Evolving Market for New Lawyers in the 21st Century, unpublished draft, Dec. 30, 2013; William Henderson & Rachel M. Zahorsky, Job Stagnation May Have Started before the Recession, and It May be a Sign of Lasting Change, ABA J., Jul. 2011; Thomas S. Clay & Eric A Seeger, Law Firms in Transition: An Altman Weil Flash Survey (2010).

④ Henderson, A Blueprint for Change, at 478; Richard Susskind, The End of Lawyers: Rethinking the Nature of Legal Services (2009).

第六章
法律教育

- 申请

随着债务负担的增加和就业前景的黯淡,越来越少的人参加 LSAT 和申请法学院。自 2010 年以来,申请已减少了 38%,并触及 30 年来的最低点。① 对于许多法学院来说,这要在接受资历较低的申请人(这将对他们在《美国新闻和世界报道》中的排名产生不利影响)还是缩减入学班级的规模(这将减少学费收入)之间作出令人不舒服的选择。2/3 的被认可的法学院在 2013 年选择减少它们的班级数量。②

此外,对法律教育的需求超过了现有的就业机会,而且不顾市场趋势,在过去 10 年中已经开办了 15 所新的法学院,尽管现有的法学院还在努力填补它们的班级。③ 这就引出了这样一个问题,即为什么有这么多的学生作出高风险的决定去上法学院。问题的部分原因在于,法学院对就业情况和薪资的披露缺乏透明度,这已经引发了集团诉讼和律师协会更严格的标准。④ 其他申请者,因为偏向于乐观,有着"奇思妙

---

① Ethan Bronner, Law School Applications Fall as Cost Rise and Jobs Are Cut, *N. Y. Times*, Jan. 30, 2013; Sloan, Enrollment Slump Continues, at A1.
② Burk, What's New about the New Normal, at 59.
③ Barton, *Glass Half Empty*; Harper, *The Law School Bubble*, at 40.
④ 这些诉讼诉称,法学院的就业率报告未能披露多少岗位要求有法律学位,或者是否由法学院资助,它们的薪酬报告未能披露回复率。*Alaburda v. Thomas Jefferson School of Law* (California Superior Ct. May 26, 2011); *Gomez-Jinenez v. N. Y. Law School* (New York Superior Court, Aug. 10, 2011); *MacDonald v. Thomas M. Cooley Law School*, No. 11-CV-00831 (转下页)

想"①。他们的假设是,他们不会像他们的同班同学那样,他们会找到高薪的工作,尽管存在不利的市场条件。在一项调查中,大多数潜在的法学院学生报告说,他们对在毕业后会找到一份法律工作感到"非常自信",但是只有16%的人对他们的大多数同学也会同样找到法律工作感到"非常自信"。② 但是,正如布莱恩·塔玛纳哈所指出的那样,考虑到在如何计算经济回报方面存在争议和不确定性,即使是最为理性的学生,也

(接上页)(W. D. Mich. Aug. 10, 2011): Staci Zaretski, Fifteen More Law Schools to Be Hit with Class Action Lawsuits over Post-Grad Employment Rates, *Above the Law*, Oct. 5, 2011. 这些诉讼中的第一个是对纽约大学法学院提起的,已经被驳回。Joe Palazzolo & Jennifer Smith, Law School Wins in Graduate Suit, *Wall St. J.*, Mar. 22, 2012, at B2. The ABA's new standards require such disclosures. Truth in Admitting, *Am. Law.*, Jul./Aug. 2011; Mark Hansen, ABA Committee Approves New Law School Disclosure requirements, *ABA J.*, Jan. 17, 2012, available at http://www.abajournal.com/news/article/aba_committee_recommends_new_law_school_disclosure_requirements/.

① David Segal, Is Law School a Losing Game? *N. Y. Times*, Jan. 8, 2011, at A1; Karen Sloan, What Are They Thinking, *Nat'l L. J.*, Jul. 12, 2010, at A1. 关于对偏向于乐观的总体描述,see Tali Sharot, *The Optimism Bias: A Tour of the Irrationally Positive Brain* (2011); Paul Brest & Linda Hamilton Krieger, *Problem Solving, Decision Making, and Professional Judgment* 405-408 (2010).

② Kaplan Survey, Despite Challenging Job Market, Tomorrow's Lawyers Appear to Have a Healthy Outlook on Their Own Job Prospects, But Not Their Classmates', Apr. 12, 2010, available at http://press.kaptest.com/press-releases/kaplan-survey-despite-challenging-job-markettomorrow%E2%80%99s-lawyers-appear-to-have-a-healthy-outlookon-their-own-job-prospects-but-not-their-classmates%E2%80%99.

很难评估法学院的长期投资价值。①

- 社会成本

不管是什么原因,许多学生无力偿还贷款,可能会造成社会和个人后果。大量违约将促使国会重新考虑是否应向法学院学生提供宽松的信贷。② 信贷市场的收紧,可能会进一步减少申请者,使法学院本已经糟糕的情况变得更糟。

法律教育的高价还有其他社会代价。不断上涨的学费,限制了那些负担不起法学院学费的毕业生能够承担哪些工作。以需求为基础的奖学金的减少,以及为提高排名更多地强调 GPA 和 LSAT 分数,阻碍了招募少数族裔申请人和使法律职业多样化的努力。高额的债务负担,使许多毕业生无法进入对服务需求最大的市场。正如第三章所指出的那样,具有讽刺意味的是,一个世界上律师最为集中的国家在向最需要的人提供帮助方面失败得很惨。律师协会的调查一直发现,超过 4/5 的低收入个人(其中大多数是中等收入者)的法律需求仍然未得到满足。③ 然而,经过 3 年的昂贵的法律教育,毕业生无法从这类工作中赚取足够的收入来还清债务并维持法律实务活动。这种违反常情的结果就是,律师供过于

---

① Tamahana, *Failing Law Schools*, at 143–145.
② Henderson & Zahorsky, Job Stagnation.
③ See Deborah L. Rhode, Access to Justice: A Roadmap for Reform, 41 *Fordham Urb. L. J.* 1227, 1228 (2014); Deborah L. Rhode, Access to Justice: An Agenda for Legal Education and Research *12 J. Legal Educ.* 531, 531 n1 (2012).

求,而法律服务却供给不足。

/ 结构 /

造成供求不对称的部分原因,包括认证标准所要求的法律教育结构。美国律师协会在 1922 年通过了第一个这样的标准,美国教育部部长随后认可美国律师协会的法律教育和准入部门的委员会作为法学院的官方认证组织。[①] 因为除少数州以外,所有州都将从一所被认可的法学院毕业作为执业的条件,委员会对法律教育的结构有重大影响。尽管对美国法学院进行某种形式的监督有强有力的理由,但是审查过程在几个重要方面是存在缺陷的。

认证制度的理论根据之一是,一个完全自由的市场不会提供足够的质量控制。作为法律教育最直接受益者的学生,对特定学校的相对费效比的信息有限,对现有信息的评估能力也有限。他们很少有根据来判断师生比等特征或者对兼职教授的依赖会如何影响他们的教育经历。此外,学生的利益不一定与公众的利益一致。教育是一种罕见的情

---

① The Higher Education Act of 1965, codified at 20 U.S.C. Section 1001 (2006),将联邦贷款对象限于教育部部长指定为认可机构的组织所认可的高等教育机构的学生。在随后的裁决中,教育部部长要求理事会要能够独立行事,不需要将最后的权力赋予美国律师协会。关于对该程序的描述,see Judith Areen, Accreditation Reconsidered, *96 Iowa L. J.* 1471 (2011).

况,即买家可能会觉得越少越好。许多学生希望花最少的钱获得学位,花最少的精力通过律师资格考试。在缺乏资格认证标准的情况下,法学院需要就那些学术水平最低的申请人展开竞争。类似的态度在主要的大学管理人员中很常见。如果没有认证机构设定的最低要求,更多的法学院可能被迫用更少的资源来对付过去,以补贴不那么富裕的其他学术院系。最后,认证要求可以为自我审查和同行评议提供有用的催化剂。

虽然这些理由支持某种形式的监督,但是目前的监督程序远远不能保护公众利益。一个门槛问题在于委员会的组成。它的多数成员是律师和法官,他们没有作为法律教育家的经验。[1] 他们也不充分独立于这个职业,而这个职业在维护其社会地位和经济利益方面有着明显的利害关系。无论如何出于善意,任何行业群体都不能够对与其自身的生计有直接牵连的事项作出超然的判断。

一个相关的问题是,该系统用对教育投入的详细规制,取代了对教育产出的更为直接的测量。它将诸如设施、资源和师生比等可观察的量度,作为教学和研究质量的极不完善的预测因素。此外,与一般高等教育认证制度不同的是,法学院的标准并不寻求提高费效比,也不因学校可能不同而允许多

---

[1] Areen, Accreditation Reconsidered, at 1492.

样化。① 相反,认可者强加了一个放之四海而皆准的结构来抑制创新,使许多学生在满足社会需要的方面既准备不足又过度准备。② 对于在可承受成本的基础上提供许多形式的常规帮助而言,毕业生的资历过高,但是在实务和跨行业技能方面往往资格不足。认证结构没有在形式上承认事实真相。法律职业活动正变得越来越专业化,要求华尔街证券律师和小镇家庭法执业者接受同样的培训,没有什么意义。在法学院学习3年并通过律师资格考试,对于许多需求最为强烈的领域(如无争议的离婚、房东—租户事务、移民或者破产)而言,既不必要也不足以保证熟练度。③ 其他国家允许非律师人员提供此类服务,也没有明显的不利影响。④ 美国法律需求的多样性要求法律教育的多样性。

/ 课程 /

范德堡(Vanderbilt)大学法学教授爱德华·鲁宾(Edward Rubin)直截了当地说:"我们现在是21世纪之初,我们使用的

---

① Areen, Accreditation Reconsidered, at 1490-1491.
② Nancy B. Rapoport, Eating Our Cake and Having It, Too: Why Real Change Is So Difficult in Law Schools, 81 Ind. L. J. 359, 366 (2006).
③ Rhode, Access to Justice, at 89, 198 n29; Herbert Kritzer, *Legal Advocacy* 193-203 (1998).
④ See Rhode, Access to Justice, at 15, 199 n29.

却是19世纪后半期发展起来的法律教育模式。"尽管"法律实务活动的性质已经发生了变化,教育理论也发生了变化",许多教员"仍然在做着我们130年前所做的同样的事情"。① 问题的一部分是,我们很少就教学艺术培训教育工作者。许多人像我一样,没有经验和训练就被扔进了教室。然后,我们就像别人对我们所做的那样对待别人,对于成人学习策略没有太多的反思或者学习。

现行的主要教学方法是讲座和苏格拉底式教学法的结合,重点是理论分析。从教育学的角度来看,这种方法很不可取。对法院判决的过分强调,往往忽略了委托人和社会背景的作用,就像是"没有岩石的地质学"②。分等级的和竞争性的课堂气氛也阻碍了许多学生,特别是女性的参与,并且没有为交互式学习、团队合作和反馈提供足够的机会。③ 常见的情况

---

① Edward Rubin, What's Wrong with Langdell's Method and What to Do About It, *60 Van. L. Rev.* 609, 610 (2007).

② Lawrence Friedman, *A History of American Law* (2nd ed., 1985).

③ 就不利影响,see Roy Stuckey et al., *Best Practices for Legal Education: A Vision and a Road Map* 3 (2007), available at http://law.sc.duc/faculty/stuckey/best_practices-full.pdf. 关于女性更低的参与率, see sources cited in Katherine Bartlett, Deborah L. Rhode, & Joanna Grossman, *Gender and Law: Theory, Doctrine, Commentary* (6th ed., 2012) 544-551. 关于无效的教学法, see Lawrence Krieger, What We're Not Telling Law Students—and Lawyers, *13 J. L. & Health* 1, 2-11 (1999); Gerald F. Hess, Seven Principles for Good Practice in Legal Education, *49 J. Legal Educ.* 367-369 (1999). 关于缺少反馈, see Erwin Chemerinsky, Rethinking Legal Education, *43 Harv. C. R. C. L. L. Rev.* 595, 597 (2008).

是,对知识的求索会成为一种对地位的争夺,而学生攀比的是哗众取宠而不是教育。

教员们普遍宣称,我们的法律教育方法教学生"像律师一样思考"。事实上,它教他们像法学教授一样思考。我们缺乏对其在实践中的效能进行验证的实证研究。① 正如论者们长期以来所指出的那样,法学院对实际技能的关注太少。② 90%的律师说,法学院没有为毕业生从事法律工作做好充分准备。③ 由于私人雇主减少了培训,这一缺陷变得更加严重。④ 尽管大多数法学院已经对这一长期批评作出了回应,增加了诊所课程和相关的行动计划,但是这些都仍处于课程的边缘。⑤ 只有3%的学校的学生需要进行诊所训练,大多数学

---

① 关于缺少实证证据,see Barnhizer, The Purposes and Methods of American Legal Education, at 7.

② 关于这一主张的最出色的文章,see Harry T. Edwards, The Growing Disjunction Between Legal Education and the Legal Profession, *91 U. Mich. L. Rev.* 34 (1992). 关于同一主题的更为新近的变化,see David Segal, What They Don't Teach Law Students: Lawyering, *N. Y. Times*, Nov. 20, 2011, at A1.

③ LexisNexis, State of the Legal Profession Survey (2009), at 7.

④ Stuckey et al., *Best Practices for Legal Education*, at 18; sources cited in Charlotte S. Alexander, Learning to Be Lawyers: Professional Identity and the Law School Curriculum, *70 Md. L. Rev.* 465, 467 n. 6 (2011). 关于委托人抵制为培训买单,see Segal, What They Don't Teach Law Students.

⑤ 关于新的行动计划,see Patrick G. Lee, Law Schools Get Practical, *Wall St. J.*, Jul. 11, 2011, at B5. 关于它们的边缘化,see Segal, What They Don't Teach Law Students, at A1; Karen Sloan, Stuck in the Past, *Nat'l Law J.*, Jan. 16, 2012, at A1 [引用了苏珊·哈克特(Susan Hackett)对这些行动计划的否定,即"未动筋骨"]。

第六章
法律教育

生在毕业时都没有接受过这样的训练。① 法律是唯一让学生在没有丰富的实践经验的情况下开始实务活动的职业,许多教育家认为他们会因此而受到损害。② 正如加州大学尔湾分校欧文·切梅林斯基(Erwin Chemerinsky)院长所说的那样,"除去做律师之外,没有其他办法能学会成为一名律师……如果从医学院毕业的医生们从未见过病人,或者说他们只是想教学生像医生一样思考,这是难以想象的。"③在全国法律就业协会和美国律师协会基金会的联合研究中,新人律师将诊所课程评为在法律行业就业之后向实践过渡的最有用的经验。④ 缺少此类课程的学生也失去了发展跨文化称职性的机会,也错失了对于法律如何对穷人发挥效能或者无法发挥效能的理解。

在整合了经验方法并针对实务导向的主题(如问题解决、营销、执业机构和项目管理、人际关系动力学和信息技术方

---

① Segal, What They Don't Teach Law Students, at A1. See also Karen Tokarz et al., Legal Education at a Crossroads: Innovation, Integration, and Pluralism Required, 43 Wash. J. L. & Pol'y 11 (2013)(发现仅有19所法学院要求诊所或者实习).

② Tokarz et al., Legal Education at a Crossroads.

③ Erwin Chemerinsky, Forward: The Benefits of Knowledge, Law School Survey of Student Engagement 5 (2012), available at http://lssse.iub.edu/pdf/2012/LSSSE_2012_AnnualReport.pdf.

④ NALP Foundation for Law Career Research & Education & American Bar Foundation, After the JD: First Results of a National Study of Legal Careers (2004).

面)的非诊所课程方面,法学院也同样薄弱。① 在一项调查中,将近 2/3 的学生和 90%的律师报告说,法学院并没有传授在当今经济中取得成功所需要的实务技能。②

太多的学校也缺乏可以使学生更好地在金融、知识产权、组织行为、公共利益和环境法等领域做好准备的系列跨学科课程。另一个空白是对于领导力的培养。虽然没有任何职业像法律这样产生了如此数量众多的领导人,并且领导力发展现在是一个 450 亿美元的行业,但是法律教育已经落后了。③ 许多法学院的宗旨包括培养领导能力,但是只有两所法学院实际上开设了领导力课程。④

虽然管理者经常承认这些差距,但他们认为纠偏措施是很奢侈的,学生负担不起。在当前的经济环境下,技能教育的代价使它难以兜售。然而,并非所有的经验性、面向实践的行

---

① Jane Porter, Lawyers Often Lack the Skills Needed to Draw, Keep Clients, *Wall St. J.*, May 20, 2009, at B5; William Hornsby, Challenging the Academy to a Dual (Perspective): The Need to Embrace Lawyering for Personal Legal Services, *70 Md. L. Rev.* 420, 437 (2011).

② Lexis-Nexis, State of the Legal Industry Survey 7 (2009).

③ 关于律师领导人,see Deborah L. Rhode, *Lawyers as Leaders* (2013); Deborah L. Rhode, Lawyers and Leadership, *Prof. Law.*, Winter 2010, at 1. 关于领导力培养的支出,see Doris Gomez, The Leader as Learner, *2 Int'l J. Leadership Stud.* 280, 281 (2007). 就法学院课程的不足,see Nitin Nohria & Rakesh Khurana, Advancing Leadership Theory and Practice, in *Handbook of Leadership Theory and Practice* 3 (Nitin Nohria & Rakesh Khurana, eds., 2010).

④ Neil W. Hamilton, Ethical Leadership in Professional Life, *6 St. Thomas L. J.* 358, 370 (2009).

动计划,都需要额外投资于昂贵的诊所课程。通过案例历史、问题、模拟、与执业者的合作项目以及跨学科协作,可以利用现有资源来完成许多工作。① 问题不在于这些方法负担不起,而在于其没有回报。课程的改进没有在排名中得到很好的反映,法律雇主也没有把实际培训作为录用的优先事项。② 正如哈佛大学教授戴维·威尔金斯所指出的那样,"法学院和职业人员就人们想要什么有很多言辞。他们说他们想要这个或者那个,但是他们最终雇用了谁?在法律审查方面工作的那些孩子。"③同样,教师没有看到教学中的卓越和创新是获得最大认可的途径。④ 要想取得重大进步,很可能需要在学术奖励结构上进行重大变革。

/ 价值观 /

法律教育的另一个困难是,它在职业责任和职业认同方

---

① 关于某些例子,see Alexander, Learning to Be Lawyers, 477-482.

② Richard Matasar, Does the Current Economic Model of Legal Education Work for Law Schools, Law Firms (or Anyone Else)? *N. Y. St. B. J.*, Oct. 2010, at 20, 24; Patrick G. Lee, Law Schools Get Practical, *Wall St. J.*, Jul. 11, 2011, at B5 (引用了 Timothy Lloyd 的观点,即实务技能并没有"造成多大区别")。

③ Sloan, Stuck in the Past (quoting Wilkins).

④ Segal, What They Don't Teach, at A22; Rubin, What's Wrong with Langdell's Method, at 614. 问题并非仅法学院才有。关于学术奖励结构中对教学的认识不足问题,see Rhode, *In Pursuit of Knowledge*, at 63, 73.

面培养或者未能培养的价值观。卡内基基金会的一份重要报告再次引起人们对法律职业伦理边缘化的长期关注。① 大多数学校仅仅将该课程归为一门必修课,通常侧重于教授律师资格考试中以多项选择方式测试的职业行为规则。② 结果是没有伦理的法律职业伦理课。③ 规则导向的课程还忽略了在规制结构、近用司法和法律执业条件方面的不足等问题。在一项调查中,大多数教授报告说,就法律职业的结构,包括歧视问题和实务活动的现实情况,没有花时间或者所花时间不到两小时;90%在公益服务上没有花时间或者所花时间不到2个小时。④

这种疏忽,反映了对职业伦理在职业教育中的重要性的根深蒂固的怀疑。许多法学院教员认为,价值观的培养超出

---

① William Sullivan et al., *Educating Lawyers: Preparation for the Profession of Law* (2007).

② Sullivan et al., *Educating Lawyers*, at145, 187; Ann Colby & William Sullivan, Legal Education Gives Ethics Training Short Shrift, *S. F. Daily J.*, Jan 18, 2007, at 6.

③ 这一主张以前就提出过。See Deborah L. Rhode, The Professional Responsibilities of Professional Schools, *49 J. Legal Educ.* 24 (1999); and Deborah L. Rhode, Teaching Legal Ethics, *51 St. Louis L. J.* 1043, 1047–1049 (2007). 关于职业伦理课程的关注点, see Andrew M. Perlman, Margaret Raymond, & Laurel S. Terry, A Survey of Professional Responsibility Courses at American Law Schools in 2009, available at http://www. legalethicsforum. com/files/pr-survey-results-final. pdf. 关于教员感到的为律师资格考试而讲授的压力, see Steven Gillers, Eat Your Spinach, *52 St. Louis U. L. J.* 1215, 1219 (2007).

④ Perlman, Raymond, & Terry, A Survey of Professional Responsibility Courses.

第六章
法律教育

了法学院的教学能力。① 尽管大多数学生报告说他们的学校强调伦理,但是只有一半的学生认为法学院已经就在实践中如何处理伦理难题对他们进行了培养,更少的人觉得他们在形成"个人价值观和伦理观"方面得到了帮助。②

关于职业责任的以规则为导向的主导方法,低估了更广泛的覆盖范围在形成伦理判断方面所能发挥的作用。在价值观问题上,法学院不可能是价值中立的。它们的课程和文化不可避免地影响着职业认同的形成和支撑它的伦理规范。③ 鉴于这一现实,法学教授需要更有意识地关注他们不可避免地要加以交流的信息。如果像美国律师协会《职业行为

---

① 关于价值观不能传授给法学院成人学生的假设, see Sullivan et al., *Educating Lawyers*, at 133; Neil Hamilton & Verna Munson, Addressing the Skeptics on Fostering Ethical Professional Formation, *Prof. Law.* (2011). 关于在多元社会里不应当传授价值观的假设,see W. Bradley Wendel, Teaching Ethics in an Atmosphere of Skepticism and Relativism, *36 U. S. F. L. Rev.* 711 (1992). 关于对法学院的能力的怀疑,see Sullivan et al., *Educating Lawyers*, at 132-133; Carole Silver et al., Unpacking the Apprenticeship of Professional Identity and Purpose: Insights from the Law School Survey of Student Engagement, *17 J. Legal Writing Inst.* 373, 376-377 (2011).

② Law School Survey of Student Engagement, Student Engagement in Law Schools: In Class and Beyond—2010 Annual Survey Results 4, 11, 12, 24, (2010). See Richard Acella, Street Smarts: Law Schools Explore Benefits of Teaching Ethics in a Clinical Setting, *ABA J.*, Jun. 2011, at 26.

③ See Wald & Pearce, Denial and Accountability; Sullivan et al., *Educating Lawyers*, at 139; Neil W. Hamilton, Assessing Professionalism: Measuring Progress in the Formation of an Ethical Professional Identity, *5 U. St. Thomas L. J.* 470, 475 (2008).

示范规则》的序言中所述的那样,律师是"对正义质量负有特殊责任的公民"①,则应在贯穿整个法学院的经验中反映和强化这一责任。

大量的证据表明,人们在处理伦理问题的基本策略上发生的重大变化,出现在成年早期。② 通过互动式教育,如问题解决和角色扮演,学生可以提高他们的伦理分析技能,并提高他们对情境压力、心理动力和规制失灵等不端行为背后的问题的认识。未能在整个课程中将职业责任问题整合在一起,会破坏其重要性。对伦理的极简主义态度,将其重要性边缘化了。课程对一些问题未讲到,这会传达强有力的信息。教师们不能把职业责任看作别人的责任。

近用司法和公益服务也是如此。就像第三章所指出的那样,关于法律服务分配的问题,在核心课程中是缺失的或者边缘化的。甚至法律专业课程的教材也常常并不讨论近

---

① ABA Model Rules of Professional Conduct, Preamble (2011).

② Rhode, If Integrity Is the Answer, What Is the Question? *72 Fordham L. Rev.* 333, 342 (2003); Sullivan et al. , *Educating Lawyers*, at 135, 154; M. Neil Browne, Carrie L. Williamson, & Linda L. Barkacs, The Purported Rigidity of an Attorney's Personality: Can Legal Ethics be Acquired? *30 J. Legal Prof.* 55, 66 (2006); Steven Hartwell, Promoting Moral Development through Experiential Teaching, *1 Clin. L. Rev.* 505, 507-508 (1995); Neil Hamilton & Lisa M. Babbit, Fostering Professionalism through Mentoring, *37 J. Legal Educ.* 102, 116 (2007); National Research Council, Learning and Transfer, in *How People Learn* 51-78 (2000).

用司法问题。① 尽管绝大多数学校都有公益项目,但是只有少数学生参与。② 只有大约10%的学校要求学生参加公益服务,而且对教员的要求更少。此外,所要求的数量有时相当少,半数的学校只规定学生服务10至20小时。③ 某些项目的质量也会受到质疑。总体来看,许多学生缺乏现场监督或者课堂机会来讨论他们的工作或者公益问题。我自己所做的全国性调查发现,只有1%的律师报告说,他们的法学院迎新计划或者职业责任课程中涵盖了公益服务,仅3%明确看到教员支持公益工作。④ 美国律师协会基金会对最近的法律毕业生进行的一次调查,在执业者认为在实践中对他们有显著帮助作用的教育体验清单中,他们将公益工作排在最后。⑤ 用美国法学院协会委员会的话说,在公益机会方面,"法学院应当

---

① Linda F. Smith, Fostering Justice throughout the Curriculum, *18 Geo. J. Poverty L. & Policy* 427 430-431 (2011).

② Law School Survey on Student Engagement, Student Engagement in Law Schools: A First Look 8 (2004). 仅仅两所法学院报告说有对教员的要求。ABA Standing Committee on Professionalism, Report on Survey of Law School Professionalism Programs 46-47 (2006).

③ ABA Standing Committee on Professionalism, Report on Professionalism Programs.

④ Deborah L. Rhode, *Pro Bono in Principle and in Practice* 161-162 (2005). 对美国律师协会的调查进行回应的人中,仅62%的人报告说得到了现场监督。ABA Standing Committee on Professionalism, Report, at 45.

⑤ Ronit Dinovitzer et al., *After the JD: First Results of a National Study of Legal Careers* 81 (2004).

做得更多。"①学校的职业责任的一部分是建立对公共服务的忠信文化。

法学院也应当做更多的工作来解决基于种族、性别、族裔、残疾、阶级和性取向的多样性和偏见问题。② 少数族裔占总人口的37%,但是在法学院课堂上,只占1/4。③ 为了解决这一差异,学校应重新考虑对法学院分数和LSAT评分的过度重视,因为这对有色人种申请者不利,而并不能准确地预测其在实务中的表现。④ 学校也应当关注风气问题。女学生(特别是有色人种女性)报告说得到教师指导的机会较少,在课堂上更

---

① AALS Commission on Pro Bono and Public Service Opportunities in Law Schools, Learning to Serve: A Summary of the Findings and Recommendations of the Commission on Pro Bono and Public Service Opportunities in Law Schools 2 (1999).

② ABA Presidential Initiative Commission on Diversity, Diversity in the Legal Profession: Next Steps (2010); Robert S. Chang &Adrienne D. Davis, Making Up Is Hard to Do: Race/Gender/Sexual Orientation in the Law School Classroom, 33 Harv. J. L. & Gender 1 (2010) (汇总了有关研究); Angela Onwuachi-Willig, Emily Hough, & Mary Campbell, Cracking the Egg: Which Came First—Stigma or Affirmative Action?, 96 Cal. L. Rev., at 1299 n126; Celestial S. D. Cassman & Lisa R. Pruitt, Towards a Kinder, Gentler Law School? Race, Ethnicity, Gender, and Legal Education, 38 Davis L. Rev. 1209, 1248 (2005); Richard Sander, Class in American Legal Education, 88 Denver U. L. Rev. 631 (2011).

③ Karen Sloan, Legal Education's Diversity Deficit, Nat'l L. J., May 12, 2014, at A1.

④ Kristin Holmquist, Marjorie Shultz, Sheldon Zedeck, & David Oppenheimer, Measuring Merit: The Shultz-Zedeck Research on Law School Admissions, 63 J. Legal Educ. 565 (2014); Marjorie M. Shultz & Sheldon Zedeck, Predicting Lawyer Effectiveness: Broadening the Basis for Law School Admission Decisions, 36 Law & Soc. Inq. 620 (2011).

不可能发言,而且与男性相比,她们有更多不满、疏离感和自我怀疑。① 在最近关于学生对多样性和法学院风气的看法的唯一的研究中,有 3/4 的人认为,非白人学生所面临的挑战,对于同样处境的白人学生来说不会发生。几乎一半的人报告说经历过因为他们的种族使他们感到不受欢迎或者不受尊重的事件。2/3 的女性同意,女学生面临的挑战,对于同样处境的男性学生来说不会发生。② 技术还为性骚扰创造了新的在线机会,并扩大了其受众。一个广为人知的案件涉及在法学院信息公告栏张贴关于女学生的猥亵和诽谤性陈述。③ 同样,女性和少数族裔在正教授和院长以及在其他有着最高地位和报酬的职位上,仍然代表性不足。④ 如果就像律师业领导人一再坚持的那样,法律职业真正忠信于多样性和包

---

① 参加下文汇总的有关研究:Mertz, Inside the Law School Classroom: Toward a New Legal Realist Pedagogy, *60 Vand. L. Rev.* 483, 509 (2007); and Adam Neufield, Costs of an Outdated Pedagogy? Study of Gender at Harvard Law School, *13 J. Gender, Soc. Pol'y, & L.* 511, 516-517, 530-539, 554-559 (2005);以及下文的研究结果:Sari Bashi & Mariana Iskander, Why Legal Education Is Failing Women, *18 Yale J. L. & Feminism* 389, 404-413, 423-437 (2006).

② Jonathan Feingold & Doug Souza, Measuring the Racial Unevenness of Law School, *15 Berkeley J. Afr. -Am. L. &Pol'y* 71, 105, 108 (2013).

③ Ellen Nakashima, Harsh Words Die Hard on the Web: Law Students Feel Lasting Effects of Anonymous Attacks, *Wash. Post*, Mar. 7, 2007, at A1.

④ ABA Section of Legal Education and Admissions to the Bar, Statistics on Legal Education (2012-13), available at http://www. americanbar. org/content/dam/aba/administrative/legal_education_ and_admissions_to_the_bar/(转下页)

容性的价值观,那么这一忠信应当在法律教育中得到更好的体现。①

法学院文化的最后一个问题是,它倾向于强化狭隘的职业成就观,以牺牲内在的自我价值量度为代价,来强调客观的成就量度。② 这种高度竞争的气氛,导致学生精神健康下降,以及药物滥用、压力、抑郁症和其他疾病比例出奇的高。③ 据估计,多达40%的法学院学生经历过严重的心理困扰,并且功能性障碍比率远远高于医学院毕业生。④ 进入法学院时,学生的心理

(接上页) statistics/ls_staff_gender_ethnicity. authcheckdam. pdf (少数族裔占终身教授的16%,法学院院长的21%;女性占正教授的30%,法学院院长的20%); Institute for Inclusion in the Legal Profession, IILP Review(2011); Vikram David Amar & Kevin R. Johns, Why U. S. News and World Report Should Include a Faculty Diversity Index in Its Ranking of Law Schools, Apr. 9, 2010, available at http://writ. news. findlaw. com/amar/20100409html.

① 关于律师协会委员会,see ABA Presidential Initiative on Diversity, Diversity in the Legal Profession; AALS Statement on Diversity.

② Kennon M. Sheldon & Lawrence S. Krieger, Understanding the Negative Effects of Legal Education on Law Students: Longitudinal Test of Self-Determination Theory, 33 Personality & Soc. Psych. 883, 884 (2007) (指出法学院学生能够从内在向外在驱动的转变,在一定程度上是因为控制性而不是支持性的风气).

③ Sheldon & Krieger, Understanding the Negative Effects.

④ Todd David Peterson & Elizabeth Waters Peterson, Stemming the Tide of Law Student Depression: What Law Schools Need to Learn from the Science of Positive Psychology, 2 Yale J. Health Pol'y, Law & Ethics 357, 359, 411-412 (2009); Lawyers and Depression, Dave Nee Foundation (2014), available at http://www. daveneefoundation. org/resources/lawyers-and-depression/. 问题是长期存在的。Andrew Benjamin et al. , The Role of Legal Education in Producing Psychological Distress among Law Students and Lawyers, 11 Law & Soc. Inq. 225 (1986).

状况类似于一般公众,但是离开法学院时,心理障碍发病率更高。① 然而,只有一所学校对此类问题制定了全面的预防措施,许多其他学校忽视了学生的需求。② 它们也未能解决执业条件和丰富学生对职业成就感的理解问题。与债务和失业率上升有关的焦虑情绪给这些关切带来更多的紧迫性。一名三年级的学生说:"我不认识任何精神不紧张的人。坦率地说,如果你不紧张,你就还没有集中注意力。"③

/ 法律评论 /

作为法律现实主义者,福瑞德·罗德尔(Fred Rodell)在75年前作出了这样的著名评论,即"几乎所有法律写作都有两个错误。一是它的风格,二是它的内容。"④学生主办的法律期刊在一定程度上要负有责任。《纽约时报》专栏作家亚当·利普泰克(Adam Liptak)直言不讳地说:"法律评论是一个进行揶揄的目标丰富的对象,取笑它们不会冒什么风险。"⑤最高法院首

---

① Lawyers and Depression.
② Peterson & Peterson, Stemming the Tide, at 374 - 375; Sheldon & Krieger, Understanding the Negative Effects, at 884.
③ Karen Sloan, The View from 3L, *Nat'l L. J.*, Jan. 26, 2009, at A1 (quoting Eric Reed).
④ Fred Rodell, Goodbye to Law Reviews, 23 Va. L. Rev. 38 (1936).
⑤ Adam Liptak, The Lackluster Reviews That Lawyers Love to Hate, *N. Y. Times*, Oct. 22, 2013.

席大法官也对此进行了抨击：

> 你知道,拿起任何一本法律评论,第一篇文章很可能是,康德对18世纪保加利亚的证据方法的影响,或者是其他什么内容,我敢肯定撰写它的学者对它很感兴趣但是对律师行业没有多大帮助。①

法律评论中刊载的大部分内容甚至对其他学者没有什么用处。关于这个问题的最新研究发现,43%的文章从未被引用过。② 大部分声称是前沿学术的东西,都是表面文章,毫无用处;它借自其他学科的华丽外衣,对非职业人员而言是令人扫兴的,与执业者也没有什么关系。很少有法官、政策制定者和执业律师定期查阅学术性法律评论,许多人根本不看它们。③

一个核心问题在于法律评论的编辑结构。与其他学科的期刊完全依赖于同行评议不同的是,法律学科将文章的选择和编辑工作主要交给了学生。这些编辑往往缺乏知识、培训、专门知识和时间来充分发挥这一作用。④ 因为法律期刊能拿

---

① Deborah Cassens Weiss, Law Prof Responds After Chief Justice Roberts Disses Legal Scholarship, *ABA J.*, Jul. 7, 2011.

② Thomas A. Smith, The Web of Law, *44 San Diego L. Rev.* 309, 336 (2007). 我自己的更早的研究发现,半数以上的文章从来无人引用。Deborah L. Rhode, Legal Scholarship, *115 Harv. L. Rev.* 1327, 1331 (2002).

③ Rhode, Legal Scholarship, at 1337; Max Stier et al., Law Review Usage and Suggestions for Improvement: A Survey of Attorneys, Professors, and Judges, *44 Stan. L. Rev.*, 1467, 1484, Table 4 (1992).

④ Robert Weisberg, Some Ways to Think about Law Reviews,(转下页)

到法学院的大量补贴,它们缺乏市场历练,许多期刊的工作质量缺乏有意义的问责。

缺乏评估投稿价值能力的编辑经常通过不完美的表象筛选稿件,例如作者的学校声望或者文献多少。脚注已成为展现这种状况的最佳场所。一个脚注可以占满五页。① 过度卖弄学识是很常见的。人们可以找到一篇490页的文章,其中有4800个脚注,专门讨论某部证券法的某个条文。② 然而,这种浮华的表象,并不是关于严谨性的可靠量度。这并不能保证作者确实阅读过所引述的资料,也不能确保他们代表了这一领域的最佳思想。而且,过度引用文献的做法,会妨害原创观点,即与他人不同的观点。虽然对教员、法官和执业者的调查一直发现,他们一直认为文章太长,脚注太重,但是这些看法对遏制这种做法帮助不大。③

(接上页) 47 *Stan. L. Rev.* 1147, 1148 (1995); Roger C. Cramton, The Most Remarkable Institution: The American Law Review, *36 J. Legal Educ.* 1, 708 (1986); Richard A. Wise et al., Do LawReviews Need Reform? A Survey of LawProfessors, Student Editors, Attorneys, and Judges, *59 Loy. L. Rev.* 1 (2013).

① Rhode, *In Pursuit of Knowledge*, 38; Arthur Austin, Footnote Skulduggery and Other Bad Habits, *44 U. Miami L. Rev.* 1009 (1990).

② Arnold S. Jacobs, An Analysis of Section 16 of the Securities Exchange Act of 1934, *32 N. Y. L. Sch. L. Rev.* 209 (1987).

③ See Stier et al., Law Review Usage, at 1499; Submissions, *Harv. L. Rev.*, http://www.harvardlawreview.org/submisssions.php; Wise et al., Do Law Reviews Need Reform? at 6. 2005年,11个法律评论发表了一个声明,表达了对40到70页之间的"更短的文章"的青睐。Wise et al., Do Law Reviews Need Reform, at 6 n18.

一个更基本的问题是,发表论文的压力是否对所有教员都有意义。不是每个天才的老师都是天才的学者。大多数研究表明,法学教授的教学效果与学术影响之间没有相关性。① 现在教员的许多精力除家人或者聘任委员会外,主要投入到可能对别人而言没有什么吸引力的论文发表上了。这些精力最好是投入到更多的教学中,或者面向执业者和一般公众的出版物上。

/ 战略 /

少了什么都不成。

——Aldous Huxley②

近30年前,《纽约时报》旗下周日杂志的一篇专题文章的题目是"美国法学院的麻烦"。③ 这篇文章突出强调了今天常

---

① Benjamin H. Barton, Is There a Correlation between Law Professor Publication Counts, Law Review Citation Counts, and Teaching Evaluations? An Empirical Study, 5 J. Emp. Legal Stud. 619 (2008). 对30多年来教学与学术之间的关系的近30个研究的综述发现,2/3没有任何关系。James Axtell, The Pleasures of Academe 241 (1998); Philip C. Wankat, The Effective, Efficient Professor: Teaching, Scholarship and Service 211 (2001).

② Aldous Huxley, Island 163 (1962).

③ David Margolick, The Trouble with America's Law Schools, N. Y. Times Mag., May 22, 1983.

第六章
法律教育

见的许多课程问题,特别是缺乏实务培训、对职业责任问题的漫不经心以及法学院上层学生的脱离群众。这些关切的背后,是教员的惰性和自大。正如一位斯坦福教授所说的那样,"目前的结构非常适合我们……对我们的学生感到厌倦这一事实我们并非无动于衷,但是在另一方面,对我们来说法学院运转得很好。"①

这种态度仍然是普遍的,并且是有理由的。对于大多数教师来说,他们的职位的薪资、工时和工作保障都令人羡慕。② 在一项调查中,93%的法律学者报告满意或者非常满意,这是所公布的所有法律行业中最高的满意度。③ 美国法律教育中的一个基本问题是,教师对于存在根本性问题或者是他们有责任解决的根本性问题缺乏共识。法学院有着抵制改革的漫长而不体面的历史。④ 只有当来自学生、认证机构、捐

① Margolick, The Trouble with America's Law Schools (quoting William Cohen).
② Tamahana, *Failing Law Schools*, at 47, 51 (引用的数据表明,法学教授的薪酬是学者中第二高的,大多数人的收入处于律师收入中上 1/4 的位置).
③ Yale Law School Career Development Office, Job Satisfaction Survey 5 (2001–2005).
④ See Edward Rubin, The Future and Legal Education: Are Law Schools Failing and, If So, How? *39 Law & Soc. Inq.* 499, 500 (2014); Robert W. Gordon, The Geologic Strata of the Law School Curriculum, *60 Vand. L. Rev.* 339 (2007); Susan Sturm & Lani Guinier, The Law School Matrix: Reforming Legal Education in a Culture of Competition and Conformity, *60 Vand. L. Rev.*, 515, 519 (2007); Erwin Chemerinsky, Legal Education Must Change, But Will It?, *Nat'l L. J.'s L. Sch. Rev.*, Nov. 1, 2011. See also Richard A. Matasar, Defining Our Responsibilities: Being an Academic Fiduciary, *17 J. Contemp. Legal Issues* 67, 71 (2008) (指出课程仍然注重的是老师想要讲授的,而不是学生想要学习的).

赠者和法院的外部压力要求改变时,才可能发生变革。

• 财务

从许多教职员和学生的角度来看,法律毕业生的财政困难要求再分配性的解决方案。例如,扩大贷款减免、增加公共补贴、放宽破产规则以允许免除学生的债务。但是这些方案面临的障碍是巨大的。律师不是一个深受美国纳税人爱戴的群体,他们的民选代表很可能会反对政府承担额外的负担来帮助这个行业。无论如何,鉴于目前律师的供过于求和法学院学费的过度上涨,降低学费可能比提高宽松信贷更具有意义。[1]

不太有争议的改革,如增加对就业安置和薪酬的披露,已经在进行之中。然而,还需要做更多的工作。平等正义工作(Equal Justice Works)执行主任戴维·斯特恩(David Stern)建议,每所学校都为学生提供个性化的财务咨询服务,以及要有一个网页,分别列出入学费用、就业安置、薪资信息和贷款负担。[2] 就像他所指出的那样,现在,学生在把这些信息凑在一起并将其应用到复杂的联邦学生贷款系统时,遇到了不必要的困难。

学校还需要寻找更多的方法来降低成本,使收入来源多

---

[1] Paul Campos, Stop Unlimited Loaning to Law School Students, *New Republic*, Jul. 23, 2013.

[2] David Stern, The Avoidable Sticker Shock of Student Loan Repayment, *Nat'l L. J.*, Sept. 23, 2013, at 39.

样化。开设更多的非律师人员、本科生、执业律师和外国研究生的课程,是显而易见的选项。① 也可以通过允许学生在大学3年级后就读法学院,来减轻学生的债务负担,就像一些法学院现在所做的那样。②

● 结构

另一种至少能降低某些法学院的费用的方法,是由州最高法院取消只有来自美国律师协会认证的法学院的毕业生才可以参加律师资格考试的要求。蒙大拿州最高法院的一项裁决驳回了加利福尼亚州一所未经认证的法学院的毕业生参加律师资格考试的申请,两位持异议的大法官指出,"没有经验数据表明,美国律师协会标准与法律教育的质量存在关联。显而易见的是,赋予这个私营行业协会为法学院制定标准的垄断权,增加了法律教育的成本,[并]让新成员有了债务负担,限制了他们的职业和公共服务的选择……"③正如布莱恩·塔玛纳哈所主张的那样,如果大量的州取消了美国律师协会对法律教育进行认证的要求,结果很可能是迫使排名较低的法学院和未经认证的学校之间(其现在的成本是前者的

---

① Matasar, Does the Current Economic Model Work? at 26; Elizabeth Chambliss, Law School Training for Licensed "Legal Technicians"; Implications for the Consumer Movement, 65 *S. Car. L. Rev.* 579 (2014).

② Tamahana, *Failing Law Schools*, at 173; Matasar, The Viability of the Law Degree, at 1579, 1618.

③ *In re Petition of Culver*, slip op. at 7 (Mont. 2002) (Trieweiler, J., dissenting).

1/3)进行更为激烈的价格竞争。① 虽然未经认证的学校的毕业生比经过认证学校的毕业生的考试及格率要低得多,但是很难知道有多少差异是由学生的素质和教育质量造成的。无论如何,未经美国律师协会认证的学校的毕业生中有相当大的比例最终会通过律师资格考试,而这种取得资格的方法是使财力有限人员负担得起法律教育的一种方式。②

如果《美国新闻和世界报道》排名系统的影响力受到质疑,如果对认证要求进行重大削减,那么更普遍地降低法律教育的价格就会变得容易得多。法学院可以与律师协会合作,建立一个评价结构,不将经费支出和含糊的声誉调查作为教学质量的表象。认证机构不能对所有学校实行同样的要求,而是要考虑到学校的不同宗旨和优先事项。就像美国律师协会法律教育的未来工作小组指出的那样,

> 法律教育体系将会更好,为不同的模式提供更多的空间。多样性和鼓励多样性的文化,可以促进项目和服务的创新,增加学生的教育选择,减少地位竞争,帮助法

---

① Tamanaha, *Failing Law Schools*, at 177.

② 例如,2012年7月的加利福尼亚州律师资格考试,来自该州认可的法学院的学生中,仅31%的首次参加考试者和10.5%的重复参加考试者通过了考试。See General Statistics Report July 2012 California Bar Examination, available at http://admissions.calbar.ca.gov/Portals/4/documents/gbx/JULY2012STATS.122112_R.pdf. 与此形成对比的是,来自美国律师协会认可的法学院的学生中,76.9%的首次参加考试者和24%的重复参加考试者通过了考试。在未经认可的法学院的毕业生中,22.2%的首次参加考试者和12.4%的重复参加考试者通过了考试。

第六章
法律教育

学院适应变化的市场和其他外部条件。①

就像高等教育提供了从社区学院到精英常春藤联盟学校这一系列的选择那样,法律教育应当提供更大的多样性。为此,认证机构可以取消诸如设施、兼职教授教学、远程学习和教员研究支持等方面的统一标准。② 机构可以因其所提供的专业、对低成本兼职教授和在线教程的依赖,以及它们对实务技能和法律学术的重视程度而异。给学生更多的选择,可能会弱化当前结构的负作用的一面,即当前这种结构因对研究进行补贴和减轻相对富裕的教师的教学负荷,造成了沉重的债务负担。

学校也可以根据1年、2年、3年的学位课程提供各种学位选择。州可以允许一年制的毕业生提供例行的法律服务。美国律师协会工作组向这一方向迈出了一步,他们建议州当局就受限制的涉法服务制定颁照制度,同时认证机构为培养受限服务提供者的项目制定标准。③ 州还可以许可律师两年后在税务、家庭或者刑法等专业领域执业。实际上,律师协会可以进一步效仿医学等其他职业,根据培训的程度,对从业人员

---

① American Bar Association Task Force on the Future of Legal Education, Report and Recommendations, at 24.
② 关于类似的建议,see Tamahana, *Failing Law Schools*, at 173.
③ ABA Task Force on the Future of Legal Education, Report and Recommendations, at 24–25.

进行认证。①

关于法律教育多样化的建议并不新鲜。阿尔弗雷德·里德(Alfred Reed)在1921年向卡内基基金会提交的一份出色的报告中就建议采用一个双层系统。全日制项目将培训高素质的律师,为公司和政府委托人服务;非全日制项目和夜校将培养综合执业者,以满足日常性法律需要。② 通过将这一划分制度化,该职业可以兼顾可近用性和高质量两方面的问题。1972年,卡内基基金会又发表了另一份报告,仿照了保罗·加灵顿(Paul Carrington)对美国法学院协会提出的建议。它提出了一个为期2年的标准课程,供大学就读3年后的学生使用。它将为毕业生在核心科目上打好基础,并就职业技能提供强化教学的机会。可以为想要读3年的学生提供高级课程,学生也可以在离开法学院后间断完成1年的课程。③ 美国律师协会断然拒绝了里德和加灵顿的提议。④ 经过认证的学校现在

---

① Laurel A. Rigertas, Stratification of the Legal Profession: A Debate in Need of a Public Forum, *J. Prof. Law.* 79, 100–110 (2012).

② Michael Schudson, The Flexner Report and the Reed Report: Notes on the History of Professional Education in the United States, *55 Soc. Sci. Q.* 347 (1974).

③ The AALS report, Training for the Public Professions of the Law, appears as an appendix to the Carnegie report. Herbert L. Packer & Thomas Ehrlich, *New Directions in Legal Education* (1972).

④ Thomas Morgan, *The Vanishing American Lawyer* 196–197 (2010); Preble Stolz, The Two-Year Law School: The Day the Music Died, *25 J. Legal Educ*. 37 (1973).

第六章
法律教育

提供为期2年课程的唯一方法,是将3年的学时压缩为2年。这样的学校像3年制的院校一样,收取相同的学费,这大大减少了缩短项目时间所可节约的成本。

2年制学位的提案最近再次浮出水面,最著名的提出者是奥巴马总统。在一个讨论如何使教育更能被负担得起的市政厅会议上,奥巴马说,"法学院将学制定为2年而不是3年可能是明智的……(学生)在第3年做法官助理或者在律师事务所执业,经济状况会更好,即使他们没有得到多少报酬,但是这一步就会降低学生的成本。"在承认取消第3年可能会损害学校的财务的同时,总统补充道:"现在的问题是,法学院能否保持质量,留住优秀的教授,并在没有第3年的情况下撑下来?我的怀疑是,如果他们就此进行创造性思考,他们可能会撑下来。"[①]这一建议引起了越来越多的论者的共鸣,他们建议让学生在法学院学习两年后参加律师资格考试,或者以在非营利组织或者政府机构中学徒或者实习取代第3年。[②]

这些提议引发了强烈的抗议。乔治敦大学法学教授菲利

[①] Peter Lattman, Obama Says Law School Should Be 2, Not 3, Years, *N. Y. Times*, Aug. 24, 2013, at B3.

[②] 关于两年的建议,see Samuel Estreicher, The Roosevelt-Cardozo Way: The Case for Bar Eligibility after Two Years of Law School, *15 N. Y. U. Rev. Legis. & Public Pol'y* 599 (2012). 关于学徒制,see David Lat, Bring Back Apprenticeships, *N. Y. Times*, Feb. 2, 2012. 关于实习,see Alan Dershowitz, Make Law School Two Years-Plus, *New Republic*, Jul. 23, 2013; Paul M. Barrett, Do American Lawyers Need Less Law School? *Bloomberg Businessweek*, Sept. 3, 2013 (描述了"为美国人服务的律师"实习项目)。

普·施拉格(Philip Schrag)担心,"新的律师将只学到基本的调查课程,并且得不到他们的未来委托人所需要的职业培训。"①加州大学尔湾分校的欧文·切梅林斯基院长预测,"如果法学院学制是 2 年,首先要削减的是诊所教育和跨学科课程,而这些是我在 20 世纪 70 年代中期读法学院以来最好的创新。"②耶鲁大学法学教授布鲁斯·阿克曼同样声称,缩短学位要求,将会

降低美国公共生活的质量。一旦 2 年制的毕业生开始执业,他们将无法充分处理反托拉斯、知识产权或者公司法这些实用问题,更不用说应对公民权利或者环境法的挑战了。认为这些律师会在工作中掌握这些关键技能,这太过轻率。社会科学和统计学需要系统的培训,而不是针对特定问题的速成课程。一项为期 2 年的课程有望在 2050 年把法律职业变得呆头呆脑。③

就像专栏作家保罗·利珀(Paul Lippe)所回应的那样,

---

① Barrett, Do American Lawyers Need Less Law School? (quoting Schrag).
② Erwin Chemerinsky, ABA Report Lacking Solutions for Law Schools, *Nat'l L. J.*, Feb. 10, 2014, at 30.
③ Bruce Ackerman, Why Legal Education Should Last for Three Years, *Wash. Post*, Sept. 6, 2013; Bruce Ackerman, Three Years in Law School Are Barely Enough! *Balkinization*, Sept. 9, 2013, available at http://balkin.blogspot.com/2013/09/three-years-in-law-school-arebarely.html and http://works.bepress.com/marjorie_shultz/14/.

事实上，我同意 Ackerman 教授所说的一些法学院应当强调的事情，但是我在他的文章中却没看到他说明这些事情不能在 2 年制课程中加以解决，或者债务缠身的法学院学生应当继续交叉补贴奖学金，以至于牺牲其长期的财务偿付能力，或者耶鲁模式应当强制适用于所有学校，这将是一个看待市场选择是什么的很好的命令和控制的方式。①

根本的问题不是第 3 年的培训是否有益。问题是这些好处是否如此重要，以至于所有学生都必须承担成本。根据 2/3 的应届毕业生的说法，传统的 3 年法学院教育可以压缩成 2 年，而不会对新律师的执业顺畅性产生负面影响。② 如果律师资格考试相应地压缩，仅测试更少的教义性科目，那么缩短法学院学制将会更容易。③ 即使在现有的情况下，1 年或者 2 年的课程也足以为未得到满足的法律需求最为旺盛的领域培训毕业生。在其他国家，这些需求中有许多是由法律培训程度低于律师的其他专业人员有效地满足的。④

----

① Paul Lippe, Yale Law Prof Falls Short in Challenging Obama's 2 Year JD Idea, *ABA J.*, Sept. 11, 2013, available at http://www.abajournal.com/legalrebels/article? Profs_op-ed_opposing_a_two-year_jd/.

② Rachel Van Cleave, Assessing the Value of Lawyers, *San Francisco Daily J.*, Sept. 24, 2013.

③ James E. Moliterno, The Future of Legal Education Reform, *40 Pepp. L. Rev.* 423, 433 (2013).

④ 参见第三章的讨论。

此外，正如联邦法官、法学教授理查德·波斯纳（Richard Posner）所说的那样，让法学院面对进一步的创新和不同模式之间的竞争，可能会产生更好的教育经历。① 法学院将面临更大的压力，他们被要求证明其特定方法的费效比，而不是简单地断言。如果雇主们认为2年和3年制项目的毕业生在质量上有差异，或者在培养他们的学校之间存在差异，学生将会作出相应的反应。

- 课程

法学院结构的根本性变革，会促进对其课程进行类似的根本性变革。教育工作者应当考虑哪些能力是法律实务活动所必需的，然后相应地调整需求，而不是把现有的核心课程视为理所当然。这样的做法将要求对实务技能的进一步关注。② 正如诊所式法律教育协会所建议的那样，作为最低标准，所有学生在毕业前都必须至少完成一门诊所课程或者实习。③ 如果学校拒绝设定这样的要求，州最高法院可以代替它

---

① See Richard Posner, Let Employers Insist if Three Years of Law School Is Necessary, *San Francisco Daily J.*, Dec. 15, 1999, at A4（指出缺少实证或者理论来说明为什么3年的法学教育是必要的）; Mitu Gulati, Richard Sander, & Robert Sockloskie, The Happy Charade: An Empirical Examination of the Third Year of Law School, *51 J. Leg. Educ.* 235（2001）（探讨了法学院第3年所面临的挑战）.
② See Sullivan et al., *Educating Lawyers*, at 29–45.
③ Karen Sloan, ABA Pressed to Boost Law Students' Practical Training, *Nat'l L. J.*, Jul. 2, 2013.

们设定这样的要求。①

更多的面向实务的行动计划的模式是现成的。② 西北大学法学院对法律雇主所期望的"基本核心能力"进行了自己的分析,并制定了一项为期 2 年的计划,强调项目管理、团队合作、沟通、领导能力和定量分析。③ 新罕布什尔州在唯一的州立法学院实施为期 2 年的以实务为导向的课程后,已经开始向那些被认证为"委托人准备就绪(client ready)"的学生发放执照。④ 他们要参加谈判、咨询、审判和审前诉辩等方面的课程,以及在证据、税务和商业协会等领域的诊所教育或者实习

---

① 加利福尼亚州律师协会的一个工作组走得更远,它建议应当要求学生完成 15 个学分的以实务为基础的体验课程。See State Bar Cal. Task Force on Admission Reg. Reform, Phase 1 Final Report, Jun. 24, 2013, available at http://www. calbar. ca. gov/portals/0/documents/bog/bot_ExecDir/.

② The ABA's MacCrate report identified critical skills: ABA Task Force on Law Schools and the Profession, Legal Education and Professional Development—An Educational Continuum (1992) (MacCrate Report). 最近,马约莉·舒尔茨(Marjorie Shultz)和谢尔登·左德克(Sheldon Zedeck)就旨在改善准入标准但是也可以指导课程改革的实务技能进行了实证研究:Marjorie M. Schultz & Sheldon Zedeck, Final Research Report: Identification, Development, and Validation of Predictors for Successful Lawyering (2008), available at http://www. law. berkeley. edu/finesLSACREPORTfinal-12. pdf.

③ 该项目需要 5 个学期,收取与 3 年项目同样的学费,仅录取有至少两年工作经历的学生。See Northwestern Law Accelerated JD Bulletin 3, available at http://www. law. northwestern. edu/academics/ajd/AJD. pdf.

④ Clark D. Cunningham, Should American Law SchoolsContinue to Graduate Lawyers Whom Clients Consider Worthless? 70 Md. L. Rev. 499, 511 – 513 (2011).

和选修课。① 其他学校在第 3 年进行了一些变革,试图扭转在这一年中出现的预习不充分和出勤率下降的趋势。② 改革包括主题课程、经验性课程和旨在向实践过渡的顶层课程。③ 还有很多法学院通过本地伙伴或者在线协作者共享课程,还有很多法学院在整合跨学科材料。④ 尽管在设计这些行动计划时付出了巨大的努力,但是无法得到对其有效性的系统性评价。这种评估应是致力于学校课程改革的优先事项。

- 价值观

然而,就讲授伦理分析而言,有大量的研究可以指导它的改革。它指出了体验、互动和以问题为导向的方法的价值。⑤ 诊所是一种特别有效的法律职业伦理教学方法,当学生

---

① Cunningham, Should American Law Schools Continue to Graduate Lawyers, at 509-510.

② Gulati, Sander, &Sockloskie, The Happy Charade.

③ Lee, Law Schools Get Practical(描述了 Washington and Lee 法学院的由执业律师运行的基于案例的模拟课程);New York City Bar Association Task Force on New Lawyers in a Changing Profession, Developing Legal Careers and Delivering Justice in the 21st Century 117-134 (2013).

④ 一个最为雄心勃勃的例子,是迈阿密大学法学院开创的"没有围墙的法律"课程,参与的学生来自美国和外国的许多学校。

⑤ Sullivan et al., *Educating Lawyers*, at 135; Hartwell, Promoting Moral Development, at 505; Jane Harris Aiken, Striving to Teach Justice, Fairness, and Morality, *4 Clin. L. Rev.* 1, 23-25 (1998); James E. Moliterno, Legal Education, Experiential Education, and Professional Responsibility, *38 Wm. & Mary L. Rev.* 71, 81 (1997); Russell Pearce, Teaching Ethics Seriously: Legal Ethics as the Most Important Subject in Law School, *29 Loy. L. Rev.* 719, 734 (1998).

面对有着真正问题的真人时,参与度往往是最大的。① 在这样的背景下,进行伦理判断所需要的,不仅仅是有关规则和原则的知识;它还要求有能力了解这些规则是如何应用的以及哪些原则在具体背景下最为重要。② 当诊所涉及来自处于劣势背景的委托人时,学生可以获得跨文化的能力,并理解穷人的正义是什么。③ 尽管诊所课程必然要涉及在学习中出现的伦理问题,但是并非所有的诊所人员都有时间、兴趣或者专业知识来全面涵盖职业责任。增加诊所时间或者就诊所设立单独课程可能是必要的,这样才能确保这种覆盖面。无论职业责任核心课程选择什么样的方法,它不应当是进行持续的伦理分析的唯一所在。如果全体教员也这样做,学生更有可能认真对待职业义务。每所法学院都应提供激励和问责,以便将伦理问题贯穿于整个课程。

---

① David Luban & Michael Millemann, Good Judgment: Ethics Teaching in Dark Times, *9 Geo J. Legal Ethic*s 31, 39 (1995); Robert P. Burns, Legal Ethics in Preparation for Law Practice, *75 Neb. L. Rev.* 684, 692-696 (1998); Peter A. Joy, The Law School Clinic as a Model Ethical Law Office, *30 Wm. Mitchell L. Rev.* 35 (2004); Alan M. Lerner, Using Our Brains: What Cognitive Science and Social Psychology Teach Us about Teaching Law Students to Make Ethical, Professionally Responsible Choices, *23 Quinnipiac L. Rev.* 643, 694-695 (2004); Joan L. O'Sullivan et al., Ethical Decision Making and Ethics Instruction in Clinical Law Practice, *3 Clin. L. Rev.* 109, (1996). For examples, see Richard Acello, Street Smarts, *ABA J.* Jun. 2011, at 26.

② Luban & Millemann, Good Judgment, at 39.

③ Aiken, Striving to Teach Justice, at 24-27.

就支持近用司法和公益服务，学校应当承担类似的责任。关注这些问题应当是核心课程的一部分。得到充分支持的课外公益服务项目可以提供广泛的实用技能，同时使学生了解未得到满足的法律需要的紧迫性。出于这些原因，美国法学院协会适当地建议学校为每一个法律学生至少提供一次受监督的公益服务机会，要么要求学生必须参与，要么想方设法鼓励绝大多数学生自愿参加。① 学校也应当做更多的工作，为学生的就业提供足够的支持，并鼓励和展示教师的公共服务。② 正如对利他主义的研究所表明的那样，榜样比劝告更能使人学习。③ 如果法学院希望激发未来的执业者对公益工作的忠信，那么教授们需要带头而行，法律学术界则需要奖励这样做的人。如果法学院不采取行动，法院可以扮演这个角色。纽约州已经树立了一个榜样，作为准入条件，该州要求律师资格的申请者完成50小时的公益服务，加利福尼亚州也准备效

---

① AALS Commission on Pro Bono and Public Service Opportunities in Law School, Learning to Serve, at 2.
② Cindy Adcock et al., Building on Best Practices in Legal Education— Pro Bono, in *Best Practices in Legal Education* (Roy Stucky et al., eds., 2d ed., 2011); Melissa H. Weresh, Service: A Prescription for the Lost Lawyer, *2014 J. Prof. Law.* 45, 75.
③ 关于角色榜样的重要性，see Rhode, *Pro Bono in Principle*, at 63. 就法学院教师作为榜样的重要性，see David Luban, Faculty Pro Bono and the Question of Identity, *49 J. Legal Educ.* 58 (1999).

仿这一做法。①

学校还需要做更多的工作,创造一种在实践上和原则上都重视包容性的文化。每所法学院都应有一个正式的机构,负责处理多样性问题。这一机构的责任,应当包括收集关于学生和教员的体验的信息,以及影响他们的与多样性有关的政策。② 帮助教师创造更具包容性的课堂环境或者教学行动计划,应当是优先事项。

所有这些课程改革的努力都需要包括对变革的激励。他们应当奖励那些整合了伦理问题、提供了足够的学生反馈并使用已经被证明最为有效的教学方法的教师。③ 年度报告、同行评估和学生评价,可被用来就教育体验的质量对教师问责,而现在往往在理论中更重视这些,而不是在实践中。

通过推行旨在帮助学生应对法律教育和法律实务活动的压力和竞争的战略,法学院也将受益。这方面的努力在许多机构已经开始。④ 需要进行更多的创新和评估。鉴于1/3的

---

① Rules of the Court of Appeals for the Admission of Attorneys and Counselors at Law, Part 520. 16 (2013); Don J. DeBenedictis, State Bar Announces Members of Skills Training Task Force, *San Francisco Daily J.*, Dec. 6, 2013.

② Deborah L. Rhode, Midcourse Corrections: Women in Legal Education, *53 J. Legal Educ.* 475, 487 (2003). 关于其他变革的讨论,see ABA Presidential Initiative Commission on Diversity, Diversity in the Legal Profession.

③ 关于有效的教学策略,see Michael Hunter Schwartz, Gerald F. Hess, & Sophie M. Sparrow, *What the Best Law Teachers Do* (2013).

④ Peterson & Peterson, Stemming the Tide, at 384, 408-415.

律师有心理健康或者滥用药物的问题,法律教育者不能忽视在法学院学习时就已经开始的机能失调。①

- 法律评论

对学生办刊所带来的挫折感的一个明显回应,是鼓励更多同行评议的替代品。然而,鉴于学术出版的经济挑战,以及学校对于资助对学生有教育价值的期刊的兴趣,这似乎不太可能。假设目前的模式仍然占据主导地位,最近一项对法学教授、学生编辑、律师和法官的实证研究发现了改进编辑过程的方法。一是学生编辑要依靠盲审,并且在选择文章发表时征求教师的意见。② 另一个是就选稿和编辑工作为学生编辑提供更多培训。这样的培训有助于减少过长篇幅的文章和文章中对于非学术读者而言令人扫兴的引用。

这不是一个简单的议程。这也不是一个"少了什么都行"的情形。③ 现代法律教育的成本、设计和报酬结构,对教师来说是合理的,但是在满足学生和社会的需要方面,却存在严重不足。最近的"危机论"甚嚣尘上,这应当提醒我们,我们有义务做得更好。

---

① See sources cited in Deborah L. Rhode, David Luban, & Scott Cummings, *Legal Ethics* 961(6th ed., 2013).

② Wise et al., Do Law Reviews Need Reforms?, at 62.

③ Huxley, *Island*, at 163.

07
Chapter

第七章
结 论

我对职业规制和近用司法的研究兴趣跨越了40个年头。作为耶鲁大学法学院的学生,在20世纪70年代,我卷入了一场关于非法执业问题的论战。我在一个法律援助办公室实习,这个办公室被例行的离婚案件淹没了。该办公室的战略是每月只有1天接办新的案件,这使得绝大多数的穷人没有律师,也没有体面的选择。对于一个标准的无争议离婚案件,私人执业律师收取的费用为2000美元至3000美元,以填写3份表格和出席平均4分钟的听证会。① 在法律援助办公室准备成套材料之前,没有可供试图自行代理的诉讼当事人使用的材料。作为回应,当地律师协会的官员威胁要提起非法执业控告。根据当时的判例,他们获胜的机会很大。就法律援助办公室而言,这一事情就此结束了。我被激怒了,开始了一项实证研究,以挑战律师协会禁止自助式帮助的理由。在接下来的几十年里,我持之以恒地研究了这个问题。② 很多事情已经发生了很大的变化,但是仍有太多的事情未曾改变。现在,成套材料和表格处理服务很容易

---

① Ralph C. Cavanagh & Deborah L. Rhode, Project: The Unauthorized Practice of Law and Pro Se Divorce: An Empirical Analysis, *86 Yale L*. 104, 123-129 (1976).

② 我最近的努力是:Deborah L. Rhode & Lucy Ricca, Protecting the Public or the Profession? Rethinking Unauthorized Practice Enforcement, *82 Fordham L. Rev.* 2587 (2014).

得到。然而盛行的做法仍然禁止提供个人化的建议,包括纠正明显的错误和遗漏。① 数以百万计的美国人在例行而迫切的需求方面,仍然因为高价格而不能获得法律服务。

在法律职业如何处理这些问题方面,任何人在提出根本性的改革建议时,对于阻碍这一进程的一切都不应当过于天真。律师协会是一个保守的实体,牢牢控制着它对自己的规制权。尽管律师收钱为委托人解决问题,但是他们在面对自己职业中的问题时,却出奇的消极被动。他们独立于公众的参与和问责,这使得他们无需竞争和创新。这本书的中心前提是,这个行业不能再有这种狭隘的观点,公众也不能再将对律师的规制权完全留给律师协会了。

应对当代挑战所必需的改革分为两大类。一项涉及优先事项。在塑造执业条件和近用司法方面,金钱要发挥不那么重要的作用。就像第二章指出的那样,在评估个人满意度时,许多律师高估了财务成功的重要性。在像美国这样的金钱至上的文化中,这一理念可能很难推销。但是律师行业对利润的关注给生活质量造成了巨大的损失,而实现更大成就感的关键,在于重新评估职业回报结构。多样性、工作与家庭的平衡以及公益服务的机会,都应当更为优先。最重要的是,法律职业需要变得更加开明,更能反思构成职业满意度的

---

① 关于一个重要判例,see *Florida Bar v. Brumbaugh*, 355 So. 2d 1186 (Fla. 1978)。

条件,而不是去适应那些不符合标准的工作场所。

在关于近用司法的辩论中,资金也需要被更多地考虑。贫困的刑事和民事诉讼当事人当前的困境,是所有文明国家的尴尬,更不用说一个认为自己是世界法治领导者的国家了。在为刑事辩护和民事法律援助提供资金方面,社会和法律职业的忠信是无法替代的。律师行业的公益服务水平不高是没有任何借口的,尤其是对美国的主要律师事务所而言。至少,每位律师都应符合美国律师协会每周1小时公益服务,或者与此相当的财力的最低标准。在涉及人类基本需求的案件中,法院应当承认获得民事律师帮助的权利,并确保提供资金支持。49个国家承认了这一权利,因此并不缺少可借鉴的模式。

第二组改革涉及律师规制结构的变革。我们既需要更少的监督,也需要更多的监督。在非律师人员提供者、跨司法辖区和多行业执业、非律师人员投资和法学院认可等问题上,更少的限制是合适的。尽管所有这些问题都需要一些规制,但是应当给市场竞争以更大的自由度。非律师人员提供者应当遵守颁照规定,确保基本称职性和遵守伦理规则。从事跨司法辖区实务活动的律师,应当受其来源州的规制,但是应当用开放边界政策取代对在其他州进行的活动的保护主义禁令。在遵守合理条件的情况下,应当允许多行业执业和非律师人员对律师事务所投资。在所有这些问题上,律师协会应当借鉴其他已经成功地实施了这些改革的国家的经验。

法律教育也将得益于更多的创新和竞争。目前的放之四海而皆准的认证模式，不适合当代实务活动的现实。律师工作的多样性应与其教育准备的多样性相匹配。应当允许1年、2年和3年的学制，并且应当允许法学院在它们的优先事项和教学与学术之间的平衡上百花齐放。

相比之下，对于律师惩戒和继续法律教育，更严格的规制是必要的。律师协会应当加强对普通委托人投诉的监督，并应当要求律师购买不当执业保险。惩戒制度应更加积极主动，更注重不当行为的原因，而不仅仅是症状。应当更加认真地对待继续法律教育。对于新律师和有不端行为的律师，应当有强制性的继续教育计划，同时要与面向其他律师的更为严格的自愿性认证制度相结合。

这不是一个简单的议程，而且存在重大障碍。州最高法院宣称对法律实务活动的规制有固有的权力以及它们对律师职业利益的顺从，仍然是改革的主要障碍。但是，最近法律市场的变化和法学院面临的日益增加的挑战，使此刻成为重新思考现行规范的绝佳时机。鉴于律师的不满意度和功能障碍的程度、法律教育的入学率的下降和费用的不断上升，以及来自律师业内外的猛烈批评，改革显然恰当其时。律师们也有能力应付这种局面。在这个国家的历史上，他们一直站在每一场社会正义运动的前列。现在他们该把更多的精力转向内部了。他们必须有一个更能满足他们对个人成就感和公共服务的最高期望的职业要求。

重要译名对照表

access to justice 近用司法
accountability 问责制
American Bar Association 美国律师协会
American Bar Foundation 美国律师协会基金会
associate 非合伙律师
baby boomer 婴儿潮一代
billable hour 计费工时
Civil Rights Act《民权法》
commitment 忠信 承诺
conflict of interest 利益冲突
continuing legal education（CLE）继续法律教育
cost-effectiveness 费效比
diversity 多样性
Enron-type accounting standards 安然型会计准则
income partners 收入合伙人
incorporated legal practices 公司化法律执业机构

Lake Woebegon 沃博艮湖
law firm 律师事务所
Legal Services Commissioner 法律服务专员
Legal Services Corporation 法律服务公司
LSAT 法学院入学考试
malpractice claim 不当执业索赔
misrepresentation 不实陈述
Model Provisions for the Legal Profession《法律职业示范规定》
Model Rules of Professional Conduct《职业行为示范规则》
moral turpitude 道德败坏
multijurisdictional practice 跨司法辖区执业
National Association of Law Placement 全国法律就业协会
nonlawyer investment 非律师人员投资
of counsel 特邀律师
offshore legal service provider 离岸法律服务提供者
old-boy network 老同学关系网
one-shot player 一次性参与者
permanent associate 永久非合伙律师
plea bargain 辩诉交易
practice 执业实务
pro bono service 公益服务
professional satisfaction 职业满意度

public defender 公共辩护人

Queen Bee syndrome 蜂王综合征

ranking 排名

self-regulation 自我规制

self-representation 自行代理

Solicitors Regulation Authority 事务律师规制局

substance abuse 药物滥用

supervising attorney 监督律师

U. S. News and World Report《美国新闻和世界报道》

unauthorized practice of law（UPL）非法执业

undocumented immigrant 无证移民

World Justice Project 世界正义项目

著作权合同登记号　图字：01-2019-7993
图书在版编目(CIP)数据

律师的麻烦：美国律师的职业困境／（美）德博拉·罗德著；王进喜译. —北京：北京大学出版社，2024.2
ISBN 978-7-301-34771-3

Ⅰ.①律… Ⅱ.①德…②王… Ⅲ.①律师业务—美国 Ⅳ.①D971.265

中国国家版本馆CIP数据核字（2024）第019234号

ⓒ Oxford University Press 2015
The Trouble with Lawyers was originally published in English in 2015. This translation is published by arrangement with Oxford University Press. Peking University Press is solely responsible for this translation from the original work and Oxford University Press shall have no liability for any errors, omissions or inaccuracies or ambiguities in such translation or for any losses caused by reliance.

《律师的麻烦——美国律师的职业困境》英文版于2015年出版。此翻译版由牛津大学出版社授权出版。北京大学出版社负责原著的翻译。对于译文可能出现的任何错译、漏译、不准确或歧义，以及由此带来的相关损失，牛津大学出版社不承担责任。

书　　　名	律师的麻烦——美国律师的职业困境 LÜSHI DE MAFAN——MEIGUO LÜSHI DE ZHIYE KUNJING
著作责任者	〔美〕德博拉·罗德(Deborah L. Rhode)　著　王进喜　译
责 任 编 辑	田　鹤
标 准 书 号	ISBN 978-7-301-34771-3
出 版 发 行	北京大学出版社
地　　　址	北京市海淀区成府路205号　100871
网　　　址	http://www.pup.cn　http://www.yandayuanzhao.com
电 子 邮 箱	编辑部 yandayuanzhao@pup.cn　总编室 zpup@pup.cn
新 浪 微 博	@北京大学出版社　@北大出版社燕大元照法律图书
电　　　话	邮购部 010-62752015　发行部 010-62750672 编辑部 010-62117788
印 刷 者	北京中科印刷有限公司
经 销 者	新华书店
	850毫米×1168毫米　32开本　9.625印张　191千字 2024年2月第1版　2024年2月第1次印刷
定　　　价	59.00元

未经许可，不得以任何方式复制或抄袭本书之部分或全部内容。
版权所有，侵权必究
举报电话：010-62752024　电子邮箱：fd@pup.cn
图书如有印装质量问题，请与出版部联系，电话：010-62756370